Troubleshooting

Microsoft

Windows XP

Stephen W. Sagman

PUBLISHED BY
Microsoft Press
A Division of Microsoft Corporation
One Microsoft Way
Redmond, Washington 98052-6399

Library of Congress Cataloging-in-Publication Data
Sagman, Stephen W.
      Troubleshooting Microsoft Windows XP / Stephen W. Sagman.
            p. cm.
      Includes index.
      ISBN 0-7356-1492-X
      1. Microsoft Windows XP.   2. Operating systems (Computers)   I. Title.

  QA76.76.O63 S34118   2001
  005.4'4769--dc21   2001055819

Printed and bound in the United States of America.

1 2 3 4 5 6 7 8 9   QWT   7 6 5 4 3 2

Distributed in Canada by Penguin Books Canada Limited.

A CIP catalogue record for this book is available from the British Library.

Microsoft Press books are available through booksellers and distributors worldwide. For further information about international editions, contact your local Microsoft Corporation office or contact Microsoft Press International directly at fax (425) 936-7329. Visit our Web site at www.microsoft.com/mspress. Send comments to *mspinput@microsoft.com*.

Acquisitions Editor: Alex Blanton
Project Editor: Aileen Wrothwell
Technical Editor: Jack Beaudry
Manuscript Editor: Gail Taylor

Body Part No. X08-41925

Acknowledgments

This book is the product of a very talened and dedicated team whose efforts I've truly appreciated and admired over the course of a number of projects. Gail Taylor, manuscript editor, and Jack Beaudry, technical editor, made enormous contributions to the material and offered invaluable suggestions all along the way. Sharon Bell, of Presentation Desktop Publications, who has worked with me on many books, created the lovely layouts with her usual great eye and careful attention to every detail. Julie Kawabata, another veteran of several Studioserv projects, created the great index.

At Microsoft Press, I'd like to thank Aileen Wrothwell, project editor for this book, along with the team of editors and designers who devised and perfected the Troubleshooting series, and Alex Blanton, for giving me the wonderful opportunity to create this book. As always, they are all a true pleasure to work with.

Quick contents

Connections   2

The desktop   12

Desktop icons   20

Disasters   30

The display   40

Downloading files   50

E-mail   58

Files   72

Folders   82

Games   92

Hard disks   102

Hardware   114

Internet connections   126

Internet Explorer   138

Laptops   152

The mouse   162

Multiple users   170

Networks, home   180

Networks, office   200

Optimizing   212

Printing   224

Programs   234

Setting up Windows   244

Sound and pictures   254

Start menu   266

Startup   276

The taskbar   292

Glossary   303

Quick fix index   313

Index   315

Contents

Acknowledgments . . . . *iii*
About this book . . . . *xiii*
Troubleshooting tips . . . . *xv*
    Privileges and permissions . . . . *xv*
    Windows XP in large organizations . . . . *xvi*
    If you're still stuck . . . . *xvi*

Connections   2

    Quick fix   I don't know how to protect my child's privacy on line 3
I can't sign in to Windows Messenger 4
I can't use Remote Assistance in Windows Messenger 6
Internet Connection Firewall is blocking the connection in
    my communications program 8
I'm frequently interrupted by instant messages from others 10

The desktop   12

    Quick fixes   Unexpected Web pages open on my desktop •
    I need to restore the old Windows look 12
Familiar items are missing from the desktop 14
The desktop doesn't show my favorite picture 16
The picture on the desktop is sized incorrectly or off center 18

Desktop icons   20

    Quick fixes   My desktop icons have become enormous •
    I don't see the icons on the taskbar that I use to start my
    favorite programs 20
The desktop is too cluttered 22
Icons are not where I left them 24
Icon labels are too large or too small 26
The My Network Places icon won't appear on my desktop 28
My desktop icons are missing or in disarray 29

Disasters   30

    Quick fix The power at my location goes out periodically 31

The display ... *(no)*

Windows won't start 32

I'm encountering inexplicable error messages after installing a program 34

My computer might have been infected with a virus 36

My hard disk has crashed 38

The display   40

    Quick fixes The colors on my display momentarily distort
    when I change Web pages • The Windows desktop doesn't fill
    the display on my LCD monitor 41

The display has an annoying flicker 42

My monitor type is incorrect so I can't choose the proper display settings 44

My screen shuts off too quickly 46

The screen saver appears too soon 47

I don't know how to get multiple monitors working 48

Downloading files   50

    Quick fix Downloading is very slow 51

I can't find the files I've downloaded 52

Windows opens downloaded files before I can choose to save them 54

Downloading stops or shows an error message 56

I can't start downloading a file by clicking a Web page link 57

E-mail   58

    Quick fixes The Inbox doesn't show all my e-mail messages •
    I get a Relay error from my ISP when I try to send a message 58

I get a *Host could not be found* error message 60

My message is undeliverable 62

My messages go out from the wrong account 64

I can't format the text in messages 66

The file I want to attach is too large 68

Outlook Express won't wait and send my messages all at once 69

Outlook Express automatically dials my ISP when I don't want it to 70

Files   72

    Quick fixes I can't open a file after I rename it • I can't see
    all the details about files in My Computer 73

The file I want is missing 74

The files for a project are scattered in different folders 76

Contents

I can't find a document I've saved 78
The file I've double-clicked won't open 79
I can't tell whether dragging a file will create a shortcut or move the file 80

Folders   82

Quick fixes   Folders don't show all the information about
my files • I can't open or modify a folder or its contents •
I have Mscreate.dir files in a lot of my folders 83
Every folder window shows a different view 84
Too many folder windows open on the screen 86
My folder isn't set up for the type of files I want it to hold 88
I have to enter a path for a file or folder 90

Games   92

Quick fixes   I can't play Internet games through my network •
I can't connect to other players on my home network 93
The graphics in my game are slow or jerky 94
I don't know which games are appropriate for my kids 97
My game doesn't sound right 98
Multiplayer Internet games run too slowly 100

Hard disks   102

Quick fix   I hear my hard disk working even when I'm not
at my computer 103
My hard disk is getting full 104
I can't compress the contents of a hard disk 108
I get a *Data Error Reading Drive*, an *IO Error*, or a *Seek Error* message 110
A disk I've added has changed my drive letters 111
The Disk Defragmenter keeps starting over 112

Hardware   114

Quick fixes   I get a message about permissions when I try to
install a new device • I installed a new driver for a device and
now the device doesn't work 115
A new device I've installed doesn't work 116
A device doesn't work after I install Windows XP 121
An older device doesn't work after I install it 122
My IDE device won't work 124
My SCSI device won't work 125

Internet connections 126

Quick fixes   I don't know how to make my full-time Internet connection secure • My modem dials too slowly 126
I don't have an Internet service provider 128
I can't connect to my Internet service provider anymore 130
Connecting takes a long time 132
I frequently lose my connection to the Internet 134
An automatic dialer keeps popping up 136
I can't connect to Web sites or use e-mail on my high-speed Internet connection anymore 137

Internet Explorer 138

Quick fixes   When I search for a site, Internet Explorer goes directly to a site without showing me alternatives • I can't change the home page on my office computer • The text on Web pages is too small to read easily 139
I get a message saying *The page cannot be displayed* 140
Web pages don't show pictures or play sound 143
Web sites don't remember me 144
Internet Explorer crashes 146
My browser doesn't start at the page I want 148
I get a message saying *You are not authorized to view this page* 149
I need to view a Web page when I can't go on line 150

Laptops 152

Quick fix   I don't want to forget to print a document when I return home or to my office 153
The battery runs down too fast 154
My laptop won't come out of standby 156
I can't transfer files between my desktop and my laptop 158
A hotel room phone line or an office phone line won't work with my laptop 160

The mouse 162

Quick fix   The mouse is too sensitive 163
The pointer doesn't move when I move the mouse 164
The mouse pointer is too hard to see 166
The buttons are backwards because I'm left-handed 167
Double-clicking doesn't work 168

Contents

Multiple users   170

    Quick fix   A folder I want to make secure doesn't have
    a Security tab in its Properties dialog box 171

Others in my home or office keep changing my settings 172

Another user can't access the files on my computer 174

Others can view the files I want to keep private 176

My e-mail messages are mixed in with everyone else's 178

Networks, home   180

    Quick fix   The host computer won't hang up an Internet
    connection when a client computer is done with it 181

I can't connect to other computers on the network 182

I don't know how to set up a home network 186

I can't share an Internet connection 190

The Internet Connection Sharing host computer won't dial the ISP when
    a client computer needs an Internet connection 194

I don't know how to set up a Windows 98 or Windows Me computer
    to connect with a Windows XP computer 195

I can't get to the Internet from computers on the network 196

Networks, office   200

    Quick fix   I can't find a computer in My Network Places 201

I can't log on to the network 202

I can't see other computers on the network 204

Other computers can't connect to my resources 208

I can't connect to my desktop remotely 210

Optimizing   212

    Quick fixes   My computer seems slow at drawing graphics •
    I never know when an update is available from Windows Update 213

Scheduled maintenance tasks won't run 214

My hard disk has slowed down 216

Windows is becoming sluggish 218

Web browsing is slow 220

Printing   224

> **Quick fix** Windows doesn't get status information
> from my printer 225

I can't print a document 226
The photos I print aren't clear 228
I can't print using a network printer 230
It takes a long time to print a document 232
My document wasn't printed the way I expected 233

Programs   234

> **Quick fixes** A program starts in a window that's the wrong
> size • A program used to work correctly but now it doesn't
> in Windows XP 235

A program has stopped responding 236
It takes too many steps to start my favorite programs 238
A program I've removed still shows error messages 240
The wrong program starts when I double-click a file 242

Setting up Windows   244

> **Quick fix** I don't know whether to convert my disk
> to NTFS during setup 245

I can't set up Windows because I can't use the CD-ROM drive 246
Setup stops responding 248
I need to uninstall Windows XP because it doesn't work correctly 250
I still need to be able to use my previous version of Windows 252

Sound and pictures   254

> **Quick fix** I get an error message saying *No wave device that*
> *can play files in the current format is installed* 255

I don't hear sound 256
My CD or DVD drive won't play music CDs 258
I can't hear music CDs with my USB speakers 259
The volume or balance is wrong 260
I can't assign sounds to Windows events 261
My digital camera isn't supported by the Scanner and Camera Wizard 262
I can't print my pictures the way I want 264

Contents

Start menu   **266**

    Quick fixes   The Start menu doesn't show my shortcuts •
    I can't get used to the new Windows XP Start menu 267
    My Start menu is too long or too disorganized 268
    The entries I want aren't on the Start menu 270
    The shortcuts I add are listed at the top of the Start menu 272
    The My Recent Documents list shows a file I don't want others to see 273
    Windows won't shut down 274

Startup   **276**

    Quick fix   Windows no longer displays a menu of users
    at startup 276
    Programs start automatically, without my approval 278
    Startup takes too long 280
    Folder windows open whenever Windows starts 282
    I get an error message about a file at startup 283
    The modem dials whenever Windows starts .284
    Windows 98 or Windows Me starts instead of Windows XP 285
    Windows hangs at startup 286

The taskbar   **292**

    Quick fixes   The Quick Launch toolbar isn't visible • I can't
    make the Quick Launch toolbar wider to see all its icons 293
    The taskbar is missing or in the wrong place .294
    The taskbar buttons are too narrow 296
    The notification area near the clock shows mysterious icons 298
    I need quick access to a folder or mobile device 300
    The Quick Launch toolbar doesn't show icons for the programs I want 301

Glossary   **303**

Quick fix index   **313**

Index   **315**

About this book

Troubleshooting Windows XP offers a new way to diagnose and solve the problems you might encounter while using Microsoft Windows XP. Whether you're a beginning user of Windows XP or you've upgraded from an earlier version of Windows, you'll be able to quickly determine the source of a problem without having to delve into all the technical mumbo-jumbo, and then fix it quickly so you can get right back to work (or play).

How to use this book

Although *troubleshooting* sounds like a task for a team of white-coated lab technicians, it's something you can tackle yourself without a degree in computer science. With the help of this book, you can quickly diagnose a problem, get a basic understanding of its source, and then get just the information you need to fix it and be on your way. The step-by-step instructions tell you where to start and what to do to zero in on and resolve the trouble.

You don't have to go through this book from cover to cover or even read its chapters in any particular order. The problems covered in the book are grouped into chapters that are presented alphabetically, like any good reference book. And the chapter titles are simple, so you'll know at a glance what topics each chapter contains.

Within each chapter, you'll find two specific elements: a flowchart and a set of solutions.

The flowchart

Your first stop in each chapter is the helpful and easy-to-use flowchart. The flowchart asks carefully chosen questions and takes you through precise, yes-or-no answers to help you diagnose a problem. If the solution to a problem requires only a handful of steps, you'll find the steps right in a *quick fix* on the flowchart. But if the solution requires a little more explanation or a few more steps, you'll be directed to the specific solution and page number in the chapter that covers the problem. And if you don't find your problem and solution on the flowchart or in the list of solutions, the list of related chapters that appears on each flowchart can take you to another chapter that just might have the solution you need.

The solutions

The solution topics that follow the flowchart in each chapter are where you'll find the answers to the problems you've pinpointed in the flowchart. They tell you the source of the problem you're experiencing, and they show you how to fix the problem with clear, step-by-step instructions. The solutions provide plenty of screen shots, showing exactly what you should see on the screen as you move through the steps.

The solutions are designed to give you just the facts, so you can quickly fix a problem and then be on your way. But in some cases, the solutions provide additional information that you can read to understand a bit more about why a problem has occurred and, more important, how to avoid similar problems in the future. Also in solutions are tips and sidebars that contain related information and offer helpful advice and important suggestions for keeping Windows running well.

Find the right solution to your problem quickly and efficiently.

Avoid unneccessary down-time using **Quick fixes** to get you back to work.

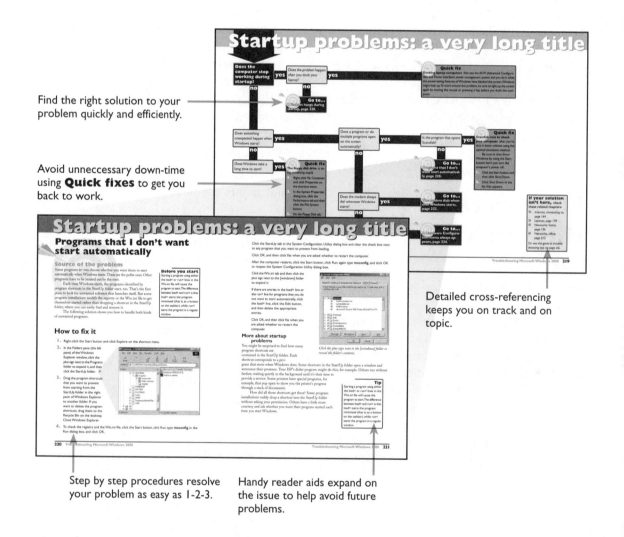

Detailed cross-referencing keeps you on track and on topic.

Step by step procedures resolve your problem as easy as 1-2-3.

Handy reader aids expand on the issue to help avoid future problems.

Troubleshooting tips

Troubleshooting a problem requires careful attention to all the circumstances surrounding the problem. If something has gone wrong, ask yourself when it began, what you were doing in Windows at the time, and what else might have been happening on the computer that might have been a contributing factor. Did the problem arise when you were trying to install a new device or program, for example? Does the trouble occur whenever Windows starts up? Has someone else been using your computer? Having a handle on these questions will help you clearly define the problem so that you can narrow it down more effectively using the flowcharts in this book.

Also consider how you would categorize the problem. Does it have to do with browsing the Internet? Sending e-mail? Playing games? Working with folders? Once you decide what category the problem falls into, you can quickly turn to the chapter in the book that's most likely to have the solution.

As you consider what led to the problem you're experiencing, remember that computers are perfectly consistent. If a problem happens once, it will almost certainly occur again under the same circumstances. This repeatability makes diagnosing problems easier because you can try something again and watch what's happening just before and just as the problem occurs. But it also means that you'll only end up at the same dead end if you try the same thing again, so there's no point in seeing if it'll work next time.

When you're in the throes of a problem, keep in mind that millions of other people are using Windows just like you. If you run into a problem, the chances are good that many others have already encountered it, and the solution might be readily available in updated software, either in an update that you can download from the Windows Update Web page or in an updated driver or program that you can download from a manufacturer's Web site. In fact, frequently in this book, you'll be prompted to make sure you've downloaded and installed all the latest updates for Windows and your programs.

Privileges and permissions

Windows XP is designed to give you easy access to its workings, as long as you have the right and the authority to get in and muck around a little bit with your system settings. Depending on what you're trying to change, you might need to be logged on using the Administrator account or an account that has administrator privileges.

The first account that you establish when you set up Windows XP is an administrator account, which has the privileges and permissions to allow you to make any change to your own computer, including creating additional user accounts and installing and removing hardware and software. If you get an error message while trying to make a change saying that you do not have security privileges, you'll need to either log on using the administrator account or appeal to the person who owns that account to make the change for you.

Windows XP in large organizations

Many of the solutions in this book assume that your computer is either on a home or small office workgroup network or even operating as a stand-alone. But if you're operating Windows XP on a computer in a large organization, your ability to make changes to your settings might be severely restricted by the network administrator who has authority over your computer. In large organizations with complex domain networks, network administrators can set policies that protect Windows from users who know just enough to be dangerous to their own computers, or to the network. If you find that you're unable to make a change

suggested in this book, you'll probably need to turn to the network administrator or help desk in your organization for assistance.

If you're still stuck

If the steps provided in this book don't solve your particular problem, or if your specific problem is not covered in a chapter, here are a few resources you can turn to for help:

- **Windows Help And Support** Click Help And Support on the Start menu to open the Help And Support Center, which offers built-in help, troubleshooters, and links to help resources on line.

- **Microsoft Knowledge Base** (*search.support.microsoft.com*) Technical support information for all Microsoft products. The best place to search for help with questions about problems with specific hardware devices and software programs.

- **Microsoft Windows XP home page** (*www.microsoft.com/windowsxp*) The home page for Windows XP information on the Microsoft Web site.

- **Windows XP Expert Zone** (*www.microsoft.com/windowsxp/ expertzone*) An online community of Windows XP experts with columnists, expert tips, and access to the Windows XP newsgroups where you can ask questions of others.

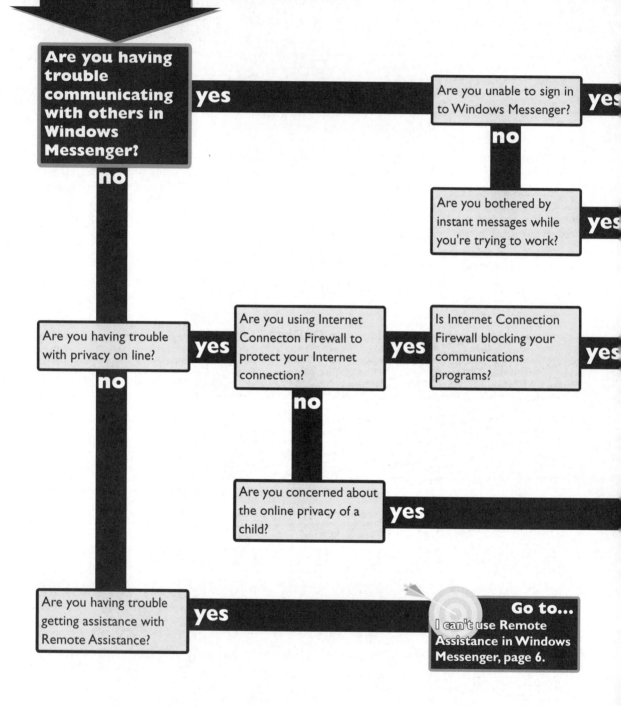

Are you having trouble communicating with others in Windows Messenger?

yes → Are you unable to sign in to Windows Messenger? yes

no

Are you bothered by instant messages while you're trying to work? yes

Are you having trouble with privacy on line? yes → Are you using Internet Connecton Firewall to protect your Internet connection? yes → Is Internet Connection Firewall blocking your communications programs? yes

no

no

Are you concerned about the online privacy of a child? yes

Are you having trouble getting assistance with Remote Assistance? yes

Go to...
I can't use Remote Assistance in Windows Messenger, page 6.

Connections

Go to...
I can't sign in to Windows Messenger, page 2.

Go to...
I'm frequently interrupted by instant messages from others, page 10.

Go to...
Internet Connection Firewall is blocking the connection in my communications program, page 8.

Quick fix

I don't know how to protect my child's privacy on line By signing your child up for a free Kids Passport account, you can prevent Web sites and the companies behind them from collecting personal information about your child. Web sites that participate with Kids Passport can't collect or disclose personally identifiable information about your child without your permission. To obtain a Kids Passport account, follow these steps:

1. Go to *kids.passport.com*.
2. On the Kids Passport Web page, click Parents' Point.
3. On the Parents' Point page, click Set Up A Kids Passport Account.
4. Follow the steps on the screen to create a new Kids Passport Account.

If your solution isn't here, check these related chapters:

- E-mail, page 58
- Internet connections, page 126
- Internet Explorer, page 138
- Programs, page 234

Or see the general troubleshooting tips on page xv.

I can't sign in to Windows Messenger

Source of the problem

To sign in to Windows Messenger to send instant messages, make voice and video calls, or collaborate on a task with someone else, you need both an active Internet connection and a .NET Passport. If you don't have either of these, you won't be able to sign in.

Each user account in Windows XP can have its own associated .NET Passport, so to sign in to Windows Messenger, you need only log on to Windows with your user account, and your .NET Passport will be used automatically in Windows Messenger. But each Windows user account can have only one passport, so several people can't use Windows Messenger simultaneously because they can't be logged on simultaneously. Instead, each person must sign in to Windows Messenger using a separate Windows user account. For more information about creating and maintaining user accounts, see "Multiple users," on page 170.

Here's how to correctly sign in to Windows Messenger, and to set up a .NET Passport if you don't already have one.

How to fix it

1. Log on to your user account in Windows XP.

   Either click your name at the Welcome screen or enter your user name and password in the Log On To Windows dialog box. If Windows is already running, click Start, and examine the name at the top of the Start menu to determine which account is active. If someone else is logged on, click Log Off on the Start menu, and log on with your own account.

2. In the notification area next to the clock on the taskbar, double-click the Windows Messenger icon.

3. If the Windows Messenger icon isn't visible, click the Show Hidden Icons button in the notification area, and then double-click the Windows Messenger icon. ▶

> **Tip**
>
> If your .NET Passport is not recognized, try going to the Passport site (*www.passport.com*) where you can sign in and see if you are recognized there. If so, the messaging servers might be temporarily out of service. Try again in a little while.

Windows Messenger icon ⌐

If the Windows Messenger icon still doesn't show up, click Start, point to All Programs on the Start menu, and click Windows Messenger. After Windows Messenger opens, click Options on the Tools menu, and then, on the Preferences tab of the Options dialog box, select the Run This Program When Windows Starts check box and click OK.

4. In the Windows Messenger window, click Click Here To Sign In. ▶

5. Enter your .NET Passport e-mail address and password.

   If you don't have a .NET Passport, see "Getting a .NET Passport," next.

Getting a .NET Passport

1. Click Start, and click Control Panel on the Start menu.

2. Click User Accounts in Control Panel, click Change An Account, and then click your account on the Pick An Account To Change page.

3. Click Set Up My Account To Use A .NET Passport. ▶

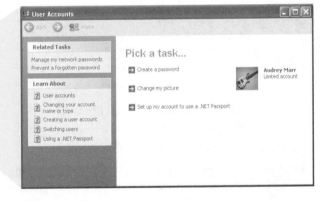

4. In the .NET Passport Wizard dialog box, click Next.

5. On the next page of the wizard, click Yes if you want to use an existing e-mail address or click No. Please Open A Free MSN.com E-mail Account For Me if you'd like to create a new e-mail account, and click Next.

   If you have an existing e-mail address (provided by your ISP, Hotmail, or MSN.com), you can click Yes to use it for your .NET Passport so you won't have to create a new e-mail mailbox to check and manage.

6. If you clicked Yes in step 5, enter your e-mail address in the next page of the wizard, click Next, enter the password for the e-mail address, and click Next. Make sure the Save My .NET Passport Information In My Windows XP User Account check box is selected before you click Next.

   If you clicked No in step 5, follow the steps of the .NET Passport Wizard to create an MSN.com e-mail address and password.

7. Click the Sign In link in Windows Messenger to connect.

I can't use Remote Assistance in Windows Messenger

Source of the problem

If you've ever heard the exasperated sighs of a friend to whom you're describing a computer problem over the phone, you'll love the new Remote Assistance feature in Windows XP. Remote Assistance allows you to invite someone who's more computer knowledgeable than you to connect to your computer and actually view your screen while offering suggestions and corrections. And if you're willing, you can even let someone else take temporary control of your machine to fix the problem while you watch.

But if you're unable to establish a Remote Assistance connection or allow someone else to control your computer, here's what to do.

How to fix it

1. Click Start, right-click My Computer on the Start menu, and click Properties on the shortcut menu.

2. On the Remote tab of the System Properties dialog box, select the Allow Remote Assistance Invitations To Be Sent From This Computer check box.

3. If you also want to allow someone else you've turned to for assistance to operate your computer remotely, click Advanced, select the Allow This Computer To Be Controlled Remotely check box, and click OK.

4. Click OK to close the System Properties dialog box.

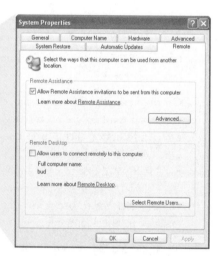

Now you can establish a Remote Assistance connection by following these steps:

1. Make sure that both you and the person who'll be helping you are on line and signed in to Windows Messenger.

2. Double-click the Windows Messenger icon in the notification area on the taskbar to open the Windows Messenger window.

   If the Windows Messenger icon is not available, click Start, point to All Programs on the Start menu, and click Windows Messenger.

3. In the Online list in the Windows Messenger window, right-click the name of the person you'd like to ask for assistance.

4. Click Ask for Remote Assistance on the shortcut menu. ▶

5. If your friend agrees to help you and accepts your invitation, click Yes in the message that asks whether you want to let your friend view your screen and chat with you.

6. In the Remote Assistance window, type messages in the Message Entry area, and click Send.

     If your computer is equipped with a microphone and speakers, you can also click Start Talking to communicate by voice.

     While you're connected, your friend can watch everything that appears on your screen and offer corrections or assistance by typing messages or talking to you. Your friend can also take control and operate your computer by clicking Take Control. To regain control at any time, press the Esc key or click Stop Control in the Remote Assistance window. To terminate the connection, click Disconnect in the Remote Assistance window.

Using e-mail to invite someone to help you

If someone from whom you'd like to request assistance is not available on line and signed in to Windows Messenger, you can send a request for remote assistance by e-mail:

1. Click Start, and click Help And Support on the Start menu.

2. In the Help And Support Center window, click Invite A Friend To Connect To Your Computer With Remote Assistance.

3. In the Remote Assistance window, click Invite Someone To Help You.

4. In the Or Use E-Mail area of the Remote Assistance window, enter the e-mail address of the person you'd like to turn to for help, and click Invite This Person.

5. In the Message box in the Remote Assistance – E-Mail An Invitation window, enter your request for help and a description of the problem, and click Continue.

6. On the next page, set an invitation expiration duration, type a password for the person to use when contacting you with help, and click Send Invitation.

     You'll be notified when the invitation has been sent successfully.

7. When the remote assistant accepts your invitation, you'll be connected through Remote Assistance.

Internet Connection Firewall is blocking the connection in my communications program

Source of the problem

Internet Connection Firewall is designed to secure Windows XP against others on the Internet who seek to gain access to your computer or the computers on your home network. But while it does a wonderful job of protecting your system, especially when your computer is attached to a cable or DSL modem, it can also block legitimate Internet communications programs on your computer, such as teleconferencing software, Internet games, and even your Web server, from establishing contact with the outside world. If you find that a communications program such as AOL Instant Messenger won't work when you have Internet Connection Firewall enabled, you need to instruct Internet Connection Firewall to allow specific openings in its security net, called TCP ports, to permit certain types of traffic to pass through. Here's how to do it.

How to fix it

1. Determine which specific TCP ports your non-working program needs open by examining the program's documentation, checking the manufacturer's Web site, or contacting the manufacturer's technical support.

    For example, AOL Instant Messenger requires that TCP ports 443, 563, and 5190 be open. Microsoft NetMeeting requires the following ports be open: 1731, 1720, 1503, 522, and 389.

2. Click Start, click Run, type **cmd** in the Open box, and click OK.

3. At the command prompt in the window that opens, type **ipconfig**, and press Enter.

4. Make a note of the IP address shown for your Internet connection.

    If you're connected to the Internet through a cable or DSL modem, make a note of the IP address of the Ethernet adapter that's connected to the modem.

5. Type **exit** and press Enter to close the command prompt window.

Now that you have all the information you need, open the ports required by your communications program by following these steps:

1. Click Start, and click My Network Places on the Start menu.

2. In the Network Tasks list in the My Network Places window, click View Network Connections.

3. In the Network Connections window, right-click the connection you use for the Internet.

4. Click Properties on the shortcut menu.

5. On the Advanced tab in the Properties dialog box for the Internet connection, click Settings. ▶

6. On the Services tab in the Advanced Settings dialog box, click Add.

7. In the Service Settings dialog box, enter a name of the service to appear in the list of services on the Services tab. ▶

8. In the Name Or IP Address box, enter the IP address of your computer that you noted in step 4 in the procedure on the opposite page.

9. In both the External Port Number and Internal Port Number boxes, enter the TCP Port number, and make sure TCP is selected.

In most cases, you enter the same number in both the External Port Number and Internal Port Number boxes.

10. Click OK.

11. Repeat steps 6 through 10 if you need to add additional ports.

Tip

Some programs require that you open UDP ports in addition to TCP ports. To accomplish this, enter the UDP port number in the External Port Number and Internet Port Number boxes, and click UPD rather than TCP in step 9 of this procedure.

I'm frequently interrupted by instant messages from others

Source of the problem

If Windows Messenger is set to start and connect to the Internet whenever you start Windows, you're a sitting duck for friends, acquaintances, and associates who feel they can interrupt you with an instant message that you'll be compelled to respond to, if only out of courtesy.

Being always accessible might be just what you have in mind, but if it's not, you can take steps to hide yourself on line from others, making yourself appear to be away or busy. Another option is for you to block everyone so you can't receive messages, or to selectively block only particularly annoying correspondents. Here are the steps to follow to make your presence on line invisible.

How to fix it

1. Click the Windows Messenger icon in the notification area on the taskbar, and point to My Status.

   If the Windows Messenger icon doesn't appear in the notification area, click the Show Hidden Icons button next to the notification area.

2. Click Appear Offline. ▶

   You can also click Busy, which will still display the instant message but not notify you by flashing the message window or playing the instant message sound. The sender of the message will see a notification that you might not reply because you're busy.

   If you choose Away, Windows Messenger will display incoming instant messages and play the instant message sound, but senders will see a notification that you might not reply because you're away.

> **Note**
>
> After you've blocked someone, you might still find yourself in a conversation with the blocked person if someone else invites you both into a conversation.

More drastic measures

If setting your status as Busy or Away is not enough of a deterrent and you're still getting unwanted instant messages, you can go so far as to block others, which prevents them from both seeing you and contacting you.

1. Right-click the name of someone in the Windows Messenger window.

2. Click Block on the shortcut menu. ▶

If someone you want to block is not on your list but you know the e-mail address of that person, follow these steps:

1. On the Tools menu in Windows Messenger, point to Send An Instant Message, and then click Other.

2. In the Send An Instant Message window, type the e-mail address of the person you want to block. ▶

3. Click OK.

4. In the new Conversation window, click Block.

For greater control, and to unblock people you've blocked, follow these steps:

1. On the Tools menu in Windows Messenger, click Options.

2. On the Privacy tab of the Options dialog box, select someone in the My Allow List and click Block to move that person to the My Block List.
   You can also select someone in the My Block List and click Allow to move that person to the My Allow List. ▶

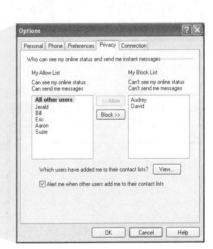

3. Click OK to close the Options dialog box.

Does the desktop look incorrect? **yes**

no

Do unexpected windows appear on the desktop? **yes**

no

Quick fix

Unexpected Web pages open on my desktop You can remove unexpected Web pages by disabling them on the Active Desktop:

1. Right-click the desktop, and click Properties on the shortcut menu.
2. On the Desktop tab of the Display Properties dialog box, click Customize Desktop.
3. On the Web tab of the Desktop Items dialog box, clear the check boxes for the Web pages that you'd like to remove from the desktop.
4. Click OK, and click OK again.

Is the problem with the picture on the desktop? **yes**

no

Do you want to return to the old Windows look? **yes**

Quick fix

I need to restore the old Windows look To restore Windows so it looks like Windows 98 or Windows 2000, follow these steps:

1. Right-click the desktop, and click Properties on the shortcut menu.
2. On the Appearance tab of the Display Properties dialog box, click the Windows And Buttons down arrow.
3. Click Windows Classic Style in the list, and click OK.

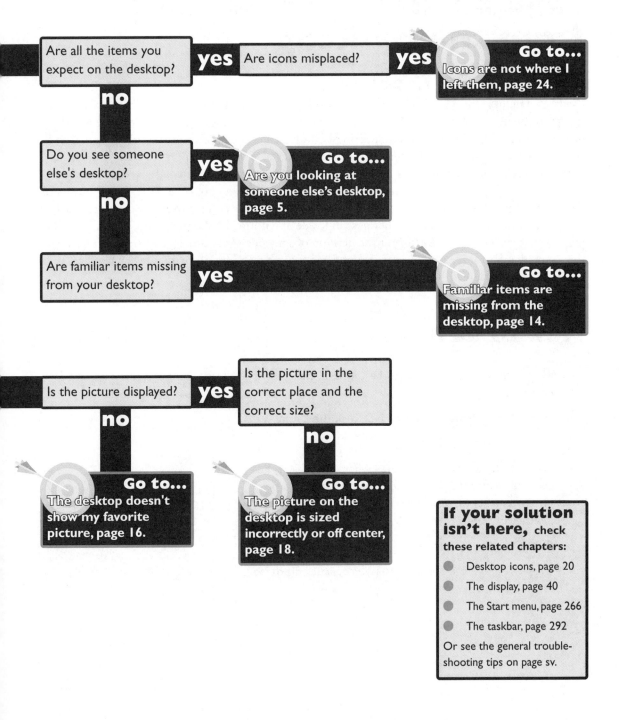

Are all the items you expect on the desktop? **yes** **Are icons misplaced?** **yes** **Go to...** Icons are not where I left them, page 24.

no

Do you see someone else's desktop? **yes** **Go to...** Are you looking at someone else's desktop, page 5.

no

Are familiar items missing from your desktop? **yes** **Go to...** Familiar items are missing from the desktop, page 14.

Is the picture displayed? **yes** **Is the picture in the correct place and the correct size?**

no **no**

Go to... The desktop doesn't show my favorite picture, page 16.

Go to... The picture on the desktop is sized incorrectly or off center, page 18.

If your solution isn't here, check these related chapters:
- Desktop icons, page 20
- The display, page 40
- The Start menu, page 266
- The taskbar, page 292

Or see the general trouble-shooting tips on page sv.

Familiar items are missing from the desktop

Source of the problem

Finding a familiar screen with all your trusted desktop items is part of the comfort and stability you expect. But when some of those desktop items are missing, don't let yourself be thrown. Instead, be confident in your ability to restore missing items by using the procedures described here.

Why do desktop items disappear? Well, they'll never hide or disappear on their own, but in some circumstances, they can seem to vanish. For example, the first time you start Windows XP can be bewildering, because the familiar desktop items you've come to depend on are just not there. Also, Windows XP has some easy-to-change settings that remove items from the desktop to help you to reduce desktop clutter. Another possibility, dealt with in "Desktop cleanup," on the opposite page, is that you're actually looking at the desktop of someone else who's logged on to Windows on this computer. Fortunately, it's easy to switch back to your own identity, with all your familiar desktop settings. Here's how to handle all these possibilities.

How to fix it

1. Right-click the desktop, and on the shortcut menu, click Properties.

2. In the Display Properties dialog box, click the Desktop tab.

3. Click Customize Desktop.

4. In the Desktop Icons area of the General tab, select the check boxes for the desktop icons you'd like to restore: My Documents, My Computer, My Network Places, and Internet Explorer. ▶

5. Click OK.

6. Click OK again to close the Display Properties dialog box.

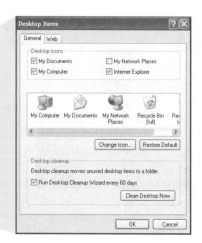

If that didn't restore the item you're missing, you might need to restore some Web content to the Active Desktop by following these steps:

1. Right-click the desktop again, and on the shortcut menu, click Properties.

2. In the Display Properties dialog box, click the Desktop tab.

3. Click Customize Desktop.

4. Click the Web tab in the Desktop Items dialog box.

5. Select the check boxes in the Web Pages list for each item you want to restore to the desktop. ▶

6. Click OK, and click OK again to close the Display Properties dialog box.

Are you looking at someone else's desktop?

Because Windows XP makes it so easy to switch among multiple users, the desktop you're looking at might actually belong to someone else who's logged on to Windows. Don't worry, Windows XP won't automatically bring up the wrong desktop when it starts, but someone else in your household or office might have logged on while you were away from the computer.

The quick and easy to way to check whose desktop you're viewing is to click Start and look at the top of the Start menu to see whose name is shown. If your user name isn't there, follow these steps:

1. Click Log Off at the bottom of the Start menu.

2. In the Log Off Windows dialog box, click Switch User. ▶

3. Click your user name on the Welcome screen.

Desktop cleanup

Periodically, the Desktop Cleanup Wizard moves unused desktop icons to the Unused Desktop Shortcuts folder right on the desktop. To restore any shortcut in the folder, drag it back to the desktop.

The desktop doesn't show my favorite picture

Source of the problem

If everyone else's desktop has a cool picture but yours doesn't, you can add a favorite picture of your child, your pet, your car, or your sweetheart, just like theirs.

You can either scan a picture to use as your desktop background or use a picture you already have in a picture file, such as a picture you've taken with a digital camera. In Internet Explorer, you can also grab a picture from any Web page to use as wallpaper. Here's how to use a picture from any source.

How to fix it

1. Right-click an empty area of the desktop, and click Properties on the shortcut menu.

2. In the Display Properties dialog box, examine the Background list. ▶

3. If None is selected, no picture is displayed. Select a picture in the list, and then click OK.

   You can also click Browse to browse for and select a picture file in a folder on your hard disk.

How to fix it (by scanning a picture)

1. Follow your scanner's software directions to scan a picture, and save it in the My Pictures folder.

2. Right-click an empty area of the desktop, and click Properties on the shortcut menu.

3. On the Desktop tab in the Display Properties dialog box, click the Browse button, open the folder where you saved the picture file, select the picture file, and click Open.

4. Click OK to close the Display Properties dialog box.

If the picture is the wrong size or if it's not centered properly on the screen, see "The picture on the desktop is sized incorrectly or off center," on page 18.

How to fix it (with a picture file)

Using a picture that's already on your hard disk is even easier than scanning a picture. Let's say the picture you want is in the My Pictures folder. Here's what to do:

1. Click Start, and click My Pictures on the Start menu.

2. In the My Pictures window, click Thumbnails on the View menu.

3. Right-click the picture you want, and click Set As Desktop Background on the shortcut menu. ▶

   The easiest way to view pictures is by choosing Filmstrip from the View menu. Then you can click a thumbnail in the row at the bottom of the My Pictures window and see its enlargement above.

How to fix it (with a picture from the Web)

When you find a picture on a Web page that would be perfect for your desktop, follow these steps to borrow it indefinitely:

1. Right-click the picture in Internet Explorer.

2. Click Set As Background on the shortcut menu. ▶

   If you right-click the desktop, click Properties on the shortcut menu, and then inspect the Background list on the Desktop tab in the Display Properties dialog box, you'll see the image now listed as *Internet Explorer Wallpaper*.

The picture on the desktop is sized incorrectly or off center

Source of the problem

Windows might not properly adjust the size of a picture on the desktop—it just stretches it to fill the screen. Fortunately, resizing a picture so it looks the way you want requires just a few steps, as you'll learn in the solution below.

If the background picture is already the correct size but it's not in the middle of the screen, look for a border on the picture that's wider along one of the picture's edges. When you scan a picture and also scan a little of the area surrounding the picture, the background that you've included can act as a border on one side and push the image off center. If you still have the picture, you can rescan it without the border. Otherwise, you can remove the border by following the instructions in "Chopping off a border to center a picture," on the facing page.

How to fix it

1. To determine the size of the desktop, right-click an empty area of the desktop, click Properties on the shortcut menu, and in the Display Properties dialog box, click the Settings tab. ▶

   The Screen Resolution area shows the desktop size in *pixels* (screen dots). Typical sizes are 800 by 600 pixels (800 dots horizontally by 600 dots vertically) or 1024 by 768 pixels.

2. Close the Display Properties dialog box.

3. Open the picture you want to use on the desktop in an image editing program, such as Microsoft Photo Editor.

   If you don't have an image editing program, see "Resizing the background in Microsoft Paint," on the facing page.

4. In the image editor, find the command that lets you change the overall size of an image, often called Resize. (Microsoft Photo Editor lets you easily resize an image by choosing Resize from the Image menu.)

5. Enter dimensions in pixels that are the same as your screen area dimensions, or if you want to leave a border around the image as a space for desktop icons, enter a size that's about 150 pixels smaller horizontally and about 200 pixels smaller vertically (leaving extra vertical space for the taskbar).

6. In the image editor, click Save on the File menu, and save the image as a .jpg or .bmp file.

After you've modified the picture, the picture on the desktop isn't automatically updated, so you need to right-click the desktop, click Properties on the shortcut menu, and reselect the picture on the Desktop tab of the Display Properties dialog box.

Chopping off a border to center a picture

Most image editing programs (including Microsoft Paint, a built-in accessory in Windows for working with picture files) let you *crop* a picture—that is, chop off excess around the edges. If a picture you've placed on the background is off center, try opening the picture in your image editor and cropping everything outside the actual image area. In Microsoft Paint, you can click the Select tool, drag a handle on the side of a picture toward the center of the picture, and then save the file. If you find there's more to crop on one side than on the facing side, you've found the reason the picture was off center on the desktop.

> **Tip**
>
> If a background picture is not centered, right-click the desktop, click Properties on the shortcut menu, and on the Background tab in the Display Properties dialog box, make sure Position is set to Center rather than Tile.

Resizing the background in Microsoft Paint

In Microsoft Paint, you don't have the precise control over image size that you get in many image editing programs. You can't easily resize an image to exact dimensions in pixels. But working in Paint can be even easier because the image in Paint is the same size as it will be on the desktop.

1. Click Start, click All Programs, point to Accessories, and click Paint.

2. In Paint, open the picture file, and on the Image menu, click Stretch/Skew.

3. In the Stretch area in the Stretch And Skew dialog box, type percentages in the Horizontal and Vertical boxes, and click OK to see the newly resized image.

To reduce the picture to half its current height, for example, type **50** in the Vertical box. If the result doesn't look correct, click Undo on the Edit menu to return to the original size, and try a different percentage. If you don't use Undo, the next percentage you enter will be percentage of the current size rather than the original size.

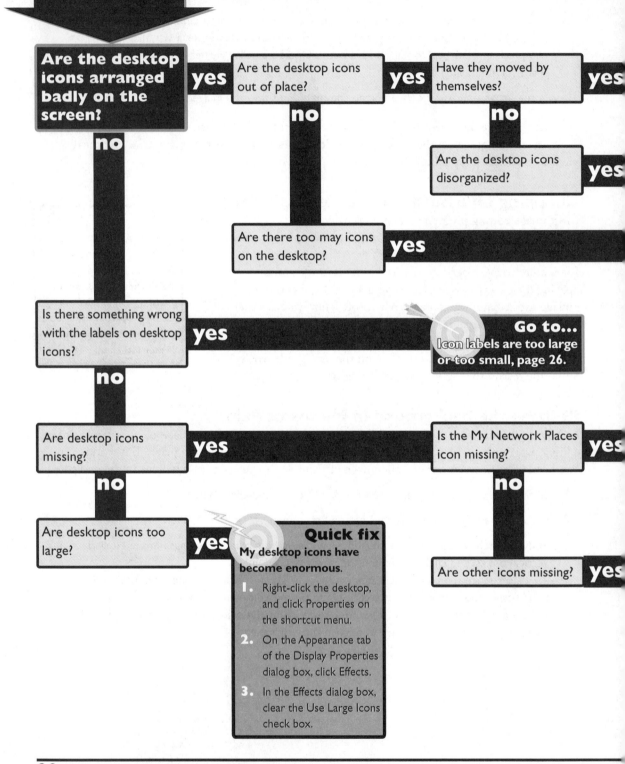

Are the desktop icons arranged badly on the screen?

yes → Are the desktop icons out of place?

yes → Have they moved by themselves?

yes

no (from "Have they moved by themselves?") → Are the desktop icons disorganized?

yes

no (from "Are the desktop icons out of place?") → Are there too may icons on the desktop?

yes

no (from "Are the desktop icons arranged badly on the screen?")

Is there something wrong with the labels on desktop icons?

yes →

Go to...
Icon labels are too large or too small, page 26.

no

Are desktop icons missing?

yes → Is the My Network Places icon missing?

yes

no

Are desktop icons too large?

yes →

Quick fix

My desktop icons have become enormous.

1. Right-click the desktop, and click Properties on the shortcut menu.

2. On the Appearance tab of the Display Properties dialog box, click Effects.

3. In the Effects dialog box, clear the Use Large Icons check box.

no (from "Is the My Network Places icon missing?") → Are other icons missing? yes

Go to...
Icons are not where I left them, page 24.

Go to...
My desktop icons are missing or in disarray, page 29.

Go to...
The desktop is too cluttered, page 22.

Go to...
The My Network Places icon won't appear on my desktop, page 28.

Do you normally use the missing icons to start your favorite programs?

yes

no

Go to...
My desktop icons are missing or in disarray, page 29.

Quick fix
I don't see the icons on the taskbar that I use to start my favorite programs.

1. Right-click the taskbar.

2. Point to Toolbars.

3. Make sure Quick Launch is selected on the Toolbars list.

If your solution isn't here, check these related chapters:

- The desktop, page 12
- The display, page 40
- Programs, page 234
- The taskbar, page 292

Or see the general troubleshooting tips on page xv.

The desktop is too cluttered

Source of the problem

The Microsoft Windows desktop is a convenient place for you to drop everything, from documents you want to keep handy, to shortcuts, to project files and programs. As time goes by, though, the desktop becomes more and more cluttered. It's just too easy to leave documents lying around the Windows desktop, just as you might on a real desktop.

In addition, many software setup programs drop shortcuts onto your desktop without even asking. Remember, it's your desktop and your work space, not an advertising billboard. Here are some ideas for cleaning up not only your own desktop icon mess, but also clutter produced by the desktop background image, trash deposited on your desktop by other users, and the Active Desktop, which displays Web pages on the desktop.

How to fix it

1. Check to see whether the programs that have desktop icons also have commands on the Start menu. Most do.

   If you don't mind using the Start menu to start programs, you can delete duplicate desktop shortcuts (especially those whose main job is to advertise software products).

2. Right-click each desktop icon and click Delete on the shortcut menu for a program or service you don't need. ▶

   Every 60 days the Desktop Cleanup Wizard will ask whether you want to remove desktop icons that you haven't used during the previous 60 days. You can run the wizard at any time by right-clicking the desktop, pointing to Arrange Icons By on the shortcut menu and clicking Run Desktop Cleanup Wizard.

3. Drag the desktop icons of the two or three programs you use most to the Quick Launch toolbar, located just to the right of the Start button, to get them off your desktop. ▶

   Windows XP hides the Quick Launch toolbar by default. To show it, right-click the taskbar, point to Toolbars on the shortcut menu, and click Quick Launch.

Desktop icons

4. Remove unwanted Web pages and Web windows: Right-click the desktop, click Properties on the shortcut menu, and, on the Desktop tab, click Customize Desktop. On the Web tab in the Desktop Items dialog box, clear the check box for each Web page or Web window you want to remove from the desktop and click OK. ▶

5. Drag loose documents on the desktop into the My Documents folder, or create folders on the desktop for groupings of documents and programs and drag documents and programs into these folders. ▶

   Create folders for documents and programs by project, by task, by type, or by whatever sorting scheme makes sense for your needs. Create a new folder by right-clicking a blank area of the desktop, pointing to New on the shortcut menu, clicking Folder, and then typing a folder name.

   Keep in mind that your programs aren't closed. You can click a program's taskbar button to reopen its window.

6. Turn off the background by right-clicking the desktop and, on the Desktop tab of the Display Properties dialog box, clicking None in the Background list. Yes, your background is an adorable picture of your little pooch, but it's taking up valuable screen space and making it harder to see the icons you want.

7. Drag icons to the far corners of the desktop rather than leaving them all bunched up against the left edge.

8. If you can, increase your screen area: Right-click the desktop, click Properties on the shortcut menu, click the Settings tab, drag the Screen Resolution slider one notch to the right, and click OK. This gives you more desktop area to work with.

   As you increase the screen resolution, everything on the screen becomes smaller, so you might be limited by the legibility of items on the screen.

Tip

You can quickly clear the desktop by right-clicking the taskbar and clicking Show The Desktop on the shortcut menu. Every open window is minimized to a button on the taskbar, and desktop shortcuts and documents that were hidden beneath other windows are revealed.

Icons are not where I left them

Source of the problem

One of the nifty aspects of using Windows is that you can customize the desktop so that it looks just the way you want. You can change the desktop's color, change the font and size of the labels under icons, and put the desktop icons wherever you like them—or so you'd think.

If the icons on your desktop seem to have a mind of their own and won't stay where you put them, several circumstances might be to blame. You might have Windows set to automatically arrange the desktop icons. There's an easy fix for that. Another possibility is that you you're looking at someone else's desktop! Or maybe someone else has inadvertently modified your user profile while trying to customize the desktop. Here's how to fix these situations.

How to fix it

1. Right-click an empty area of the Windows desktop, point to Arrange Icons By, and take a look at the drop-down menu.

2. If there's a check mark next to Auto Arrange, clear the Auto Arrange check mark. ►

Now you can drag icons wherever you want them and they won't scoot back into a grid at the left side of the desktop.

3. Click Start, and look for your user name at the top of the Start menu.

If someone else's name is there, you're looking at someone else's desktop. That explains why the icons on the desktop are missing or rearranged. Follow the rest of these steps to restore your own desktop.

4. On the Start menu, click Log Off.

5. In the Log Off Windows dialog box, click Switch User.

If the only options in the Log Off Windows dialog box are Log Off and Cancel, Windows is not set to use the Welcome screen. Click Log Off, and then enter your user name and password in the Log On To Windows dialog box.

6. On the Welcome
   screen, click your user
   name. ▶

Managing multiple users

When Windows has multiple
user profiles, which allows
several people to have individual sets of desktop icons,
you should enforce a simple
rule to maintain order around
the desktop. Anyone who
wants to modify how the
desktop looks must log off
and then log back on using
the correct user name. That
way, any changes will be part
of that person's user profile, not yours.

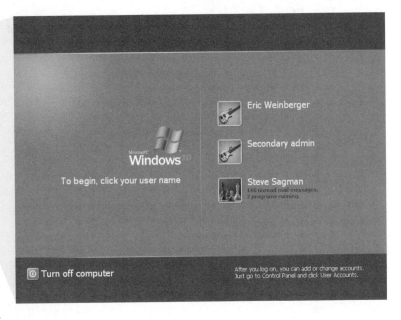

Give people these directions for logging off and logging back on with the correct user name:

1. On the Start menu, click Log Off.

2. In the Log Off Windows dialog box, click Log Off or Switch User, depending on whether Windows is set to show the Welcome screen.

3. If the Welcome Screen appears, click your user name. If the Log On To Windows dialog box opens, enter your user name and password.

If you'd rather not force people to log off and then back on, an alternate approach, not quite as foolproof, is to ask them to check that the correct user name shows at the top of the Start menu before making changes.

Tip

Saving documents on the desktop makes them handy, but it contributes to desktop clutter. One useful alternative is to drag documents to the My Documents folder on the desktop, where they'll be nearly as easy to get to.

Icon labels are too large or too small

Source of the problem

An obvious way to save desktop space is by resizing the text labels under the icons. But it's easy to make that text the wrong size. If you make the labels too small, they can be hard to read. Conversely, if you make them too big, they can get truncated (an impress-your-friends term for chopped off). Here's how to resize icon labels so they'll fit well on the desktop.

How to fix it

1. Right-click an empty area of the Windows desktop, and click Properties on the shortcut menu.

2. On the Appearance tab of the Display Properties dialog box, click Advanced.

3. In the Advanced Appearance dialog box, click the Item down arrow, and then click Icon. ▶

4. Choose a new size from the Size list to the right of the Font list and click OK. (The Advanced Appearance dialog box has two Size options, so take care to choose the correct one.)

5. Click Apply and take a look at the icon text. If it's not the size you want, repeat steps 2 through 4 and try a different size.

6. Click OK when the size is correct.

My icon labels are getting cut off like th...

You can't tell when an icon label will be chopped off and replaced with an ellipsis (...)—at least, you can't tell until it's too late. But when you see it happen, you can try two methods for fixing things. One is to reduce the text size, as described above, and the other is to increase the spacing between icons. Follow the steps 1 through 3 in the procedure above, but in step 3, click Icon Spacing (Horizontal) rather than Icon in the Item list. Gradually increase the value in the item Size list, clicking Apply after each change, until the space surrounding each icon is large enough to contain the entire icon label.

Changing other desktop items

On the Themes tab of the Display Properties dialog box, you can choose a theme to personalize the look of your desktop or download more themes from the Windows Media Technologies Web page.

After you choose a theme, you can refine individual items on the desktop—the colors and sizes of icons, menus, and text in message boxes—by clicking Advanced on the Appearance tab of the Display Properties dialog box and modifying items from the Items list. The trick is to know which item controls which part the screen. Here's some help:

- The Icon item controls the size and font of the text under icons, and it also controls the size of the text used for the file and folder listings in My Computer and Windows Explorer. This is good to know if the text in My Computer becomes too small when you try to reduce just the icon label size.

- The Menu item controls the size and font of the text on the Start menu (along with menus within My Computer, Windows Explorer, and other programs). The Menu and Selected items (the regular entries on menus and those that are selected) are linked: You can give them different colors, but not different sizes.

- This one is not so obvious. The size of the text for Active Title Bar item controls the size of the text on taskbar buttons. This makes sense if you think of a taskbar button as a shrunken title bar for a program that's running. ▶

Downloading More Themes

To download new themes from the Windows Media Technologies Web page, click More Themes Online in the Theme list on the Themes tab in the Display Properties dialog box.

- One more thing: The Active Title Bar and Inactive Title Bar items are linked, so changing the size of one changes the size of the other (although you can make them different colors).

The My Network Places icon won't appear on my desktop

Source of the problem

If the My Network Places icon won't appear on the desktop, it's probable that all the Windows networking components aren't installed on your computer. If the Windows setup program doesn't find a network adapter in your computer, it doesn't install these components. In this case, the solution is to install a network adapter.

The My Network Places icon also won't appear when you have no *client* installed, such as the Client For Microsoft Networks. A client allows your computer to join the network and communicate in the same language as the other computers. If you remove the client, Windows won't display the My Network Places icon. You no longer need it because you can't connect to a network without a client. If you've just discovered that the My Network Places icon is missing, you can restore the icon by following these steps to reinstall the client.

How to fix it

1. Click Start, and click Control Panel.

2. In Control Panel, click Network And Internet Connections, and then click Network Connections.

3. In the Network Connections window, right-click your LAN connection, and click Properties.

4. On the General tab of the Local Area Connection Properties dialog box, click Install.

5. In the Select Network Component Type dialog box, click Client, and click Add.

6. In the Select Network Client dialog box, click Client For Microsoft Networks, and click OK. ▶

7. Click Close to close the dialog box, and click Yes if you're asked whether you want to restart your computer.

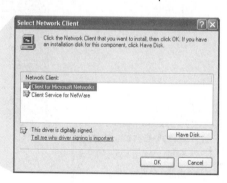

My desktop icons are missing or in disarray

Source of the problem

Neatness counts, but the more you use Windows, the more desktop icons you'll have. If your desktop icons are in disarray, you have several options for organizing them in a tidy arrangement. You can drag them wherever you want, creating neat little groupings according to their purpose, or you can let Windows organize them into neat columns by name, size, or type. If your desktop icons are missing altogether, the solution below offers a quick way to get them back, too.

How to fix it

If the icons are in disarray, follow these steps:

1. Right-click the desktop.

2. Point to Arrange Icons By on the shortcut menu.

3. Make sure Align To Grid is selected.
   To have the icons sorted by name, by file size, or by type, also select Name, Size, or Type on the shortcut menu. The fourth option, Modified, organizes the icons by when their files were last changed.

If the desktop icons are missing altogether, follow these steps:

1. Right-click the desktop.

2. Point to Arrange Icons By on the shortcut menu.

3. Make sure Show Desktop Icons is selected on the shortcut menu. ▶

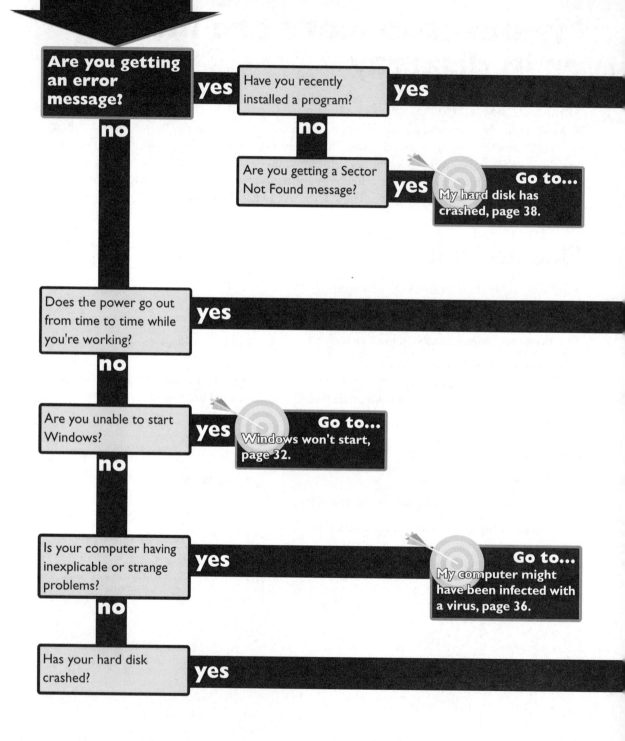

Are you getting an error message?

yes → Have you recently installed a program? → **yes**

no ↓

Have you recently installed a program? → **no** ↓

Are you getting a Sector Not Found message? → **yes** → **Go to...** My hard disk has crashed, page 38.

Does the power go out from time to time while you're working? → **yes**

no ↓

Are you unable to start Windows? → **yes** → **Go to...** Windows won't start, page 32.

no ↓

Is your computer having inexplicable or strange problems? → **yes** → **Go to...** My computer might have been infected with a virus, page 36.

no ↓

Has your hard disk crashed? → **yes**

Disasters

Go to...

I'm encountering inexplicable error messages after installing a program, page 34.

Quick fix

The power at my location goes out periodically To keep your computer running for a short time even when the power fails, you can buy and install an uninterruptible power supply (UPS). You plug the UPS into the wall outlet and plug the computer and monitor into the UPS. A UPS is like a giant battery. It stores power when the power is on and dispenses power to your system starting the instant the lights go off. If the power just flickers, the UPS can keep your computer running so you won't lose any work. If the power goes off for longer, the UPS gives you a while to save open documents, and then shut down the computer.

If your solution isn't here, check these related chapters:

- Hard disks, page 102
- Hardware, page 114
- Setting up Windows, page 244

Or see the general troubleshooting tips on page xv.

Go to...

My hard disk has crashed, page 38.

Windows won't start

Source of the problem

Nothing's more disconcerting than a computer that won't start up after you flick on the power. If Windows can't get to the Log On dialog box or the Welcome screen, how will you be able to repair it with the tools within Windows?

Fortunately, you have some immediate options. First, you can start the computer using the "last known good configuration," which restores the computer to its state when it last started successfully. And if that doesn't work, you can use Safe Mode to get Windows up and running, and then use System Restore to return Windows to its state at a time when it was working fine. Here's how to use these two options.

How to fix it

1. Turn off the power to the computer, wait a few seconds, and then turn on the power.

2. After the routine messages that tell you about the BIOS and the amount of RAM in your computer, press F8.

   If a menu appears giving you a choice of operating systems to start, press F8.

3. On the Windows Advanced Options Menu, press the up arrow or down arrow key to move the highlight to Last Known Good Configuration, and press Enter. ▶

4. If another menu appears asking which operating system to start, move the highlight to Microsoft Windows XP Home Edition or Microsoft Windows XP Professional, depending on your version of Windows XP, and press Enter.

```
Windows Advanced Options Menu
Please select an option:

     Safe Mode
     Safe Mode with Networking
     Safe Mode with Command Prompt

     Enable Boot Logging
     Enable VGA Mode
     Last Known Good Configuration (your most recent settings that worked)
     Directory Services Restore Mode (Windows domain controllers only)
     Debugging Mode

     Start Windows Normally
     Reboot
     Return to OS Choices Menu

Use the up and down arrow keys to move the highlight to your choice.
```

If Windows fails to start even after you choose Last Known Good Configuration, follow these steps:

1. Turn off the power to the computer, wait a few seconds, and then turn on the power.

2. After the routine messages that tell you about the BIOS and the amount of RAM in your computer, press F8.

   If a menu appears giving you a choice of operating systems to start, press F8.

3. On the Windows Advanced Options Menu, press the up arrow or down arrow key to move the highlight to Safe Mode, and press Enter. ▶

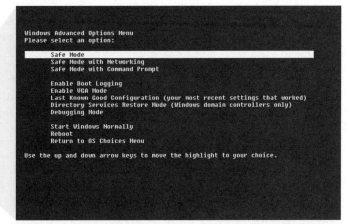

```
Windows Advanced Options Menu
Please select an option:

    Safe Mode
    Safe Mode with Networking
    Safe Mode with Command Prompt

    Enable Boot Logging
    Enable VGA Mode
    Last Known Good Configuration (your most recent settings that worked)
    Directory Services Restore Mode (Windows domain controllers only)
    Debugging Mode

    Start Windows Normally
    Reboot
    Return to OS Choices Menu

Use the up and down arrow keys to move the highlight to your choice.
```

4. If another menu appears asking which operating system to start, move the highlight to Microsoft Windows XP Home Edition or Microsoft Windows XP Professional, depending on your version of Windows XP, and press Enter.

5. When Windows reports that your computer is running in Safe Mode, click No so you can use System Restore to restore the computer to an earlier configuration, when it was starting properly. ▶

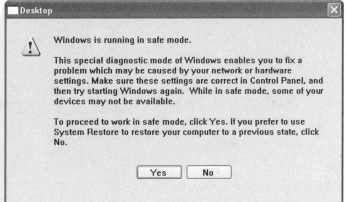

Desktop ☒

⚠ Windows is running in safe mode.

This special diagnostic mode of Windows enables you to fix a problem which may be caused by your network or hardware settings. Make sure these settings are correct in Control Panel, and then try starting Windows again. While in safe mode, some of your devices may not be available.

To proceed to work in safe mode, click Yes. If you prefer to use System Restore to restore your computer to a previous state, click No.

[Yes]   [No]

6. In the System Restore window, make sure Restore My Computer To An Earlier Time is selected, and click Next.

7. On the Select A Restore Point page of System Restore, click a recent bold date in the calendar when your system was working.

8. On the same page, click a restore point in the list of restore points, and click Next.

9. After System Restore warns you to close programs and files, click Next.

   System Restore restores the crucial system files from the date you specified, restarts the computer, and shows a message saying that the system restore was completed.

I'm encountering inexplicable error messages after installing a program

Source of the problem

Programs that sport a "Designed for Windows XP" logo on their packaging shouldn't impose problems on Windows XP. And while it would be unusual for any Windows program produced since 1995 to cause serious errors, anything can happen, especially when you begin bogging down a Windows XP installation with dozens of applications, utilities, games, and other software.

Here are the steps to take if you begin encountering grim-sounding error messages such as *Illegal Operation* after you've installed a new program.

Before you start

Troubleshooting error messages caused by programs requires two steps. The first is to remove the program to see whether the error stops. The second is to restore Windows to an earlier time, before you installed the program. Neither procedure will remove or damage any of your data files, but you might not be able to use programs or devices that you recently installed until you reinstall them.

How to fix it

1. Click Start, and click Control Panel on the Start menu.

2. Click Add Or Remove Programs.

3. Select the program you installed before the error messages started, and click Change/Remove. ▶

4. Follow the steps shown on the screen to remove the application.

5. Restart the computer, and see whether the error messages have stopped appearing.

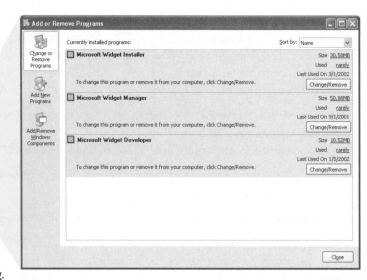

If removing the application hasn't fixed the operation of your computer, use System Restore by following these steps:

1. Click Start, point to All Programs, point to Accessories, point to System Tools, and click System Restore.

2. In the System Restore window, make sure Restore My Computer To An Earlier Time is selected, and click Next.

3. On the Select A Restore Point page of System Restore, click a recent bold date in the calendar when your system was working. ▶

4. On the same page, click a restore point in the list of restore points, and click Next.

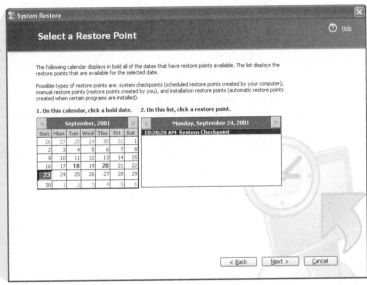

5. After System Restore warns you to close programs and files, click Next.

System Restore restores the crucial system files from the date you specified, restarts the computer, and shows a message saying that the system restore was completed.

More about restore points

System Restore creates a restore point whenever it detects a significant change to your computer, such as the installation of a new device. It also creates a restore point to match the way you use your computer. If you use your computer daily, it creates a daily restore point. And if you'd like, you can create a restore point at any time by running System Restore and clicking Create A Restore Point.

You don't need to manage or monitor the System Restore feature because it works quietly in the background, but you can reduce the number of restore points that are maintained to decrease the amount of hard disk space used. To reduce the number of restore points, follow these steps:

Control Panel → System → System Restore

1. Click Start, right-click My Computer on the Start menu, and click Properties on the shortcut menu.

2. On the System Restore tab in the System Properties dialog box, select your hard disk, and click Settings.

3. In the drive Settings dialog box, drag the slider to the left, and click OK twice to close the dialog boxes.

System Restore will be suspended if you have less than 200 MB of free hard disk space.

My computer might have been infected with a virus

Source of the problem

A *virus* is a malicious program that infects your computer through a file you get across the network, from the Internet, or through an e-mail message. While some viruses are relatively benign, displaying a "gotcha" message on the screen, others are very harmful. They can't physically damage your computer, but they can damage or delete your data, and they can replicate and transfer themselves from your computer to other computers. One type of virus can even send itself to everyone in your e-mail address book.

Not every computer problem is a symptom of a virus, but these symptoms might indicate that your computer has been infected:

- Some files or programs are suddenly missing.

- A program doesn't work properly.

- Unusual messages appear on the screen, or you hear unusual sounds or music playing unexpectedly.

- Files that you haven't created appear on your computer.

The most important measure you can take to protect yourself is to obtain antivirus software that can both remove viruses from your computer and shield your computer from new viruses. Here's how to rid your computer of an existing virus and to protect yourself from future attack.

How to fix it

1. Obtain and install an antivirus program.

   Buy an antivirus program from a well-known software manufacturer that will provide updates to the software as new viruses are discovered. The leading antivirus programs are always available on the Web in trial versions that you can download and use immediately until you have the full version of the software. Visit www.symantec.com and www.mcafee.com, for a start.

2. Run the antivirus program and use its scanning feature, which can detect viruses in the computer's memory and on the hard disk.

3. If the antivirus program detects a virus in a file, select the program's clean or disinfect option. If the file can't be cleaned or disinfected, delete the file, and be sure to empty the Recycle Bin.

4. Contact any people with whom you've recently exchanged files, e-mail attachments, or Zip disks to let them know that you've found a virus and that they should check their computers for viruses too.

Hoaxes

Almost as widespread as jokes in e-mail messages are warnings from well-meaning friends about new viruses. Fortunately, many rumors about viruses are hoaxes, so you'd be doing a disservice to other people by passing the warnings on. To determine which viruses are real and which are hoaxes, you can visit several sites on the Web that track hoaxes. Among these are *antivirus.about.com/compute/antivirus/library/blenhoax.htm* and *www.symantec.com/avcenter/hoax.html*.

Protecting your computer from viruses

Even though your goal is to detect and remove viruses you might have already received, it's just as important to also protect yourself from new viruses by taking these steps:

● Run the antivirus program's real-time monitoring service, which scans incoming files and e-mail messages as they arrive.

● Scan floppy disks and removable disks, such as Zip disks, that you receive from others.

● Don't open attachments in e-mail messages from strangers, unless the attachments are .jpg pictures or .txt text files.

● Don't leave floppy disks or removable disks in your computer's drives—that way, they won't become infected with a new virus.

● Update your antivirus software frequently by visiting the software manufacturer's Web site and downloading updates that will eliminate new viruses.

    All well-known antivirus software makers publish frequent updates that can identify and remove new viruses that have appeared since the last update of the program.

● After you've scanned your system and found it clear of viruses, back up all your important files to be sure you have spare copies in case your computer becomes infected later.

● Create an ASR (automated system recovery) disk that you can use to restore your system. Click Start, point to All Programs, point to Accessories, point to System Tools, and click Backup. In the Backup Or Restore Wizard, click Advanced Mode. In the Backup Utility window, click Automated System Recovery Wizard and follow the steps of the wizard to create an ASR disk. Store this disk in a safe place.

Tip

Even though you've purchased and installed an antivirus program from a major manufacturer, you might want to download, install, and scan your system with a trial version of another manufacturer's antivirus program to get a second opinion. After you run the scan, you should uninstall the second program, because using both programs for ongoing monitoring can be too taxing on your system's resources.

My hard disk has crashed

Source of the problem

Usually a hard disk starts making odd sounds—grinding or banging noises—before it gives out. It also might become reluctant to start when you turn on the computer. You might need to flip the power switch a few times before you hear the whine of the disk as it begins to spin. This is your signal to immediately back up your data before you lose it. But occasionally hard disk problems manifest themselves as increasingly common error messages, such as *Sector not found*, when you try to open files or start programs.

If the problem with a disk is mechanical, there might be little you can do but replace the disk. Most computer manufacturers or disk drive manufacturers will replace a disk rather than repair it if it's still under warranty. But if the symptom is repeated error messages, you should use Check Disk, the disk maintenance program in Windows, to repair the disk. If Check Disk can't repair the problem, you might need to reformat the hard disk and restore Windows from your backed up data. These options are covered here.

How to fix it

1. Click Start, My Computer on the Start menu, and right-click the hard disk.

2. On the shortcut menu, click Properties, and on the Tools tab in the Properties dialog box, click Check Now in the Error-Checking Status area.

3. In the Check Disk dialog box, select the Automatically Fix File System Errors check box, select the Scan For And Attempt Recovery Of Bad Sectors check box, and then click Start.

Are hard disks reliable?

Most components in your computer—the processor, the video adapter, the sound card, even the monitor—are electronic, without moving mechanical components. But the hard disk in your computer is both electronic and mechanical. The heads that read and write data move rapidly across the surface of disk platters that are rotating thousands of times per minute. So even though a hard disk is extraordinarily reliable, and rated to work for hundreds of thousands of hours before failing, it is the component in your computer that's most likely to break down and have a mechanical failure. One of the oldest adages in computing: It's not *if* your hard disk breaks down, it's *when*. Take every precaution to back up your data so that you'll be prepared for that day.

> **Tip**
>
> If a drive appears to be dead and it contains essential data that you don't have backed up, you can contact a data recovery company, which may be able to recover your critical files. This service is extremely expensive, however, so it's really only an option for organizations whose critical data is at risk.

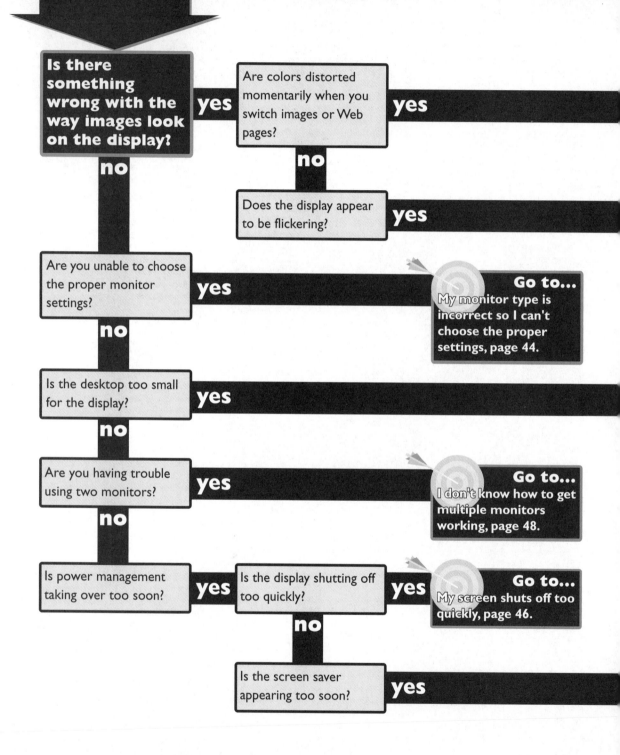

Is there something wrong with the way images look on the display?

yes → Are colors distorted momentarily when you switch images or Web pages?

yes →

no ↓

Does the display appear to be flickering?

yes →

no ↓

Are you unable to choose the proper monitor settings?

yes → **Go to...** My monitor type is incorrect so I can't choose the proper settings, page 44.

no ↓

Is the desktop too small for the display?

yes →

no ↓

Are you having trouble using two monitors?

yes → **Go to...** I don't know how to get multiple monitors working, page 48.

no ↓

Is power management taking over too soon?

yes → Is the display shutting off too quickly?

yes → **Go to...** My screen shuts off too quickly, page 46.

no ↓

Is the screen saver appearing too soon?

yes →

The display

Go to...
The display has an annoying flicker, page 42.

Quick fix

The colors on my display momentarily distort when I change Web pages If your display is set to show only 256 colors, you might find that the colors in pictures become distorted for a moment when you switch images or Web pages. This happens when Windows needs to change from one set of 256 colors to the colors in the new image. To avoid these color shifts, set your display adapter to use more than 256 colors by following these steps:

1. Right-click the desktop, and click Properties on the shortcut menu.

2. On the Settings tab in the Display Properties dialog box, click the Colors down arrow, click Medium (16 bit) or Highest (32 bit), and click OK.

Quick fix

The Windows desktop doesn't fill the display on my LCD monitor Unlike a regular monitor, which can display a flexible number of pixels, or dots, an LCD display (the display in your laptop or a flat-panel LCD screen) has a fixed number of dots. So if the Screen Resolution setting is lower than the LCD's screen area (for example, 800 by 600 pixels when the LCD has 1024 by 768 pixels), the Windows desktop won't fill the screen, or the image may be stretched to fit the larger screen area and look jagged. To fix this problem, follow these steps:

1. Right-click the desktop, and click Properties on the shortcut menu.

2. On the Settings tab in the Display Properties dialog box, drag the Screen Resolution slider to the same setting as the actual resolution of the LCD display. To determine this resolution, consult the documentation for the display or laptop.

If your solution isn't here, check these related chapters:

- The desktop, page 12
- Desktop icons page 20
- Hardware, page 114
- Laptops, page 152

Or see the general trouble-shooting tips on page xv.

Go to...
The screen saver appears too soon, page 47.

The display has an annoying flicker

Source of the problem

The image on your computer screen should be rock steady. But if you've recently hooked up a larger monitor or installed a new video adapter, you might find that the screen appears to be flickering rapidly instead, as if it's vibrating. Some people are unaware of flicker until it's removed. Others are maddened by it. Either way, flicker will ultimately tire your eyes and make your time in front of the computer less enjoyable, so eliminating it is well worth the effort.

How to fix it

1. Right-click the desktop, and click Properties on the shortcut menu.

2. In the Display Properties dialog box, click the Settings tab, and click Advanced.

3. On the Monitor tab in the Properties dialog box, note the monitor type. ▶

    If the monitor type is incorrect, or if the monitor type is "Default Monitor," see "My monitor type is incorrect so I can't choose the proper display settings," on page 44. After you've set the correct monitor type, return to this procedure and continue with step 4.

4. In the Monitor Settings area of the Monitor tab, click the Screen Refresh Rate down arrow if it's available, and click a refresh rate higher than 60 Hertz.

    The refresh rate is the number of times the screen is revised each second, measured in hertz (Hz). You can select any value in the list, but to avoid flicker, select a value greater than 60 Hz. (A rate of 70 to 80 Hz is fast enough to eliminate flicker.)

    Some video adapters come with configuration programs that you use to change their refresh rates. With these video adapters, you might not find a Screen Refresh Rate list in the Properties dialog box.

5. Click OK. The screen might go dark for a second until the new refresh rate kicks in.

6. In the Monitor Settings dialog box, click Yes if the refresh rate change appears to have fixed the problem, or click No and return to step 4 to select another refresh rate.

If the screen becomes completely unreadable, just wait for a few seconds. The display settings will revert to their previous values so you can again use your monitor.

7. Click OK to close the Display Properties dialog box.

Fixing a distorted display

If you're still having display problems of any type after you verify the driver and refresh rate, try adjusting the hardware acceleration, which disables features of the display adapter that could be causing the problem you see. To do so, follow these steps:

1. Right-click the desktop, and click Properties on the shortcut menu.

2. On the Settings tab in the Display Properties dialog box, click Advanced.

3. On the Troubleshoot tab in the Properties dialog box, drag the Hardware Acceleration slider one notch to the left, and click OK. ▶

4. Click OK in the Display Properties dialog box.

5. Click Yes if you are asked whether you want to restart your computer.

Now use the computer as you normally do and see whether the problem goes away. If it doesn't, drag the slider another notch to the left and try again. If you can fix the problem only by dragging the slider all the way to None, consider replacing your video card with a newer model.

What's flicker?

The image on your screen is updated many times each second. The speed of those updates is called the *refresh rate*. When the refresh rate is high enough, the updates occur faster than the eye can see. But if the refresh rate is too low, your eye detects the updates as *flicker*. To remove flicker, you need to make sure the correct driver is installed for your monitor, and to increase the refresh rate until your flicker is gone.

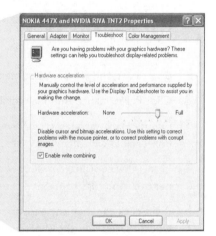

My monitor type is incorrect so I can't choose the proper display settings

Source of the problem

Windows XP can detect the make and model of most popular monitors, but if your monitor is a bit older or a bit unusual, Windows might not know about your display (it might not have the correct driver for your monitor). In this case, Windows will fall back to the generic choices of either Default Monitor or Plug And Play Monitor.

The problem with the Default Monitor and Plug And Play Monitor drivers is that they don't contain any knowledge of the display settings that your own monitor can actually support. The proper driver for your monitor contains a list of the refresh rates that the monitor can use and can display only those rates in the Screen Refresh Rate list.

Here's how to help Windows when it can't figure out on its own which monitor you're using.

How to fix it

1. Click Start, and on the Start menu, click Control Panel.

2. Click Performance And Maintenance, and click System.

3. On the Hardware tab of the System Properties dialog box, click Device Manager. ▶

4. In the Device Manager window, click the small plus sign next to Monitors to expand the Monitors list.

5. Right-click the monitor shown in the list, and click Update Driver on the shortcut menu.

6. On the first page of the Hardware Update Wizard, click Install From A List Or Specfic Location, and click Next.

7. On the next page of the Hardware Update Wizard, click Don't Search. I Will Choose The Driver To Install and click Next.

8. In the list of Models, click your monitor model. If your model is not listed, clear the Show Compatible Hardware check box, and click the monitor manufacturer in the Manufacturer list and the monitor model in the Model list. ▶

9. Click Next.

10. When the Hardware Update Wizard reports that it's finished installing the software for your monitor, click Finish.

11. Close the Device Manager window, close the System Properties dialog box, and close the Performance And Maintenance window.

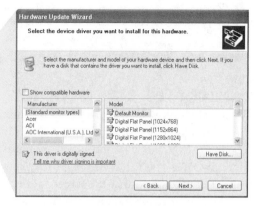

You can now verify that the correct monitor is selected by right-clicking the desktop, clicking Properties on the shortcut menu, and checking to see which monitor is listed as the Display on the Settings tab of the Display Properties dialog box. Click OK to close the Display Properties dialog box.

I've downloaded the Windows XP driver for my monitor or have it on disk

If you obtained the driver for your monitor by downloading it from the manufacturer's Web site, or if your monitor came with a disk containing a Windows XP driver, follow the procedure above, but at step 7, leave Search For The Best Driver In These Locations selected, and follow these steps:

1. Select the Include This Location In The Search check box if you downloaded the driver. ▶

2. Click Browse to find and open the folder that contains the driver.

3. When the Hardware Update Wizard finds the driver for your monitor, continue with step 9 in the procedure above.

My screen shuts off too quickly

Source of the problem

Whether you're working on a desktop computer or a laptop, power management in Windows can help lower your electricity bill or save your computer's batteries. After a period of inactivity, which can range from a few minutes to a few hours, power management can turn off the screen, which not only saves power but also helps keep a warm computer room from getting still warmer.

But if you find that the screen is shutting down prematurely, while you're just taking short breaks or making phone calls, you can instruct power management to wait longer before activating itself, or you can simply turn off power management until you're ready to use it again. Here's how to change the power management settings in Windows.

How to fix it

1. Right-click the desktop, and click Properties on the shortcut menu.

2. On the Screen Saver tab in the Display Properties dialog box, click Power in the Monitor Power area.

3. On the Power Schemes tab in the Power Options Properties dialog box, click the Turn Off Monitor down arrow, and click a longer interval in the list. ▶

   To disable the power management of your screen so that the screen always stays on, click Never in the list.

4. Click OK, and click OK again to close the Display Properties dialog box.

By making this change, you've modified the power scheme that's currently in effect, as shown in the Power Schemes section of the dialog box. In the Power Schemes list, you can choose other power schemes to enable different sets of options.

The screen saver appears too soon

Source of the problem

If you have a screen saver enabled, the screen saver will appear whenever Windows detects that you haven't moved the mouse or touched the keyboard for a certain length of time. If the screen saver appears too frequently, this interval is simply too short for your liking. You can easily lengthen it by following these steps.

How to fix it

1. Right-click the desktop, and click Properties on the shortcut menu.

2. On the Screen Saver tab in the Display Properties dialog box, click the up arrow in the Wait box to increase the number of minutes that will elapse before the screen saver is activated. ▶

   If you find that the little arrow in the Wait box is difficult to click, press Tab repeatedly or click in the box until the current number in the box is highlighted, and then type a different number.

3. Click OK.

I don't know how to get multiple monitors working

Source of the problem

When you use two video cards in one computer attached to two monitors placed side by side, you can increase your work area by extending the Windows desktop across the two monitors. You can actually double the amount of screen space you have to work with, and open different program windows on each screen. But to make multiple monitors work, you must have the right display adapters installed in your computer in the correct way. You also need to make Windows aware of how the monitors are physically arranged. Using multiple monitors is not difficult, though, and it can be a huge enhancement to the way you work. To install multiple monitors, follow these steps.

How to fix it

1. Obtain a second display adapter and monitor.

    The second display adapter must support multiple monitors.

2. Turn off the computer, and install the second display adapter and monitor.

    If you have two PCI cards (most display adapter cards plug into either PCI or AGP slot in the computer, as listed on their packaging or in their documentation), the computer will choose one to be the primary adapter. You probably want this to be the better of the two adapters, because its image will be on your primary monitor. If you'd rather use the other PCI card as the primary adapter, turn off the computer and switch the order of the cards in the slots. If you have one PCI card and one AGP card, the PCI card will be the primary adapter, unless the setup program for your computer's BIOS allows you to choose the primary adapter.

3. Start Microsoft Windows and, when you are prompted, install the driver for the display adapter. Click Yes if you are asked whether you want to re-start the computer.

4. Right-click the desktop, and click Properties on the shortcut menu.

5. Click the Settings tab in the Display Properties dialog box. ▶

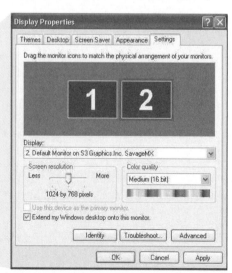

6. On the Settings tab in the Display Properties dialog box, click the Display down arrow and click the secondary display adapter in the list.

7. Select the Extend My Windows Desktop Onto This Monitor check box.

8. Click OK to close the Compatibility Warning message.

9. Right-click one of the monitor icons shown on the Settings tab.

10. Click Identify on the shortcut menu to determine which physical monitor corresponds to the monitor labeled 1.

11. Drag the icons of the two monitors to reposition them so that they match the physical arrangement of the two monitors in your work area.

12. Click OK.

Programs don't open on the secondary monitor

When you start Windows, the logon dialog box always appears on the primary monitor. The programs you start always open in windows on the primary monitor also. After a window opens on the primary monitor, you can always drag it to the secondary monitor.

To work on the secondary monitor, move the mouse pointer all the way across the desktop toward the secondary monitor, and continue dragging beyond the edge of the desktop until the pointer appears on the secondary monitor. To return to the primary monitor, drag the mouse pointer back.

To move a window from one monitor to the other, simply drag it there by dragging it off the edge of the first monitor's screen toward the other monitor.

> **Tip**
>
> You can't drag a window from one monitor to another if the window is maximized. You must restore the window first by clicking the Restore button (next to the Close button).

Using Dualview on a laptop

A new feature in Windows XP allows you to connect a monitor to the video output port on your connector and use both the laptop's screen and the external monitor to extend your desktop space.

> **Tip**
>
> You can't use Dualview if you have Adobe Type Manager installed. The two programs are incompatible.

When you plug in an external monitor, Windows gives you the same options you get when you have dual monitors connected to dual video cards in a desktop. If you do not see these options on the Settings tab, make sure you have the most updated video drivers installed in your laptop.

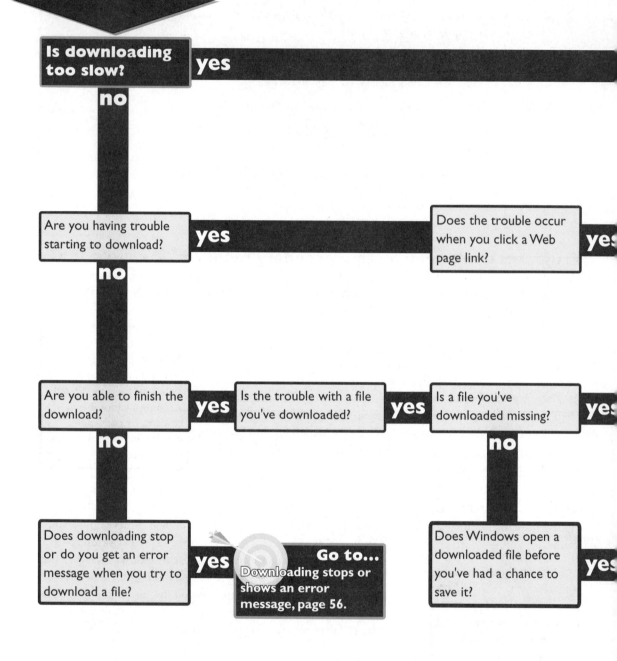

Is downloading too slow? — yes

no

Are you having trouble starting to download? — yes

Does the trouble occur when you click a Web page link? — yes

no

Are you able to finish the download? — yes

Is the trouble with a file you've downloaded? — yes

Is a file you've downloaded missing? — yes

no

no

Does downloading stop or do you get an error message when you try to download a file? — yes

Go to...
Downloading stops or shows an error message, page 56.

Does Windows open a downloaded file before you've had a chance to save it? — yes

Downloading files

Quick fix

Downloading is very slow The same problems that cause Web pages to be displayed slowly on your screen affect the transfer rate of files you download. For information about getting the best possible transfer rate, see "Web browsing Is slow," on page 220.

Go to...

I can't start downloading a file by clicking a Web page link, page 57.

Go to...

I can't find the files I've downloaded, page 52.

Go to...

Windows opens downloaded files before I can choose to save them, page 54.

If your solution isn't here, check these related chapters:

- E-mail, page 58
- Files, page 72
- Folders, page 82
- Internet Explorer, page 138

Or see the general troubleshooting tips on page xv.

I can't find the files I've downloaded

Source of the problem

When you click a link on a Web page to download a file, Windows opens a File Download dialog box that asks whether you want to open the file or save it. If you save it, you'll have it on your hard disk for use later. Clicking Save leads you to another dialog box, which asks for the destination and name of the saved file. Unless you specify a different folder, Windows uses the same folder you downloaded to last time. The hot new music file you download, for example, might end up in the folder where you downloaded an updated driver for your video card. Unless you keep track of where your files are going, they'll be as good as lost.

To avoid losing track of downloaded files on your hard disk, follow this rule: After you click a Web link to download a file and then click Save in the File Download dialog box, be sure to carefully choose a destination folder for the file in the Save As dialog box. If the file is already lost somewhere on your hard disk, here are a few ways to find it and move it where you want it.

How to fix it

1. Click the same Web page link again, or if you've closed the Web page, click any link on a Web page that will start a file download.

2. In the File Download dialog box, click Save, and click OK.

3. In the Save As dialog box, click the Save In down arrow and check to see which folder is open. The file you've downloaded is most likely in that folder. ▶

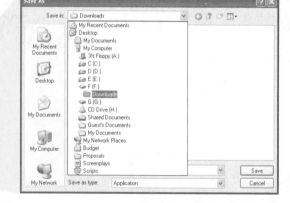

4. Click Cancel to avoid downloading the file again.

5. In My Computer, browse to and open the folder you located in the Save As dialog box.

6. Open the destination folder in another My Computer window, and drag the downloaded file to the destination folder.

Downloading files

Using Find to locate a file you've downloaded

Another way to find a downloaded file that's hiding in an unknown folder on your hard disk is to use the Search command in Windows. Ordinarily, you search for files by name, but you can also use Search to look for files by date. In this example, you'll be looking for today's files—that is, the files you added to your hard disk today.

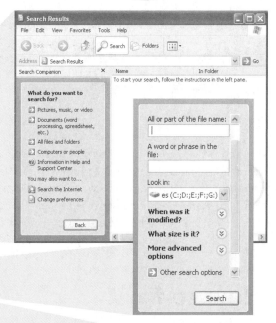

To search for today's files, follow these steps:

1. Click Start, click Search, and in the Search Companion pane, click All Files And Folders. ▶

2. Click the double-arrow button next to When Was It Modified? ▶

3. Click Specify Dates, and click Search. ▶
   Today's date is used by default.

4. In a My Computer window, open the folder in which you want to put the file, and then drag the file you want from the search results list to the destination folder.
   If you downloaded the file yesterday or a few days earlier in the week, you can change the range of search dates.

Creating a download folder

To avoid losing the files you download, create a special folder for downloaded files on your hard disk. You can create it on your desktop so it'll always be easily available. Name it anything you like.

If you always download files to this folder, you'll know where to find the files after the download is complete, and you can then drag the files you've downloaded from the download folder to their final destination in another folder on your hard disk.

Windows opens downloaded files before I can choose to save them

Source of the problem

If Windows no longer displays the File Download dialog box to ask whether you want to open or save a downloaded file, you must have cleared the Always Ask Before Opening This Type Of File check box the last time you downloaded a file of the same type (such as .zip). If you choose not to be asked, Windows remembers the previous setting and uses it to determine whether to display the File Download dialog box when you download a file. For each file type you can download, you can change whether Windows will display the File Download dialog box or skip right over it.

How to fix it

1. Click Start, and click My Computer on the Start menu.

2. On the Tools menu, click Folder Options.

3. On the File Types tab of the Folder Options dialog box, click the file type that no longer causes the File Download dialog box to appear, and click Advanced.

4. In the Edit File Type dialog box, select the Confirm Open After Download check box, and click OK. ▶

5. Click Close to close the Folder Options dialog box, and then close the My Computer window.

Organizing downloaded files

The whole point of saving the files you download rather than immediately opening them is to have them handy so that you don't have to download them all over again. Sometimes you need to reinstall programs, for example, or run their setup programs again to change options. But what's the point of saving downloaded files in folders if you can't find them or even tell what they are from their cryptic file names?

Downloading files

To organize downloaded files, create a *Downloaded files* folder and save files in it. To further organize your files, you can also create subfolders within the download folder for different programs and save downloaded files in these folders. To do so, follow these steps:

1. In the File Download dialog box, click Save, and click OK.

2. In the Save As dialog box, browse to the disk where you want to create a download folder, and click the Create New Folder button.

3. Type a name for the folder and press Enter.

4. To create a subfolder within the download folder, open the download folder in the Save As dialog box, and click the Create New Folder button. ▶

5. Type a name for the folder, press Enter, and then be sure to open the new folder you've created before clicking Save in the Save As dialog box.

Create New Folder button ⌐

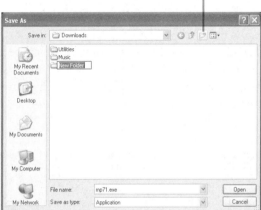

You can also change the file name in the Save As dialog box to something that'll be easier to understand. Here's a good rule of thumb: use a name for the file that will make sense when you look in the folder again a year from now. If you're downloading a software upgrade, for example, don't be afraid to use a long and descriptive name for its file name, such as *Upgrade to Version 2*. ▶

Don't worry: changing the name of an .exe or a .zip file won't prevent the program from working. But be careful not to change the file extension (.exe or .zip, for example). Changing the extension can keep a program from working.

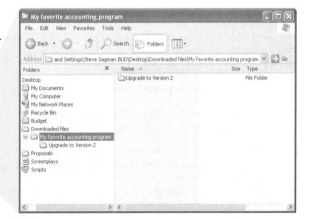

Downloading stops or shows an error message

Source of the problem

Any number of problems might cause downloading to just stop or to display an error message and then give up. But the most common causes are a busy server at the other end of the connection, a technical problem at your Internet service provider (ISP), an ISP that's overburdened with users, an Internet slowdown, or even a glitch in your phone line. The following steps will solve the problem, regardless of the cause.

How to fix it

- Try a different server. Many sites list several servers from which you can download a file. If one server won't work, try the next.

- If changing servers doesn't work, try a different file download site. In many instances, you'll find the same file at other download sites on the Web. Popular file download sites such as *www.cdrom.com*, *www.tucows.com*, and *www.download.com* often offer the same files.

- Another option is to try one of the site's *mirrors* or *affiliates*. These are sites that duplicate the primary file download site at other geographical locations. Mirrors or affiliates are often listed by location so that you can pick the closest site. But if the closest site doesn't work, try the next closest.

- You might want to try the download at a later time. Sometimes it's just a losing battle—too many people are vying for the same capacity at your ISP, on the Internet, or at the server. A few hours later, you might have no problem.

- Download a shareware FTP program for downloading files from the Internet, and then look on the Web site for information about using FTP transfers to obtain files. FTP is helpful because it lets you resume a transfer from the point at which the initial transfer failed.

- Disconnect from the Internet, reconnect, and then try the download again. You might establish a better connection the second time.

> **Tip**
> After you've been downloading for a while, you'll get an idea of your average download speed, which shows up in the download progress dialog box as the Transfer Rate. If you see an unusually slow transfer rate for a download you've started, don't hesitate to cancel the download and try again at a different file download site or server. Some sites have faster connections than others or fewer people trying to download from them.

Downloading files

I can't start downloading a file by clicking a Web page link

Source of the problem

Web pages that offer files you can download usually have a *Click here to download* link or a Download button you can click. But depending on how the Web site is designed and which Web browser version you use, you might not be able to download a file just by clicking the link to the file, even when the link is clearly labeled. Fortunately, there's an alternative method you can use to start the download, and it's described here.

How to fix it

1. Right-click the download link on the Web page.

2. On the shortcut menu, click Save Target As. ▶

3. In the Save As dialog box, click the Save In down arrow if you want to change the folder the file will be downloaded to, and click a folder in the list. ▶

4. If you want, replace the existing file name in the File Name box with a file name that you'll remember more easily.

5. Click Save.

Pulling other items off Web pages

Just as you can right-click and choose Save Target As to pull a file from a Web site, you can also right-click pictures on Web pages to download copies to your hard disk. To download a picture, right-click the picture, and click Save Picture As on the shortcut menu. In the Save Picture dialog box, choose a destination folder for the picture, and click Save. A copy of the picture will be saved in that folder. Remember, most pictures are copyrighted, so don't reuse them on your own Web site.

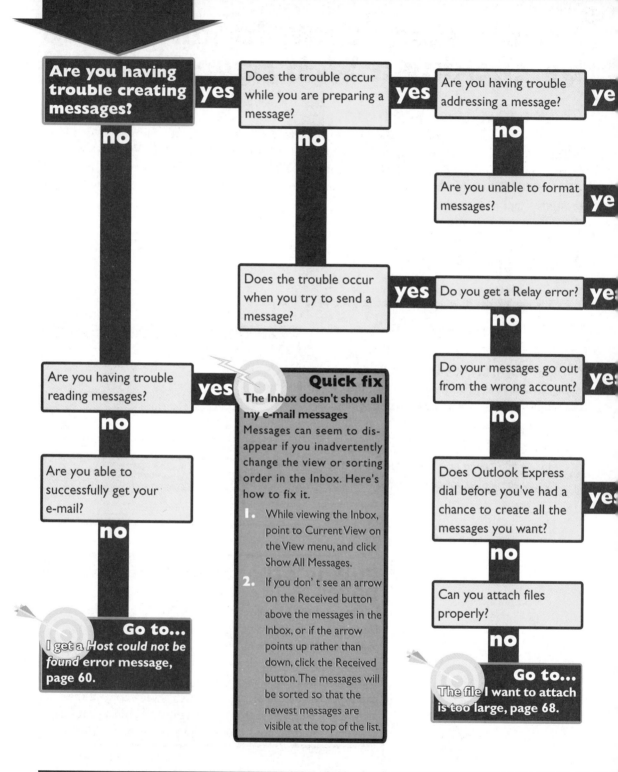

Are you having trouble creating messages? → **yes** → Does the trouble occur while you are preparing a message? → **yes** → Are you having trouble addressing a message? → **ye**

↓ no

Does the trouble occur while you are preparing a message? → no ↓

Are you having trouble addressing a message? → no ↓

Are you unable to format messages? → **ye**

Does the trouble occur when you try to send a message? → **yes** → Do you get a Relay error? → **ye**

↓ no

Do your messages go out from the wrong account? → **ye**

↓ no

Are you having trouble reading messages? → **yes** →

↓ no

Does Outlook Express dial before you've had a chance to create all the messages you want? → **ye**

↓ no

Are you able to successfully get your e-mail?

↓ no

Can you attach files properly?

↓ no

Go to...
I get a *Host could not be found* error message, page 60.

Quick fix
The Inbox doesn't show all my e-mail messages
Messages can seem to disappear if you inadvertently change the view or sorting order in the Inbox. Here's how to fix it.

1. While viewing the Inbox, point to Current View on the View menu, and click Show All Messages.

2. If you don' t see an arrow on the Received button above the messages in the Inbox, or if the arrow points up rather than down, click the Received button. The messages will be sorted so that the newest messages are visible at the top of the list.

Go to...
The file I want to attach is too large, page 68.

Is your message coming back as undeliverable?

yes

Go to...
My message is undeliverable, page 62.

Go to...
I can't format the text in messages, page 66.

Quick fix

I get a Relay error from my ISP when I try to send a message If you dial in through a different ISP, while traveling for example, but still try to use your own ISP's outgoing mail server, you might get a Relay error. To prevent unauthorized users from sending junk mail through their mail servers, most ISPs require that you have an account to send mail.

If you need to send mail through another ISP, set up a separate Outlook Express mail account with the other ISP's outgoing mail server, but change the Reply address on that account to your primary e-mail address so that responses go to your home e-mail address.

Go to...
My messages go out from the wrong account, page 64.

Does Outlook Express dial whenever it starts?

yes

Go to...
Outlook Express automatically dials my ISP when I don't want it to, page 70.

no

Go to...
Outlook Express won't wait and send my messages all at once, page 69.

If your solution isn't here, check these related chapters:

- Connections, page 2
- Internet connections, page 126
- Programs, page 234

Or see the general troubleshooting tips on page xv.

I get a *Host could not be found* error message

Source of the problem

The *host* is the e-mail server at your Internet service provider (ISP) that keeps all your e-mail until you retrieve it. If the host can't be found when you try to get e-mail, your connection isn't working, the name of the e-mail server is incorrect in your mail account settings, or the e-mail server might have a technical problem and so is not currently available.

How to fix it

1. On the Start menu, click Internet to start Internet Explorer and see whether your home page opens. If it doesn't, the problem is your Internet connection. See "I frequently lose my connection to the Internet," on page 134.

2. If you confirmed that your Internet connection is working in step 1, start Outlook Express, and on the Tools menu, click Accounts.

3. On the Mail tab of the Internet Accounts dialog box, click the mail account through which you are unable to get e-mail and click Properties.

4. In the Properties dialog box for the mail account, click the Servers tab, and examine the name in the Incoming Mail (POP3) box. The name you see should exactly match the name of the e-mail server given to you by your ISP. If it doesn't, delete the incorrect name, type the correct name, and click OK. ▶

5. Click Close to close the Internet Accounts dialog box.
     If the e-mail server name in the account Properties dialog box is correct, the e-mail server is probably unavailable at the moment. Either wait and try to get your e-mail later or contact your ISP to determine when the e-mail server will be working again.

> ### Tip
> If you're unable to receive an attachment, the attachment may be larger than the size allowed by your ISP or online service. Or the attachment might have been blocked by your corporate e-mail system as a protective measure against viruses, which often arrive hidden within attachments.

Getting your e-mail even when your ISP's mail server is down

When having constant access to your e-mail messages is critical, you might be able to forward copies of your incoming e-mail messages to another mail account, such as a free Hotmail account. ▶

    If your ISP's e-mail server is temporarily unavailable, you can check the account to which you've forwarded mail. You'll find e-mail messages that your server forwarded before it went temporarily kaput. You'll have to get the rest after the server is fixed.

    ISPs that offer e-mail forwarding as an option usually let you change preferences or options to turn on forwarding and to enter the e-mail address to which you'd like copies of all your e-mail messages sent. Forwarding e-mail messages to a Web-based e-mail service such as Hotmail or Yahoo! Mail also enables you to read your incoming e-mail from any computer that has an Internet connection. When you travel, you can read your e-mail messages at many hotel business service offices, at Web browsing terminals at airports, and at cyber cafés.

What's POP and SMTP?

E-mail is managed by a computer at your ISP called a *server*. Servers that deliver e-mail messages to you are called *Post Office Protocol (POP) servers*. Outgoing mail servers are called *Simple Mail Transfer Protocol (SMTP) servers*. Each server has a name that you need to enter on the Servers tab of your mail account's Properties dialog box. Depending on your ISP, you might use the same name for both servers, or the POP server might have a different name from the SMTP server. For example, the incoming mail server at MSN is named *pop3.email.msn.com*, whereas the outgoing server is named *smtp.email.msn.com*.

My message is undeliverable

Source of the problem

When the outoing mail server at your ISP can't deliver an e-mail message you've sent or the incoming mail server at the destination can't find the addressee, one server or the other will send a notice to your Inbox letting you know that your message is undeliverable so that you won't wait in vain for a response.

Most e-mail that doesn't arrive at its destination is simply misaddressed. A single typo in the address is all it takes to make a message undeliverable. If the outgoing mail server at your own Internet service provider can't find the domain you've put in the e-mail address (the domain is the part after the @ symbol, with an ending such as .com, .net, or .org), it won't be able to properly route the message to the addressee. If, on the other hand, the incoming mail server at the recipient's Internet service provider can't find the addressee you've entered (the name to the left of the @ symbol), it can't deliver the message properly. Either way, the message won't make it to the recipient, and you'll get an Inbox message telling you so. Here's how to fix the problem.

How to fix it

1. Start Outlook Express, and click Addresses on the toolbar.

2. On the toolbar in the Address Book window, click Find People.

3. In the Find People dialog box, click the Look In down arrow, and click one of the directory services in the list. ▶

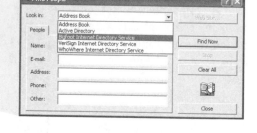

4. In the Name box, type the name of the person you're addressing an e-mail message to, and click Find Now.

5. If the directory service doesn't find the e-mail address you want, click a different directory service in the Look In list, and click Find Now again.

What are directory services?

Directory services are online databases that you can search to find someone's e-mail address, phone number, and other information that's public. The Address Book in Outlook Express is set up to connect to and search several directory services, including Bigfoot, VeriSign, and WhoWhere. ▶

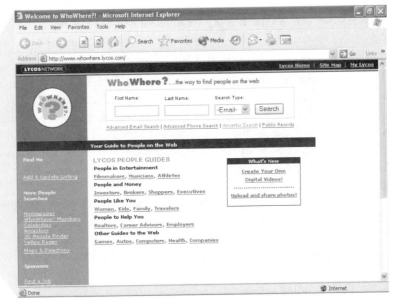

Directory services vary in the breadth of the information they collect and maintain, and they also vary in their conscientiousness about removing obsolete e-mail addresses, so you might need to try a few services to find the most current e-mail address. Directory services are usually unable to give you the e-mail addresses of individuals who reach the Internet through America Online, MSN, EarthLink, AT&T Worldnet, and other large, national ISPs. To protect the privacy of their members, many of these organizations don't release e-mail addresses.

If you work for a large organization, you might have access to the Active Directory, another option in the Look In list, which is a directory service that lists everyone in your organization. Your system administrator can tell you how to use this directory service.

Looking up e-mail addresses on line

You can also find or verify someone's e-mail address at one of the Web sites that let you search online address books. Sites such as *www.switchboard.com* and *www.infospace.com* have e-mail searches you can use in addition to their standard searches for phone numbers and regular postal addresses. Several Internet portals and search engines—for example, Yahoo!—also provide e-mail address searching.

When the problem is the attachment

If you receive a return message from a mail server complaining about the size of an attachment you've sent, you might need to remove the attachment, reduce its size, or take other measures to get a file to someone else on the Internet. For information about attachments, see "The file I want to attach is too large," on page 68.

My messages go out from the wrong account

Source of the problem

These days everyone who's anyone has an e-mail address. What's more, plenty of people have several e-mail accounts: a primary account from an ISP, a corporate account used at their office or place of business, and perhaps a free e-mail account from a Web service like Hotmail. Having a free account is great for checking your messages from airports, hotels, and Web browsers when you travel. If you want, services like Hotmail can even gather e-mail from all your other accounts so you don't have to check multiple mailboxes when you're calling from an expensive hotel room phone line.

But multiple mailboxes can be hard to track, and even though you can set up Outlook Express to retrieve mail from each and every e-mail address you have (even your Hotmail address), you run the risk and potential embarrassment of sending out a message from the wrong account. For example, you might send a message from your personal, home-based business e-mail address when you intended to use your corporate address. Here's how to make sure your e-mail goes out from the account you want.

How to fix it

1. In Outlook Express, click Create Mail on the toolbar.

2. In the New Message window, click the From down arrow.

3. In the From list, click the mail account you want to use. ▶

4. Create the new mail message, including entering the recipient's address, the subject, and the message text.

5. When you've completed your new mail message, click Send. When you click Send/Recv, Outlook Express will connect to your mail servers one by one and send the correct message through the correct server.

What if I don't specify a mail account?

One of the mail accounts you've set up in Outlook Express is the *default account*. Outlook Express sends your message through this account unless you specify a different account before you click Send. To determine which account is the default, follow these steps:

1. On the Tools menu in Outlook Express, click Accounts.

2. Click the Mail tab in the Internet Accounts dialog box.

    The default account shows *(default)* next to the account type. ▶

    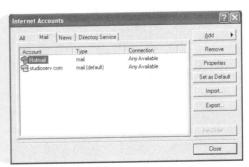

    To change the default, click a different account, and click the Set As Default button.

Changing the reply address

If you'd like to maintain the appearance that messages are coming from your desk rather than from your hotel in Aruba, follow these steps:

1. On the Tools menu in Outlook Express, click Accounts.

2. Click the Mail tab in the Internet Accounts dialog box.

3. Select the mail account whose reply address you want to change, and click Properties.

4. On the General tab in the Properties dialog box, type your business e-mail address in both the E-Mail Address box and the Reply Address box. ▶

5. Repeat steps 3 and 4 for any other account whose reply address you want to change.

6. Click OK to close the Properties dialog box, and click Close to close the Internet Accounts dialog box.

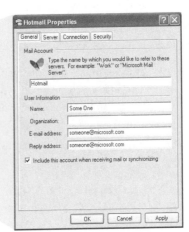

No matter which account you use to send e-mail, even if it's one of the free e-mail accounts provided on the Web, the recipient of the message will see the return address you've entered. Be aware, though, that anyone determined to pinpoint the source of an e-mail message can examine the message header, which usually reveals the origination point of the message, even after you've changed the reply address.

I can't format the text in messages

Source of the problem

You might have received messages that use large text and colorful fonts, but you can't create your own unless you switch the format of the message to Hypertext Markup Language (HTML). HTML is the language of the Web, and it's what enables Web pages to show formatted text and pictures in a designed layout. Outlook Express can interpret and produce the HTML in a message that gives the text its styling, size, color, bullet points, indents, centering, and other formatting attributes.

When you use HTML format to create a message instead of using plain text, the formatting toolbar appears in the New Message window. To apply formatting, you select the text you want to modify and click the buttons on the toolbar. Here are the steps for using HTML in a message.

How to fix it

1. On the Outlook Express toolbar, click the Create Mail button.

2. In the New Message window, on the Format menu, click Rich Text (HTML).

3. Type the message. To format the text, select the word or words you want to change, and click a button on the formatting toolbar. ▶

4. Click Send to send the message.

The recipient doesn't see my formatting

All the latest e-mail programs can interpret the HTML coding in messages and display your message with all the formatting you've applied, but some older e-mail programs don't understand HTML, so they show the coding itself rather than use it to format the text. The first time someone with such a mail program gets an HTML message from you, they'll write to complain about all the computerese in your message. In the future, you can turn off HTML and return to plain text for these people by clicking Plain Text on the Format menu in the New Message window.

When you know someone will have a problem with HTML messages, you might as well go one step further and change that recipient's entry in the Address Book so that Outlook Express will always use plain text for that person. To do so, follow these steps:

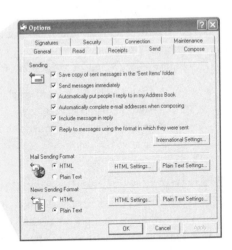

1. Click Addresses on the Outlook Express toolbar.

2. In the Address Book window, click the person's name in the list of addresses, and click Properties.

3. On the Name tab of the Properties dialog box, select the Send E-Mail Using Plain Text Only check box. ▶

4. Click OK, and then close the Address Book window.

People who have mail programs that are more current but still incapable of understanding HTML will see the message you've written in plain text accompanied by an attachment in the message that contains the HTML version. To see the attachment, they can double-click it to open it in their browser.

Switching to HTML for the long haul

If you don't see the formatting toolbar when you create a new message, HTML is not the default mail sending format. To set HTML as the default, on the Tools menu, click Options. On the Send tab in the Options dialog box, click HTML in the Mail Sending Format section. ▶

Decorating the background

In addition to formatting text, HTML can change the background color of a message and display a background picture. Be sparing when you include pictures, because pictures make messages larger and therefore more time-consuming to send and receive.

To change the background color in a message or add a picture, follow these steps:

1. Click Create Mail on the toolbar.

2. On the Format menu, point to Background, and either choose a color from the Color submenu or click Picture and then choose a picture file from a folder on your hard disk.

If you're sure that the recipient will really appreciate your originality, you can also include a sound file by clicking Sound on the submenu.

The file I want to attach is too large

Source of the problem

Even though your friends and family might welcome every one of your digitized pictures, songs, and video files, their ISPs might not be too happy when your messages arrive with huge attachments. Some ISPs limit the size of attachments they will handle to reduce the load on their mail servers. They'll bounce a message back to you when the size of an attachment exceeds their restrictions. To get around this problem, you have several options.

How to fix it

Tip

You can quickly add someone's e-mail address to the Address Book by opening a message that person has sent, right-clicking the name in the From line, and then clicking Add To Address Book on the shortcut menu.

- Attach only one file per message. Some ISPs have trouble with multiple attachments in messages anyway.

- Use a file compression program such as WinZip to compress a file before attaching it. With WinZip, you can also copy multiple files into a single .zip file, so you'll have only one file to send.

- No matter what file type your digital camera or scanner produces, send picture files as .jpg images, which are compressed, so they're a fraction of the size of other types of picture files.

- Use an image editing program to shrink the dimensions of pictures to reduce their file size. Most image editing programs have a Resize command, which reduces pictures to preset, smaller sizes. Your pictures will fit most people's screens best if they are 640 by 480 pixels or 800 by 600 pixels in size.

Sharing files in online communities

MSN (*communities.msn.com/home*) and other ISPs, such as Yahoo! (*photos.yahoo.com*), allow you to set up communities and photo albums where you can place files and photos that you want to share with others. You create photo albums, upload your photos into the albums, and then invite others to view the albums. You can create public communities or private, password-protected communities, which will only allow those you've invited.

Outlook Express won't wait and send my messages all at once

Source of the problem

If you've set the Outlook Express option to send messages immediately, Outlook Express jumps into action and dispatches each message as soon as you finish it, dialing your Dial-Up Networking connection if necessary. But if you plan to write more messages, you should have Outlook Express wait until you've composed all the messages you want to send.

You won't experience this problem if you're already connected to the Internet or you've got a full-time Internet connection such as a cable modem or a Digital Subscriber Line (DSL). Outlook Express dispatches the messages quietly and efficiently in the background.

Here's how to make Outlook Express wait until you're ready to send all the messages you've written.

> **Tip**
>
> If you find that the messages you sent don't appear in the Sent Items folder, click Options on the Tools menu of Outlook Express, click the Send tab in the Options dialog box, and select the Save Copy Of Sent Messages In The 'Sent Items' Folder check box.

How to fix it

1. In Outlook Express, click Options on the Tools menu.

2. On the Send tab of the Options dialog box, clear the Send Messages Immediately check box. ▶

3. Click OK to close the dialog box.

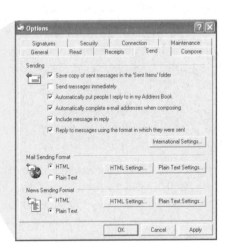

Sending a message later

If you've selected the Send Messages Immediately option, you can override it by clicking Send Later on the File menu of the New Message dialog box. The message goes to the Outbox, but it won't be sent until you specifically click Send/Recv.

Outlook Express automatically dials my ISP when I don't want it to

Source of the problem

Even if you have an unlimited use plan with your ISP, you still want to be judicious about connecting with your modem. Each call costs something, even if it's only the few cents you have to pay your local phone company. But if you have the connection set up wrong, Outlook Express dials each time it starts and dials again whenever it checks for mail, which might be too often for your needs. You should regain control of your Internet connection, dialing when you want, not when Outlook Express sees fit.

How to fix it

1. On the Tools menu, click Options, and on the Connection tab in the Options dialog box, click Change to open the Internet Properties dialog box. ▶

   The settings in the Internet Properties dialog box are shared by both Internet Explorer and Outlook Express.

2. On the Connections tab of the Internet Properties dialog box, click Never Dial A Connection, and click OK.

3. On the General tab of the Options dialog box, clear the Check For New Messages Every x Minute(s) check box, and click OK. ▶

4. On the status bar at the bottom of the Outlook Express window, double-click Working Online to change to Working Offline mode so that Outlook Express won't try to connect while you're working on a message. Double-click Working Offline to return to Working Online mode when you're ready to connect to your ISP and check for new e-mail.

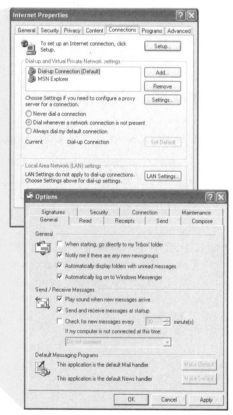

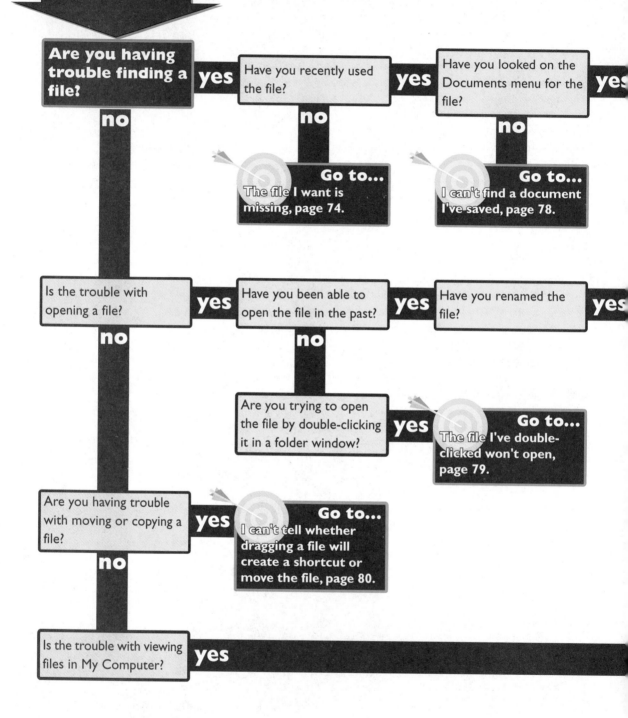

Are you having trouble finding a file?

yes → Have you recently used the file?

    yes → Have you looked on the Documents menu for the file?

        yes

    no

    Go to...
    The file I want is missing, page 74.

    Go to...
    I can't find a document I've saved, page 78.

no

Is the trouble with opening a file?

yes → Have you been able to open the file in the past?

    yes → Have you renamed the file?

        yes

    no

    Are you trying to open the file by double-clicking it in a folder window?

    yes

    Go to...
    The file I've double-clicked won't open, page 79.

no

Are you having trouble with moving or copying a file?

yes

    Go to...
    I can't tell whether dragging a file will create a shortcut or move the file, page 80.

no

Is the trouble with viewing files in My Computer?

yes

Go to...
The files for a project are scattered in different folders, page 76.

Quick fix

I can't open a file after I rename it If the Open With dialog box opens when you double-click a file you've renamed, you've inadvertently changed the file extension, which prevents Windows from telling which program to use to open the file. Here's how to restore the file and prevent the same problem in the future by hiding the file extensions so you can't easily change them.

1. Right-click the file, and click Rename on the shortcut menu.

2. Edit the file extension to restore the original, and press Enter.

3. Click View, and then click Folder Options.

4. On the View tab of the Folder Options dialog box, select the Hide File Extensions For Known File Types check box.

Quick fix

I can't see all the details about files in My Computer If text in columns is cut off in Details view in My Computer, select a file in the list and press Ctrl+plus sign (numeric keypad) to widen all the columns to best fit their contents.

If your solution isn't here, check these related chapters:

- The desktop, page 12
- Downloading files, page 50
- Folders, page 82
- Hard disks, page 102

Or see the general troubleshooting tips on page xv.

The file I want is missing

Source of the problem

It's easy to lose files in the layers of folders on your hard disk, unless you're meticulous to a fault about assigning a place to every file you save or you've hired an efficiency expert to come in and reorganize your folders and files. But if neither of these options is practical, rely on the Search command in Windows to dig up files that you'd given up for lost. This command scours your disks for folders or files by name. If you can't remember the exact name of an item, you can even enter a string of text to try to match within a file.

How to fix it

1. Click Start, and click Search.

2. In the Search Companion pane of the Search Results window, click the type of file or folder you're looking for, or click All Files And Folders to search through everything on your hard disk. ▶

3. In the Search Companion pane, enter the information requested by the Search Companion, such as a specific file type, file name, or the last time the file was modified. The more of a file name you enter the better.

   If you chose to search through all files and folders, you can click the Look In down arrow and click a specific hard disk letter or, if you have multiple hard disks, click Local Hard Drives.

4. Click Search.

5. In the search results list, double-click a file to open it, or drag the file to a program window to open it in the program, or drag the file to a folder in My Computer to put it somewhere you'll remember.

Digging deeper

When you can't remember the name of a file and the names you try with the Search command don't turn up anything, it's not time to give up, it's time to dig deeper.

In the Search Companion pane, click All Files And Folders, and then scroll down within the Search Companion pane to the advanced options, which let you limit your search to a particular time interval and a particular file type. For example, to look for a Microsoft Excel worksheet that you created last week, click When Was It Modified, and click Within The Last Week. Then click More Advanced Options, click the Type Of File down arrow, click Microsoft Excel Workspace in the list, and click Search.

Customizing the Search Companion

The Search Companion reintroduces the kind of animated assistants that you've come to love (or hate) in Microsoft Office. If you don't find them particularly helpful, you can dispense with them. You can also streamline searching if you'd rather enter search criteria all at one time rather than be prompted for them step by step. To remove the animated assistants, follow these steps:

1. Click Start, and click Search.

2. In the Search Companion pane of the Search Results window, click Change Preferences.

3. Click Without An Animated Screen Character to dispatch Rover, Courtney, Earl, or any other character you've selected. ▶

4. Click OK.

If you also want to streamline the Search Companion and perform advanced searches, follow these steps:

1. In the Search Companion pane, click Change Preferences again.

2. Click Change Files And Folders Search Behavior.

3. Click Advanced – Includes Options To Manually Enter Search Criteria. ▶

4. Click OK.

The Search Companion pane now includes boxes for file name and text within a file, along with a set of advanced options for searching for files or folders.

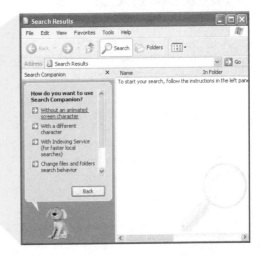

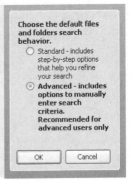

The files for a project are scattered in different folders

Source of the problem

Because programs of different types often save files in different folders, the files for a project you're working on might be scattered across your hard disk. For example, your marketing plan, budget, and project schedule, each created in a different program, might each reside in different folders.

One solution is to create a folder within My Documents for all the files for a project, and then carefully save all the project's files in the folder. But let's face it, few of us can always be that organized. So if you haven't been that scrupulous about filing away your work, here's a way to search through all the folders on your hard disk for files that contain specific project-related text.

How to fix it

1. Click Start, and click Search.

You can also click Search on the toolbar of any My Computer window.

2. In the Search Companion pane of the Search Results window, click All Files And Folders.

3. In the Search Companion pane, enter a word or phrase that relates to the project in the A Word Or Phrase In The File box. ▶

4. Click Search.

5. In the search results list, double-click the file you want to open.

You can also drag files from the search results list to a new folder you've created expressly to house project-related files. Just be sure to open the folder in My Computer and organize the Search Results and folder windows side by side.

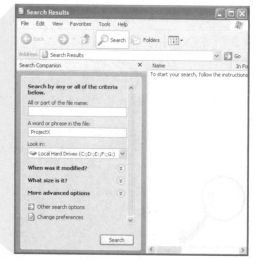

Indexing files for faster searches

By turning on Windows XP's built-in file indexing service, you can have Windows create an index (a catalog) of the files on your hard disk and their contents. The Search function can then search through the index to quickly find files rather than having to search through all the files on the hard disk. Windows builds and maintains its catalog continuously in the background, doing its hard work when the computer is idle.

Here's how to turn on the indexing service and adjust its parameters:

> **Searching for Microsoft Office files**
>
> If you use Microsoft Office, searching for text within files is faster if you use the File Open dialog box in any application. Open the File Open dialog box by clicking Find on the Tools menu. Microsoft Office provides its own file indexer, called Find Fast, which tracks the text in all your documents. When you use the File Open dialog box, Office searches its index of the text in documents, so it doesn't need to open and search each document.

1. Click Start, and click Search on the Start menu.

2. In the Search Results window, click Change Preferences in the Search Companion pane.

3. Click With Indexing Service. ▶

4. Click Yes, Enable Indexing Service.

5. Click OK.

To determine the folders whose documents are indexed, follow these steps:

1. Click Change Preferences in the Search Companion pane in the Search Results window.

2. Click Without Indexing Service in the Search Companion pane.

3. Click Change Indexing Service Settings in the Search Companion pane.

4. Double-click a catalog in the Indexing Service window, and double-click the Directories folder.

5. Double-click a folder and click either Yes or No in the Include In Index area of the Add Directory dialog box, and click OK.

6. Add new folders to index by pointing to New on the Action menu of the Indexing Service window, and then clicking Directory.

7. Specify the path to the folder, or click Browse to select the folder, and then click OK.

8. Close the Indexing Service window and the Search Results window.

I can't find a document I've saved

Source of the problem

Unless you're very conscientious about specifying a particular folder when you save a document, the file is saved in the default folder for the program you're using. Because many programs set up their own default folders, documents can become scattered around your hard disk in various default folders, and therefore hard to find.

To help you return to a document you've recently used, Windows tracks the documents you've opened most recently, listing them on the My Recent Documents submenu on the Start menu. Many applications also list, on their File menus, the last few documents you've used. But the first place to look for a missing document is the My Documents folder, which programs such as the Microsoft Office applications use as the default filing location for documents.

Here's the fastest way to find a document you've recently saved.

How to fix it

1. Click Start, and point to My Recent Documents.
2. On the My Recent Documents submenu, click the document you want to reopen. ▶

Looking on a program's File menu

You might find a list of recently used documents on the File menu in the program you used to create the file. Sometimes these files appear at the bottom of the File menu, and sometimes they're on a submenu named Recent or Recent Files.

Checking the My Documents folder

Many programs use the My Documents folder as their default storage folder for files. You can also set the My Documents folder as the default folder for saved files in all your programs. The My Documents folder is organized with subfolders named My Music, My Pictures, and My Videos, and you can create additional folders for other types of files.

The file I've double-clicked won't open

Source of the problem

Although you've gotten the hang of double-clicking files to start programs or open documents (or to do both simultaneously), you can't open every file on your hard disk by double-clicking it. Some files contain program components that you can't open, or they hold configuration settings. Other files are system files that are used by Windows. To help determine which files you can open and which you can't, follow the procedure below.

How to fix it

1. On the Start menu, click My Computer.

2. In the My Computer window, click Details on the View menu.

3. On the Tools menu, click Folder Options.

4. On the View tab of the Folder Options dialog box, click the Apply To All Folders button. ▶

5. Click Yes when you're asked whether you want to set all folders to match the current folder's view settings.

6. On the same tab of the Folder Options dialog box, in the Advanced Settings list, click Do Not Show Hidden Files And Folders.

7. In the same list, make sure Hide Protected Operating System Files is selected.

8. Double-click any folder in My Computer or Windows Explorer, and examine the description of the file in the Type column to find files described as *applications* or *documents*.

These are the files you can double-click to open.

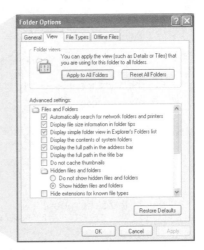

I can't tell whether dragging a file will create a shortcut or move the file

Source of the problem

Windows follows a set of rules to determine whether it will move or copy a file or folder you're dragging or whether it will create a shortcut instead. If you don't know the rules, you won't know what to expect, and if Murphy's Law holds true, whatever happens will probably be exactly the opposite of the outcome you anticipated. Here's a foolproof method for moving or copying files.

How to fix it

1. On the Start menu, click My Computer.

2. In the My Computer window, open the folder containing the file.

3. On the Start menu, click My Computer again, and open the folder to which you want to move or copy the file.

4. Point to the file or folder you want to move or copy, and then press and hold down the right mouse button.

5. Drag the file to the destination folder, and then release the mouse button.

6. On the shortcut menu, click Copy Here, Move Here, or Create Shortcuts Here. ▶

Knowing the rules

Using the right-click and drag technique described above is a surefire solution, but it requires an extra step—clicking an option on a shortcut menu. If every click matters to you, take a minute to memorize a few rules so that you'll know what to expect when you drag a file or folder by holding down the left mouse button.

- Dragging *moves* a file or folder to a folder on the *same* drive.

- Dragging *copies* a file or folder to a folder on a *different* drive.

- Dragging *creates a shortcut* when the file is an *application*.

Watching the signs

As you drag a file or folder, the mouse pointer changes appearance to show exactly what will happen when you release the mouse button. Keep an eye on the pointer to determine the result of a drag operation. ▶ Copy: ⊠ Move: ⊠ Shortcut: ⊠

When releasing the mouse button will cause the file to be copied, a small plus sign appears next to the pointer. If no plus sign appears, the file will be moved. If the file is an application and releasing the mouse button will create a shortcut, a shortcut arrow appears next to the pointer.

Forcing the issue

No matter what Windows thinks it should do when you drag a file or folder, you can override the rules by pressing either the Ctrl key or the Shift key as you drag:

- If dragging will *move* a file or folder, press Ctrl to force the file or folder to be copied.

- If dragging will *copy* a file or folder, press Shift to force the file or folder to be moved.

- If dragging will create a *shortcut* to an application, press Ctrl to copy the application file or press Shift to move the application file.

More about shortcuts

When you right-click and drag files between folders on your own computer and click Create Shortcuts Here on the shortcut menu, you create shortcuts that point to the files or folders you dragged. Shortcuts are helpful because you can have one copy of a file but point to it from several folders. For example, you can refer to a master schedule file for a project from within each of the project's folders. You don't accumulate multiple copies of the file, so you don't have to worry about discrepancies between the duplicates, and you can update the single file to which all the shortcuts point.

Using tasks to move or copy files

If your folder windows show tasks, you can also first select a file or folder, and click Move This File/Folder or Copy This File/Folder in the list of tasks and then select a destination for the file or folder.

If you don't see a tasks list in a folder, click Folder Options on the Tools menu in any folder window, and click Show Common Tasks In Folders on the General tab of the Folder Options dialog box, and then click OK.

Tip

The desktop is just another folder, so if you're dragging a file or folder to the desktop, all the rules given here apply. The desktop folder is usually on the same drive as the Windows files.

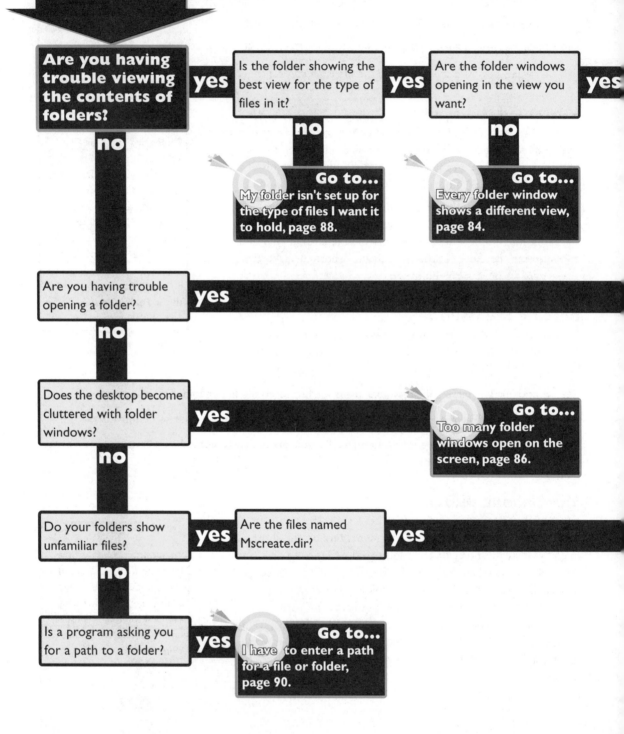

Are you having trouble viewing the contents of folders?

yes → Is the folder showing the best view for the type of files in it?

yes → Are the folder windows opening in the view you want?

yes →

no ↓ (from "Is the folder showing the best view...")

Go to...
My folder isn't set up for the type of files I want it to hold, page 88.

no ↓ (from "Are the folder windows opening...")

Go to...
Every folder window shows a different view, page 84.

no ↓

Are you having trouble opening a folder?

yes →

no ↓

Does the desktop become cluttered with folder windows?

yes →

Go to...
Too many folder windows open on the screen, page 86.

no ↓

Do your folders show unfamiliar files?

yes → Are the files named Mscreate.dir?

yes →

no ↓

Is a program asking you for a path to a folder?

yes →

Go to...
I have to enter a path for a file or folder, page 90.

Is information missing about the files in a folder? **yes**

Quick fix

Folders don't show all the information about my files If a folder doesn't show all the information you want to know about your files, such as their type and size, follow these steps:

1. Click Start, and click My Computer on the Start menu.

2. Open the folder containing the files.

3. On the View menu, click Details.

Quick fix

I can't open or modify a folder or its contents If you're unable to open a folder or make changes to the files in a folder, you might not have permission to do so. Permissions are controlled by the owner of the folder, usually the person whose computer contains the folder. On a network, a folder on someone else's computer might be accessible only to a select group of people, such as the members of a project team. Ask the folder owner to add you or your team to the list of people with access.

Quick fix

I have Mscreate.dir files in a lot of my folders In each folder it uses, a Microsoft program might place an Mscreate.dir file to indicate that the folder was created by the program's setup and that the folder can be deleted if the program is removed. These files are tiny and innocuous, so don't worry about them.

If your solution isn't here, check these related chapters:

- The desktop, page 12
- Files, page 72
- Hard disks, page 102
- Programs, page 234

Or see the general troubleshooting tips on page xv.

Every folder window shows a different view

Source of the problem

For every folder it displays, My Computer can remember the view you chose last—a great convenience if you always prefer to view a folder of program files as icons and to view a folder of picture files as thumbnails. But if you prefer the consistency in every folder rather than the excitement of giving each folder its own view, you can set all folders to be displayed in the same way. Although you can choose a different view of any folder at any time you want, here's how to maintain a uniform system with a familiar view of each folder.

How to fix it

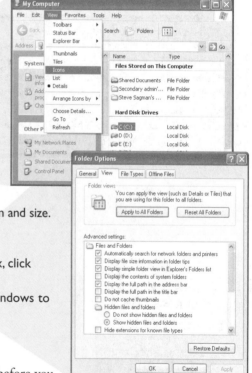

1. Click Start, and click My Computer on the Start menu.

2. Open any folder in My Computer.

3. On the View menu, click one of the views (Filmstrip, Thumbnails, Tiles, Icons, List, or Details). ▶

4. Set the position and size of the My Computer window by dragging its title bar and borders.
   Other windows will open at the same location and size.

5. On the Tools menu, click Folder Options.

6. On the View tab of the Folder Options dialog box, click Apply To All Folders, and click Yes. ▶
   Apply To All Folders sets all future folder windows to look like the current folder window.

There's more to do in Details view

In Details view, you can set a few additional defaults before you click Apply To All Folders. Drag the right edge of any heading button at the top of a column to widen or narrow the column. Click a heading button at the top of a column to sort the information according to the information in that column. For example, click the Size button to sort the listings by size from smallest to largest. Click the same button again to reverse the sort of the listings, from largest to smallest.

Resetting the View memory

If you'd like to return to the good old days when every folder had its own view, follow these steps:

1. On the Tools menu in the My Computer window, click Folder Options.

2. On the View tab of the Folder Options dialog box, click Reset All Folders and then click Yes to return the folders to the way they were displayed when you first installed Windows. ▶

3. In the Advanced Settings list on the same tab, select the Remember Each Folder's View Settings check box, and then click OK.

Advanced View settings you can save

In addition to the basic settings you can choose on the View menu or in the Details view window, you can store many more settings by selecting them in the Advanced Settings list on the View tab in the Folder Options dialog box. Here are some of the most commonly used.

● **Display The Full Path In The Address Bar** Shows the hard disk and all the folders in the path to the current folder in the Address bar of a folder window.

● **Display The Full Path In Title Bar** Shows the hard disk and all the folders in the path to the current folder in the title bar of the folder window.

● **Hidden Files And Folders** Lets you show or hide files that you designate as hidden. (To hide a file, right-click the file name, click Properties on the shortcut menu, select the Hidden check box, and click OK.)

● **Hide File Extensions For Known File Types** Prevents the file extensions of file types that are associated with programs from being displayed. Hiding them makes the file list cleaner and prevents you from changing the file extension inadvertently when you rename a file.

● **Hide Protected Operating System Files** Hides files you shouldn't modify because they're part of Windows.

● **Remember Each Folder's View Settings** Causes Windows to remember the settings for each individual folder. When you clear this check box, the folder returns to its default settings when it's closed and then reopened.

● **Show Pop-Up Description For Folder And Desktop Items** Displays a small box containing a description of any desktop or folder item you point to and pause the mouse pointer on.

Too many folder windows open on the screen

Source of the problem

If Windows opens a new folder window whenever you double-click a folder, your screen can soon become clogged with windows. When each folder opens in its own window, you can drag files and folders from one window to another—a definite advantage. But every window you open is another window to close, and lots of windows can clutter your desktop. An alternative is to have every folder you double-click open in the same window the previous folder was displayed in. The display of each new folder's contents replaces the display of the previous folder's contents. You end up with a single window on the screen, displaying the contents of the latest folder you opened. Here's how to accomplish it.

How to fix it

1. Click Start, and click My Computer on the Start menu.

2. On the Tools menu, click Folder Options.

3. On the General tab of the Folder Options dialog box, click Open Each Folder In The Same Window. ▶

4. Click OK.

Avoiding desktop clutter with Windows Explorer

Windows Explorer presents the same information as a My Computer window but adds the convenience of a second pane to the left of the folder and file listing. This pane shows the tree structure of disks and folders on your computer. ▶

If you're connected to a network, the pane also shows the computers, disks, and folders that you have access to on the network.

Opening one Windows Explorer window can provide the same benefits as opening several My Computer windows. In a Windows Explorer window, you can open a folder by clicking it in the left pane. The contents of the folder are displayed in the right pane. You can then drag a file or folder from the right pane to any other disk or folder shown in the left pane.

To start Windows Explorer rather than My Computer, right-click My Computer on the Start menu and click Explore on the shortcut menu. You can also right-click any folder in My Computer and click Explore on the shortcut menu to open a Windows Explorer window that shows the folder.

Transforming a folder window into a Windows Explorer window

Dragging a file from one folder to another can be a bit of an annoyance when you're using regular folder windows. You need to open two folder windows, one for the folder where the file is, and another for the destination folder. But rather than open a second My Computer window, you can convert the My Computer window you have open to an Explorer window, adding a second pane containing the folder list. Then you can easily drag a file from the list of files to any other folder shown in the folder list. ▶

To add a folders list, click the Folders button on the toolbar. Or, on the View menu in My Computer, point to Explorer Bar, and then click Folders. The Folders list replaces the Tasks pane, and the folder window converts to a Windows Explorer window.

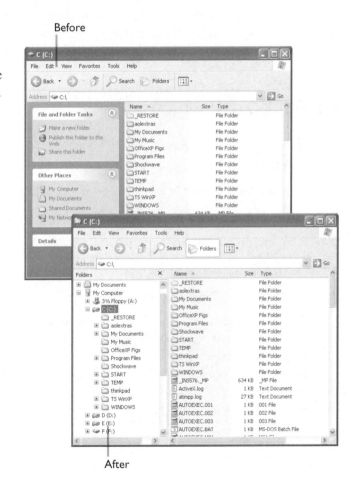

Before

After

My folder isn't set up for the type of files I want it to hold

Source of the problem

Windows gives you special folders that provide tools for working with the files inside. In folders that contain pictures, such as the My Pictures folder, you can use Filmstrip view, with which you can easily view enlargements of the images. Similarly, in the My Music folder, you can play music files or select tracks for the playlist in Windows Media Player. These special folders offer unique ways to preview files and specialized tasks that are designed for the file type they hold.

But when you create a new folder, Windows makes a generic folder without special capabilities or an identifying icon. Without these traits, the folder can't live up to its potential, offering you quick and easy ways to use files. Here's how to set up a folder for the type of files you want it to contain.

How to fix it

First, create a new folder by following these steps:

1. Click Start, and click My Computer on the Start menu.

2. Open the disk or folder in which you want to create a folder.

3. In the File And Folder Tasks list, click Make A New Folder.

4. Enter a name for the new folder, and press Enter.

   Next, customize the folder by following these steps:

1. Double-click the folder to open it.

2. On the View menu, click Customize This Folder.
   You can also right-click the folder, click
   Properties on the shortcut menu, and then click the
   Customize tab in the Properties dialog box. On the
   Customize tab, you can choose a folder type and icons
   for the folder in both Thumbnails and all other views.

3. In the What Kind Of Folder Do You Want area on the Customize tab, click the down arrow, and click the appropriate file type, such as Pictures, Music Album, or the generic type: Documents. ▶

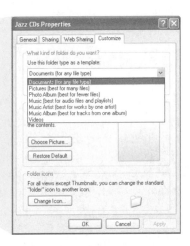

4. In the Folder Pictures area of the Customize tab, you can customize the look of the folder icon in Thumbnails view by clicking Choose Picture and selecting a picture file from any folder.

5. In the Folder Icons area, you can customize the look of the folder icon in all other views of this folder by clicking Change Icon and then clicking an icon that would appropriate for the files in the folder, such as an icon for a music folder that resembles a CD or a page with a musical note.

More about folder types

Windows XP offers these seven folder types:

- **Documents** The generic folder type that you can use to hold any file. It offers no special features.

- **Pictures** Displays the files in a folder as thumbnails (miniature versions of the pictures), and it gives you a set of picture tasks, including View As A Slide Show, Order Prints Online, and Print Pictures, which opens the Photo Printing Wizard. Also, in Thumbnail view, the icon of the folder displays miniatures of the first four photos in the folder.

- **Photo Album** Similar to Pictures, but displays the images in Filmstrip view, so you can click a thumbnail of any picture to see an enlargement.

- **Music** Displays the track title, artist, and album name next to each icon, and the tasks list gives you options to play all the tracks in the folder or shop for music on line.

- **Music Artist** Similar to the Music folder type, but displays only the track titles below file icons.

- **Music Album** Similar to the other type music folder types, but displays the file name, artist name, and album name next to each file icon.

- **Videos** Displays the first frame of the video file in Thumbnails view and, the tasks list gives you the option to play the video files in Windows Media Player.

I have to enter a path for a file or folder

Source of the problem

MS-DOS programs and even some older Windows programs don't use the Windows method of visually depicting files in folders on your hard disk. Instead, they ask you to spell out the location of a file or folder by using a line of text called a *path*, which looks something like this: *c:\program files\accessories\wordpad.exe*. When a program asks you for a path to specify the location of a file or folder, you need to translate the information in a folder window into a path.

How to fix it

1. Click Start, and click My Computer on the Start menu.

2. On the Tools menu of the My Computer window, click Folder Options.

3. On the View tab of the Folder Options dialog box, clear the Hide Extensions For Known File Types check box.

4. Select the Display The Full Path In The Address Bar check box.

5. Click OK.

6. In My Computer, open the folder that contains the file you want to specify, and make a note of the file name.

7. If the program that needs a path specified is an MS-DOS program, make a note of the text in the Address bar of the My Computer window. If the program is a Windows program, click the box in the Address bar and press Ctrl+C to copy the text. ▶

8. Start the program, and perform the task or choose the command that asks for the path.

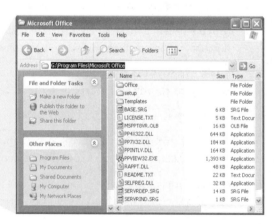

9. If the program is an MS-DOS program, type the path that you noted in step 7. If the program is a Windows program, press Ctrl+V to paste the path.

10. If you need to specify a file in a folder, type a backslash (\) immediately following the last folder name in the path, and then type the file name from step 6, including the file extension.

More about paths

You can almost always get around in Windows without entering a path, but you still see paths in the Address bar in My Computer and in dialog boxes, so you might want to understand just a little bit about them.

The files on your hard disk are organized in folders, and some of these folders are located within other folders. Windows represents this organizational scheme visually. You see folders within folders in Windows Explorer and in the Save In and Look In lists in the dialog boxes that you use to save and open files. ▶

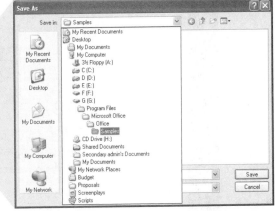

But if you're not a computer old timer, you might not know that this scheme of folders within folders predated Windows, and came from the days of DOS. MS-DOS, the operating system before Windows, gave users a way to type a line of text to describe a path to any folder on a hard disk. That path still shows up in Windows today in the Address bar. ▶

The first entry in a path is the disk name, such as *C:*. That entry is followed by a backslash (\). After that comes the first folder you need to look in, again followed by a backslash. Each subfolder you need to open is added to the text entry and followed by a backslash. The last entry on the line is the file name, if you want to be that specific. Now you see why being able to click through folders in Windows is much more convenient than typing long path names.

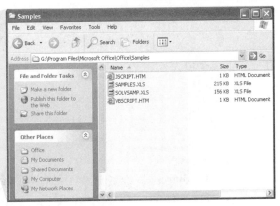

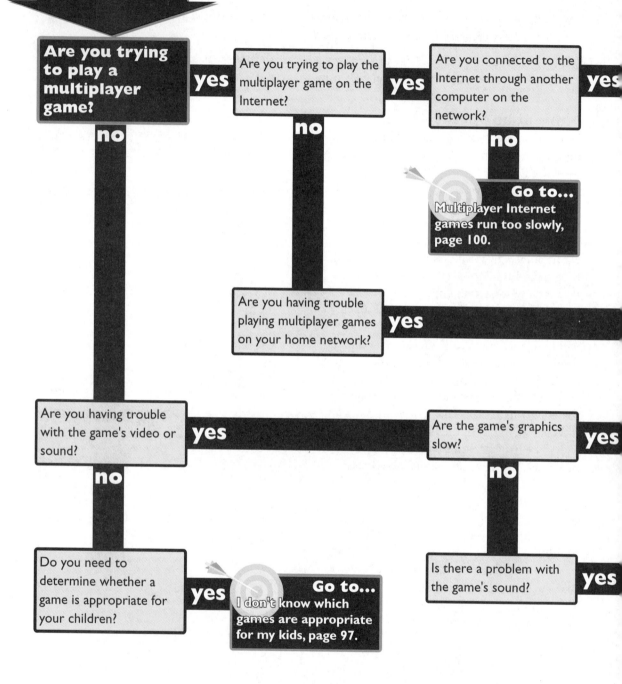

Are you trying to play a multiplayer game?

yes → Are you trying to play the multiplayer game on the Internet?

yes → Are you connected to the Internet through another computer on the network?

yes →

no ↓ (from "Are you connected to the Internet through another computer on the network?")

Go to...
Multiplayer Internet games run too slowly, page 100.

Are you having trouble playing multiplayer games on your home network?

yes →

no ↓ (from "Are you trying to play a multiplayer game?")

Are you having trouble with the game's video or sound?

yes → Are the game's graphics slow?

yes →

no ↓ (from "Are the game's graphics slow?")

Is there a problem with the game's sound?

yes →

no ↓ (from "Are you having trouble with the game's video or sound?")

Do you need to determine whether a game is appropriate for your children?

yes →

Go to...
I don't know which games are appropriate for my kids, page 97.

Games

Quick fix

I can't play Internet games through my network If your computer is connected to the Internet through someone else's computer on the network, you can't play multiplayer games on the Internet. Arrange to be connected directly to the Internet through a regular modem, cable modem, or DSL line or have your computer connected directly to a router that's providing Internet access to multiple computers on a network.

Quick fix

I can't connect to other players on my home network The same problems that prevent you from connecting to other computer on your home network prevent you from playing multiplayer games with others on your home network. For information about solving this problem, see "I can't connect to other computers on the network," page 182.

Go to...

The graphics in my game are slow or jerky, page 94.

Go to...

My game doesn't sound right, page 98.

If your solution isn't here, check these related chapters:

- Hardware, page 114
- Networks, home, page 180
- Programs, page 234
- Sound and pictures, page 254

Or see the general trouble-shooting tips on page xv.

The graphics in my game are slow or jerky

Source of the problem

The hottest action games for the PC demand a lightning-fast graphics card along with a powerful processor, such as a fast Intel Pentium III or Celeron. If either the card or the processor is feeble, the animation in your games will be slow, and movements will look jerky rather than smooth. Simulations, high-speed action games, and first-person shooters such as Quake are particularly demanding. If you plan to play against the machine, you might be fine, but if you want to play against other players on line, you won't stand much of a chance. They're just too good. So if you want to have any hope of winning, follow these steps.

How to fix it

- Download the latest update patch for your games.

    Popular games are frequently updated to fix problems and provide greater speed. To find these patches, go to the manufacturer's Web site or visit a site devoted to gaming, such as *www.gamespot.com*, or *www.bluesnews.com*.

- Download the latest driver for your graphics card.

    Graphics card manufacturers frequently release new drivers for their cards that wring every last bit of performance from the graphics chip and often provide noticeable improvements in game speed. Visit the manufacturer's Web site to download the latest driver, and follow the driver's installation instructions carefully. If you need help updating a driver, see "A new device I've installed doesn't work," on page 116.

- Tune up your computer.

    Follow the procedures in "My hard disk has slowed down," on page 216, and "Windows is becoming sluggish," on page 218, to optimize the performance of your hard disk and the speed of Windows.

- Check out Web sites devoted to gaming and gaming hardware.

    Legions of game fans depend on Web sites designed for and by gaming enthusiasts to find the latest ideas for getting the most out of their current computers or upgrading to the latest and greatest hardware.

- Upgrade your computer to a newer model if you hope to survive alien wars, the Grand Prix, or a shootout in a dark hallway of a secret underground lab.

If you have a Pentium or Pentium II, upgrade to a fast Celeron, or even better to a Pentium III. Get the fastest processor you can afford; speed is indicated by the MHz number. (1 GHz is better than 833 MHz, and so on.) In addition to getting more raw performance, which will also help in your other guise (mild-mannered business application user), your new computer is likely to come with faster components on its main circuit board (the *motherboard*), a faster and larger hard disk, and a speedier graphics card, which is powered by a newer and more advanced graphics chip.

- Replace your graphics card with a newer model.

    Next to updating to a faster processor, updating the graphics card in your computer will have the greatest effect on the speed of most games. New graphics cards based on the latest graphics chips are produced almost monthly, offering vast increases in their power to create smooth movement and realistic scenery.

    Replacing the graphics card is a fraction of the cost of replacing the entire computer. But keep in mind that the graphics card and the main processor (the CPU, such as the Pentium chip) in a computer interact, so putting the very latest graphics card in an early-model PC won't let the card run at its full speed. You'll see an improvement, but not as much as if you'd upgraded the CPU too.

    For information about the latest graphics chips, visit Web sites devoted to gaming graphics, such as *www.Tweak3D.net*.

- Keep DirectX updated. DirectX is the gaming component in Windows.

    DirectX has gone through a succession of revisions. To learn which version of DirectX is the latest, go to *www.microsoft.com/directx*.

    To determine which version you're using, click Run on the Start menu, type **dxdiag** in the Open box, and press Enter. The System tab in the DirectX Diagnostic Tool dialog box shows the current DirectX version. ▶

    To download for free the latest version of DirectX, use Windows Update by pointing to All Programs on the Start menu and clicking Windows Update.

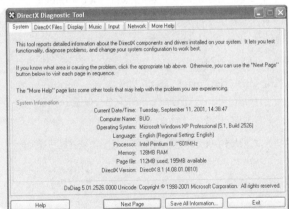

If this solution didn't solve your problem, go to the next page.

The graphics in my game are slow or jerky

(continued from page 95)

Updating a driver

If the latest driver doesn't come with specific instructions, here's the generic procedure to follow:

1. Click Start, right-click My Computer on the Start menu, and click Properties on the shortcut menu.

2. On the Hardware tab of the System Properties dialog box, click Device Manager.

3. In Device Manager, click the plus sign next to Display Adapters.

4. Right-click your display adapter, and click Update Driver to start the Hardware Update Wizard. ▶

5. Click Install From A List Or Specific Location, and click Next.

6. Click Search For The Best Driver In These Locations.

7. Clear the Search Removable Media check box. ▶

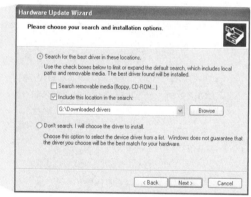

8. Select the Include This Location In The Search check box.

9. Enter the path to the folder where you downloaded the updated driver, or click Browse to browse to the folder, and click OK.

10. Click Next, and then click Yes if you're asked whether you want to use this driver.

I don't know which games are appropriate for my kids

Source of the problem

Not all games are appropriate for kids of any age. Before you let your kids buy a computer game, you can check its Entertainment Software Rating Board (ESRB) rating to determine whether the game is suitable for them. The ESRB has developed a standardized rating system that gives parents information about the content of computer games. (It also rates video games for popular gaming consoles.) Games are rated by three independent, trained raters drawn from a pool that includes, among others, retired school principals and parents.

How to fix it

Look on the game box for the ESRB rating before you purchase a game. If you can't accompany your kids to the store and check the box yourself, visit *www.esrb.org*, where you can look up game titles and check their ESRB rating. You can search for a particular game at *http://www.esrb.org/ search.asp#game*.

Rating categories provided by the ESRB include the following:

- **Early Childhood (EC)** Appropriate for ages 3 and older. No inappropriate content.

- **Everyone (E)** Appropriate for ages 6 and older. Titles may contain minimal violence, some comic mischief, or crude language.

- **Teen (T)** Appropriate for ages 13 and older. Titles may contain violent content, mild or strong language, and suggestive themes.

- **Mature (M)** Appropriate for ages 17 and older. Titles may contain intense violence and language and mature sexual themes.

- **Adults Only (AO)** Appropriate for ages over 18. Titles may include graphic depictions of sex and violence.

The ESRB rating is often accompanied by a *content descriptor*, which gives additional information about the title's content, such as "Contains scenes involving characters/animated/pixelated characters in the depiction of unsafe or hazardous acts or violent situations."

My game doesn't sound right

Source of the problem

Any devoted gamer will tell you that sound is an integral part of the gaming experience, especially when it's three-dimensional, surround sound that helps you identify the direction of an impending danger. Sophisticated sound cards can create three-dimensional sound with only two speakers, but serious gamers use four speakers for true surround sound. If your sound isn't working the way you expect, or if it doesn't sound three-dimensional, here are a few things to try.

How to fix it

1. Click Start, click Control Panel on the Start menu, click Sounds, Speech, And Audio Devices in Control Panel, and click Adjust System Volume.

2. On the Volume tab in the Sounds And Audio Devices Properties dialog box, click Advanced, and make sure the Volume sliders for Play Control, Wave, and MIDI (or Synth, Synthesizer, or SW Synth) are not at the bottom of the scale and the corresponding Mute check boxes are not selected. ▶

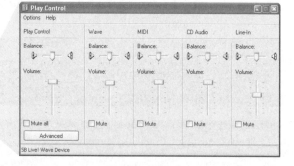

3. If your sound card has its own icon on the taskbar, double-click the icon to open the controls for the card. Look for an option with which you can enable three-dimensional sound and other features.

    If the sound card doesn't have its own icon, click Start, point to All Programs, and look for a controlling program for the card.

If the sound still isn't right, you should reinstall the sound card's drivers and accompanying programs (using the disk that came with the sound card) by following these steps:

1. Click Start, click Control Panel, and click Add or Remove Programs.

2. In the list of currently installed programs in the Add Or Remove Programs dialog box, select the sound card's software in the list, and click Remove.

3. If you're asked whether you want to restart the computer, click No. (You still have things to do.)

4. Click Start, right-click My Computer on the Start menu, and click Properties on the shortcut menu.

5. On the Hardware tab of the System Properties dialog box, click Device Manager.

6. In Device Manager, click the plus sign next to Sound, Video, And Game Controllers.

7. Right-click your sound card in the list, and click Uninstall. ▶

    Be sure to click all other entries related to your sound card, such as the joystick controller or MIDI support, and remove them too.

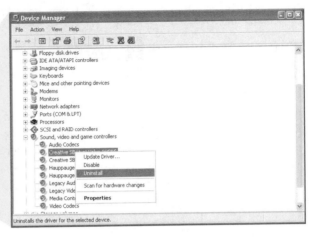

8. Close the Device Manager window and click OK to close the System Properties dialog box.

9. Restart the computer, and let it redetect the sound card and reinstall its drivers.

10. Reinstall the software for the sound card using the disk or CD that accompanied the sound card or that came with your computer.

11. Restart the computer, if necessary.

Tip
Be sure to check the sound card manufacturer's Web site for updated drivers for the sound card installed in your computer. These drivers may fix an incompatibility problem that's preventing your sound from working.

Disabling onboard sound

Some computers come with built-in sound capabilities—in the form of a chip inside the computer that can produce music and sound effects. But if you've just purchased the latest three-dimensional sound card for the ultimate gaming experience, you might need to turn off the sound capabilities in the computer so that they don't conflict with your new sound card.

Your computer's documentation should tell you whether the sound in your computer comes from an add-in board that you can easily replace or from circuitry built into the computer's main circuit board (the *motherboard*).

If you don't have the computer's documentation, shut down the computer and unplug it from the wall, and then carefully open the computer's case and look inside the computer for connections that lead from the jacks into which you plug the speakers and microphone. If these connections lead to an add-in board, you can replace the board. If they lead to plugs on the motherboard instead, you'll need to disable the sound circuitry by using the configuration program that's built into the computer. To start this program, you usually press a particular key, such as the Ctrl key, while starting the computer. Watch the screen carefully as you start the computer for a message that tells you to press a key to start the setup program.

Multiplayer Internet games run too slowly

Source of the problem

Some of the games you can play across the Internet don't require blisteringly fast connections. Online chess and strategy games work just fine at any speed. Action games, on the other hand, require not only lightning reflexes but also ultrafast Internet connections; otherwise, you'll experience dreaded *lag*—that interminable pause between the moment you move the mouse and the instant your race car begins to turn. Here are a number of steps you can take to reduce your *ping*—the time it takes for commands to get to the Internet game.

How to fix it

1. Make sure no other programs that use the modem connection are running.

2. Right-click My Network Places, and click Properties on the shortcut menu.

3. In the Network Connections window, right-click your network connection (usually named Local Area Connection), and click Properties on the shortcut menu. ▶

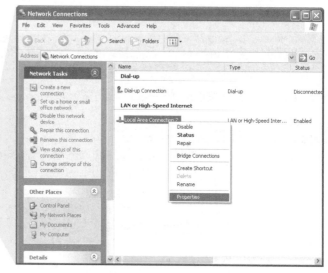

4. On the General tab in the Properties dialog box, click any IPX/SPX-Compatible Protocol entries in the network components list in turn, click Uninstall, and click OK.

5. Download and install the latest driver for your modem.

6. If you use a regular, modem dial-up connection, disable call waiting: Click Printers And Other Hardware in Control Panel, and click Phone And Modem Options. In the Phone And Modem Options dialog box, select the modem you use for your Internet connection on the Modems tab, click Properties, select the To Disable Call Waiting, Dial check box, type the disable call-waiting sequence for your area in the box, and click OK twice to close the dialog boxes.

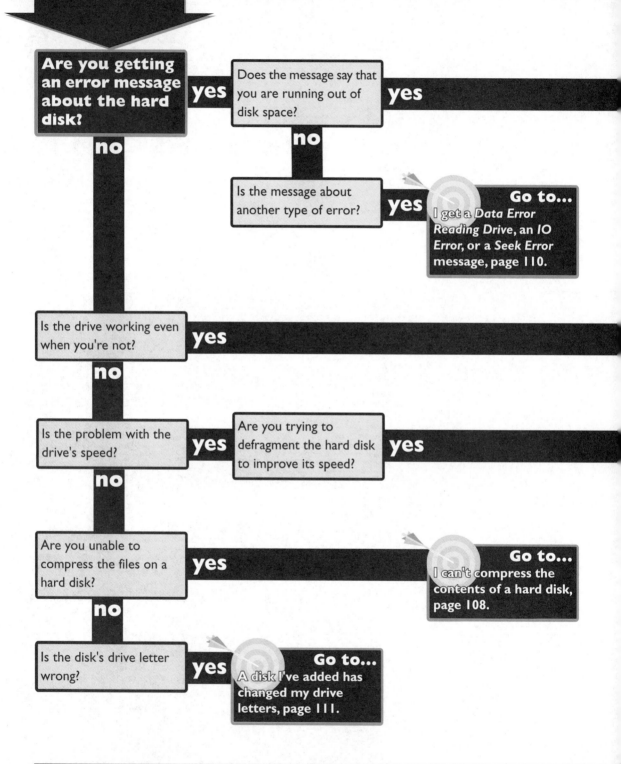

Are you getting an error message about the hard disk?

yes → Does the message say that you are running out of disk space? **yes** →

no ↓

no ↓

Is the message about another type of error? **yes** →

Go to... I get a *Data Error Reading Drive*, an *IO Error*, or a *Seek Error* message, page 110.

Is the drive working even when you're not? **yes** →

no ↓

Is the problem with the drive's speed? **yes** → Are you trying to defragment the hard disk to improve its speed? **yes** →

no ↓

Are you unable to compress the files on a hard disk? **yes** →

Go to... I can't compress the contents of a hard disk, page 108.

no ↓

Is the disk's drive letter wrong? **yes** →

Go to... A disk I've added has changed my drive letters, page 111.

Go to...
My hard disk is getting full, page 104.

Go to...
The disk defragmenter keeps starting over, page 112.

Quick fix

I hear my hard disk working even when I'm not at my computer

There's no need to worry if you hear the hard disk working even when you're not starting programs or working with files. Windows performs a number of routine, behind-the-scenes tasks even when you aren't at the computer, such as swapping data from the computer's memory to its hard disk, and indexing files to make them quickly searchable.

If your solution isn't here, check these related chapters:

- Files, page 72
- Folders, page 82
- Hardware, page 114

Or see the general troubleshooting tips on page xv.

My hard disk is getting full

Source of the problem

Just as your closets get stuffed with clothes, files fill your hard disk—almost as if your files multiply when you turn your back. Eventually, your hard disk just can't store any more, but before then, inexplicable Windows problems can crop up. Hang-ups and error messages can signal a space crunch on your hard disk even before the Disk Cleanup program in Windows pops up with a message that you're running out of hard disk space. To free up space, either take the measures described here—such as emptying the Recycle Bin and removing unused programs and files—or handle them through Disk Cleanup, as described in "Using Disk Cleanup," on page 107.

How to fix it

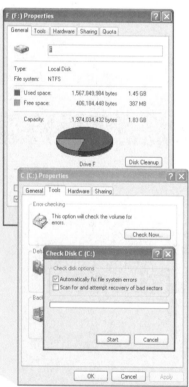

1. Click Start, and click My Computer on the Start menu.

2. Right-click the hard disk that's nearly full, and click Properties on the shortcut menu to see a pie chart showing the disk's used and free space. ▶

    Now that you've seen the specifics of your disk's free space, begin by running Check Disk, which fixes errors and removes extraneous chunks of files that were left on the hard disk by programs.

3. Click the Tools tab in the Properties dialog box, click Check Now, select the Automatically Fix File System Errors check box, and then click Start. ▶

    If a message tells you that the operation can't be performed, click Yes to schedule the check to occur when you next restart the computer.

4. Quit Check Disk, and click OK to close the Properties dialog box for the disk.

Next, empty the Recycle Bin by following these steps:

1. Right-click the Recycle Bin icon on the desktop, and click Empty Recycle Bin on the shortcut menu.

2. Click Yes to confirm the permanent deletion of the files.

More about the Check Disk tool

For more information about Check Disk, see "I get a *Data Error Reading Drive,* an *IO Error,* or a *Seek Error* message," on page 110.

Those steps help free up some disk space immediately, but for a more complete fix, you can also remove programs and components you don't need.

1. Click Start, and click Control Panel.

2. In Control Panel, click Add Or Remove Programs.

3. In the list of currently installed programs in the Add Or Remove Programs dialog box, select a program that you rarely or never use, and click Remove. ▶

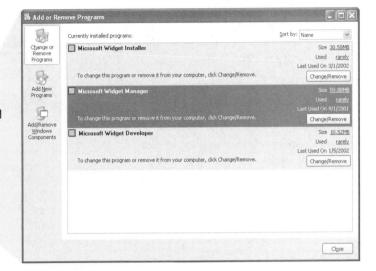

4. Follow the procedure for uninstalling the program. If you're prompted to do so, restart your computer after the removal is complete.

5. Repeat steps 1 through 4 above to remove all other programs that you use rarely or never.

6. Click Start, and click Control Panel. In Control Panel, click Add Or Remove Programs again, and in the Add Or Remove Programs dialog box, click Add/Remove Windows Components.

7. Clear the check boxes for all Windows components that you rarely or never use, and click Next to remove these components. ▶

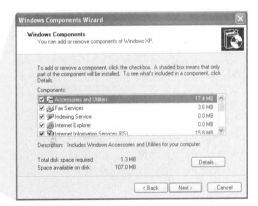

8. Click Finish to close the Windows Components Wizard.

Another method that works well, no matter what file system you have on your hard disk, is to back up and remove files you don't need to have on hand at all times: If you have a tape backup drive or a removable disk, copy old or rarely needed files to it, and then delete those files from the hard disk.

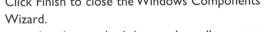
If this solution didn't solve your problem, go to the next page.

My hard disk is getting full

(continued from page 105)

To delete other files that you might not need, follow these steps:

1. Click Start, and click My Computer on the Start menu.

2. Double-click the hard disk that contains the Windows folder, and double-click the Windows folder. ▶

3. In the Windows folder, double-click the Temp folder, and delete all the files in the folder. If you get an *Access Denied* message for a file, indicating that the file is in use, delete the rest of the files.

4. Click Start, and click Control Panel.

5. In Control Panel, double-click Network And Internet Connections, and then click Internet Options.

6. On the General tab of the Internet Options dialog box, click Delete Files to delete temporary Internet files. ▶

Using Compressed Folders

Another way to conserve space on a hard disk is to use the Compressed Folders feature to create one or more compressed folders. Any files you move to these folders will be compressed, so they'll take up less space on the hard disk.

1. Click Start, click My Computer on the Start menu, and double-click the hard disk that needs more space.

2. On the File menu, point to New, and click Compressed Folder. Type a name for the folder and press Enter.

   Move files or other folders into the compressed folder to compress them and free up disk space.

Using Disk Cleanup

You can perform many of the tasks listed in the steps above by using Disk Cleanup. When you've nearly run out of disk space on a hard disk, an icon with a message about Low Disk Space appears at the lower right corner of the screen, next to the clock, but you can start Disk Cleanup at any time.

Disk Cleanup scours your hard disk for files that it can remove and then reports how much hard disk space you'll gain. Before Disk Cleanup removes files, you can approve of the categories of files it will delete, and you can even view the actual files that will be removed before making the commitment.

1. Click Start, click My Computer on the Start menu, right-click the hard disk, and click Properties on the shortcut menu.

2. In the Properties dialog box for the hard disk, click Disk Cleanup. ▶

3. On the Disk Cleanup tab of the Disk Cleanup dialog box, select the check boxes for the categories of files you want to delete, clear the check boxes for the categories of files you want to keep, and then click OK.

If you want to view the files you're about to delete or delete files selectively within a category, click the View Files button. In the folder window that opens, you can delete individual files. Then close the folder window, and clear the check box for the category. If the View Files button isn't available, you've selected a category of files that Disk Cleanup can't show you.

To free more space, you can click the More Options tab in the Disk Cleanup dialog box and use the additional options to remove Windows components and installed programs that you don't use. ▶

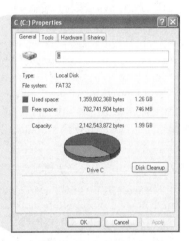

Can I compress an existing folder?

You can't compress an existing folder using the Compressed Folders feature. You can only create a new compressed folder and then move files into it from an existing, uncompressed folder.

I can't compress the contents of a hard disk

Source of the problem

If a Compress Drive To Save Disk Space option is not available when you view the properties for your hard disk, there's nothing wrong with the disk or with Windows. It's just that the disk hasn't been prepared with NTFS, which stands for NT file system.

Besides providing additional security features, such as the ability to restrict users' access to the folders you've set up for them, NTFS can also compress the files on a disk to dramatically increase the disk's capacity and encrypt files so their contents are not accessible to snoops. (The encrypt files option is not available in Windows XP Home Edition, though.)

Here's how to check to see whether your hard disk is formatted with NTFS, and how to convert it to NTFS if it's formatted instead with an older file system, either FAT or FAT32.

Before you start

If you determine in the steps below that your hard disk uses the FAT or FAT32 file system rather than NTFS, you can convert the disk's file system to NTFS, but before you do, be sure to back up your important data files. While the conversion process is safe and non-destructive to your files (and it's been carried out millions of times), you're still making a significant change to how your files are stored, which warrants the caution of a backup.

> ### Caution
> After you convert a hard disk from FAT or FAT32 to NTFS, you'll no longer be able to access the files on the disk if you also use Windows 98 or Windows Me on the same computer by dual-booting (choosing the operating system to start from a menu when the computer starts). You can't easily convert a drive from NTFS back to FAT or FAT32, so if you need to access the files on a disk with Windows 98 or Windows Me, leave the hard disk formatted with FAT or FAT32, and use compressed folders on the disk instead.

How to fix it

1. Click Start, and click My Computer on the Start menu.

2. Right-click the hard disk you're interested in, and click Properties on the shortcut menu.

3. In the Properties dialog box for the disk, note the file system, which will be FAT, FAT32, or NTFS. ▶

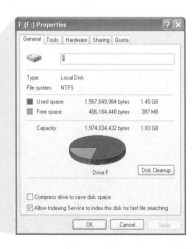

If the file system is listed as either FAT or FAT32, make a note of the volume label, which is shown in a box next to a disk drive icon at the top of the General tab, and then follow these steps to convert the disk to NTFS.

1. Click Start, point to All Programs, point to Accessories, and click Command Prompt.

2. In the Command Prompt window, type the following: **convert *drive_letter:* /fs:ntfs**, replacing *drive_letter* with the letter of the hard disk you want to convert. ▶

   For example, to convert drive D to NTFS, you'd type **convert d: /fs:ntfs**.

3. Press Enter.

4. Type the volume label that you noted earlier to confirm that you want to convert the drive, and press Enter.

   If you want to change your mind and not convert the drive, press Ctrl+C, and then type **exit** and press Enter.

Using Compressed Folders

Another way to conserve space on a hard disk is to use the Compressed Folders feature to create one or more compressed folders so you don't have to compress your entire hard disk. Any files you move to these folders will be compressed, so they'll take up less space on the hard disk. Compressed folders are actually .zip files, so you can e-mail a compressed folder to someone else who can open it with a .zip file viewer. To create a compressed folder, follow these steps:

1. Click Start, click My Computer on the Start menu, and double-click the hard disk that needs more space.

2. On the File menu, point to New, and click Compressed (zipped) Folder. ▶

3. Type a name for the folder and press Enter.

   Move files or other folders into the compressed folder to compress them and free up disk space.

I get a *Data Error Reading Drive*, an *IO Error*, or a *Seek Error* message

Source of the problem

All of these messages indicate that the hard disk either has physical damage or contains damaged files. A dropped laptop is the most common cause of a disk problem, but all mechanical components fail eventually, even well-made ones that last for years. The Check Disk tool, the disk error-checking program in Windows, can repair most files, and it can even attempt to repair files in areas of the hard disk that have been physically damaged.

How to fix it

1. Click Start, and click My Computer on the Start menu.

2. Right-click the hard disk that's reporting an error message, and click Properties on the shortcut menu.

3. On the Tools tab of the Properties dialog box, click Check Now. ▶

4. In the Check Disk dialog box, select the Automatically Fix Errors check box.

5. Also select the Scan For And Attempt Recovery Of Bad Sectors check box.

6. Click Start.
   If a message tells you that the operation can't be performed, click Yes to schedule the check to occur when you next restart the computer.

Check Disk checks the files and folders on the disk for errors and then scans the disk surface for errors. It fixes all errors it can. If it finds damaged data, Check Disk gives you the option of saving the data to a file or discarding the data.

If Check Disk is unable to fix a disk, or if you continue to get error messages after using Check Disk, contact the computer or disk manufacturer. The disk needs to be checked by a service professional or replaced.

A disk I've added has changed my drive letters

Source of the problem

Your computer assigns drive letters, such as *A:*, *C:*, and *E:*, to the floppy disks and hard disks you install, but Windows assigns drive letters to CD-ROM drives, Zip drives, USB drives, and other removable drives. If you install a program that requires a CD, for example, and then add a removable drive, the drive letter of the CD-ROM drive might change. The program will then be unable to find the CD unless you restore the original drive letter to the CD-ROM, as described here.

How to fix it

1. Click Start, click Control Panel, click Performance And Maintenance, click Administrative Tools, and then double-click Computer Management.

2. In the left pane of the Computer Management window, click Disk Management under Storage.

3. In the right pane of the Computer Management window, right-click the CD-ROM drive or removable drive, and click Change Drive Letter And Paths. ▶

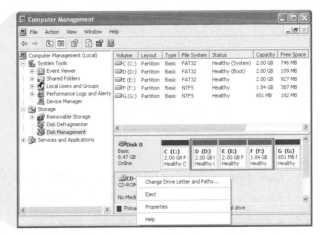

4. In the Change Drive Letter And Paths dialog box, click Change.

5. Select an available drive letter.

6. Click OK.

   If the drive letter you want isn't listed, click Change, click the down arrow in the Change Drive Letter And Paths dialog box, click a different letter, and click OK.

7. Click OK, and then close the Computer Management window.

The Disk Defragmenter keeps starting over

Source of the problem

You probably know the importance of defragmenting your hard disk regularly to keep it running well. Defragmenting takes all the chunks of files that Windows scatters across empty spots on the hard disk and reassembles them into complete files. When bits of files are scattered across the hard disk, the hard disk has to go and get each chunk to gather the complete file. But when files are contiguous so all their data is sequential on the hard disk, the hard disk can grab the file from one place, retrieving it quickly and easily.

But sometimes, when you run the Disk Defragmenter, it gets only partway through defragmenting the disk before stopping and starting over from the beginning. Defragmenting a disk isn't exactly a speedy process, so a defragmenter that keeps restarting from the beginning can make you crazy.

The solution is to stop other programs from writing to the hard disk while the Disk Defragmenter is working and to turn off the screen saver, which also makes the Disk Defragmenter loop back to the beginning.

How to fix it

1. Quit all programs that are running.

2. Press Ctrl+Alt+Delete, and in the Windows Security dialog box, click Task Manager.

3. On the Applications tab of the Windows Task Manager, click each program in the list, and click End Task.
   If the End Program dialog box opens, click End Now. Close Task Manager after you've ended all applications.

4. In the system tray, next to the clock, right-click each icon, and click Close or Exit on the program's shortcut menu. If the shortcut menu for the program doesn't have a Close or Exit command, you can leave the program as is and go on to the next icon.

Now that you've closed the programs that are running, you should also disable your screen saver by following these steps:

1. Right-click the desktop, and click Properties on the shortcut menu.

2. On the Screen Saver tab of the Display Properties dialog box, click None in the Screen Saver list

3. Click Power, and on the Power Schemes tab in the Power Options Properties dialog box, write yourself a note about the settings. Click the Turn Off Monitor and Turn Off Hard Disks down arrows, click Never in both lists, and then click OK twice to close the dialog boxes. ▶

    If you also have System Standby and System Hibernates lists in the Power Options Properties dialog box, click Never in both lists before clicking OK.

4. If you're using Microsoft Office, double-click the Find Fast icon in Control Panel. (You might need to click Switch To Classic View in the tasks list to see the Find Fast icon.) Then on the Index menu in the Find Fast window, click Pause Indexing if the command is available.

5. Click Start, and click My Computer on the Start menu, right-click the hard disk you want to defragment, click Properties on the shortcut menu, and on the Tools tab of the Properties dialog box, click Defragment Now. ▶

6. In the Disk Defragmenter window, right-click the disk to defragment, and click Defragment on the shortcut menu.

7. When the Disk Defragmenter finishes, click OK to close the Properties dialog box.

8. Repeat steps 1 and 2, but select the screen saver you want in the Screen Saver list.

9. Repeat step 3, but restore the previous settings that you noted in the Power Options Properties dialog box.

10. Click Start, click Shut Down, click Restart in the Shut Down Windows dialog box, and click OK to restart the computer.

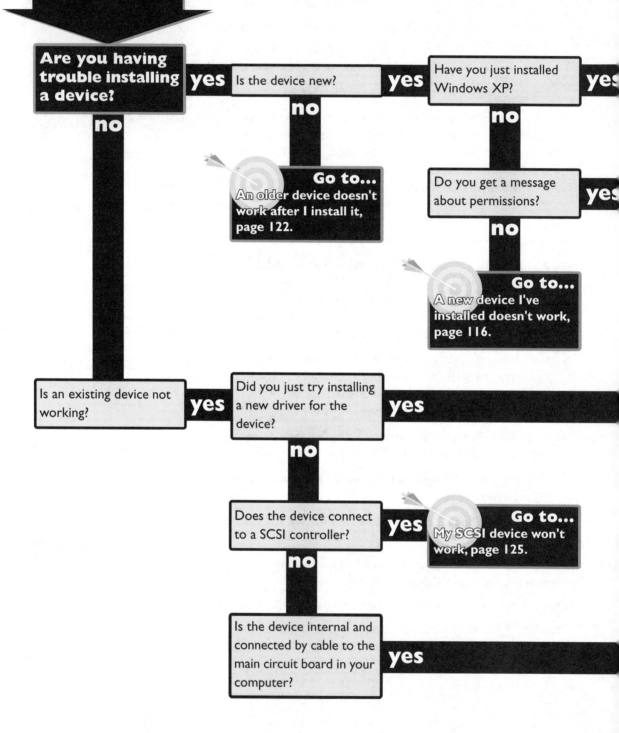

Are you having trouble installing a device?

yes → Is the device new?

yes → Have you just installed Windows XP?

yes

no ↓

Go to...
An older device doesn't work after I install it, page 122.

Have you just installed Windows XP?
no ↓

Do you get a message about permissions?

yes

no ↓

Go to...
A new device I've installed doesn't work, page 116.

Are you having trouble installing a device?
no ↓

Is an existing device not working?

yes → Did you just try installing a new driver for the device?

yes

no ↓

Does the device connect to a SCSI controller?

yes → **Go to...** My SCSI device won't work, page 125.

no ↓

Is the device internal and connected by cable to the main circuit board in your computer?

yes

Hardware

Go to...

A device doesn't work after I install Windows XP, page 121.

Quick fix

I get a message about permissions when I try to install a new device Depending on your settings, and whether you're a part of a network, you might need administrative privileges to install new hardware. You need to be the administrator for a PC or part of the Administrators group. If the computer is at home, you can probably log on as the administrator. If the computer is at an organization, you might need to consult the computer adminstrator at the organization for help.

Quick fix

I installed a new driver for a device and now the device doesn't work Windows comes with a feature that allows you to return to a previously working driver if you install a new driver that prevents a device from working.

1. Click Start, right-click My Computer on the Start menu, click Properties on the shortcut menu, and on the Hardware tab of the System Properties dialog box, click Device Manager.

2. Right-click the device that isn't working, and click Properties.

3. On the Driver tab of the properties dialog box, click Roll Back Driver, and follow the instructions on the screen.

If your solution isn't here, check these related chapters:

- Hard disks, page 102
- Laptops, page 152
- Optimizing, page 212
- Setting up Windows, page 244

Or see the general troubleshooting tips on page xv.

Go to...

My IDE device won't work, page 124.

A new device I've installed doesn't work

Source of the problem

Eight out of ten times, the solution to fixing a display adapter that won't display, a scanner that won't scan, a digital camera that won't transfer pictures, or any other device that just won't work is to remove and then reinstall the software that controls the device, called the *device driver*, or just the *driver* for short. The ninth time, the solution is to install an updated driver from the manufacturer that fixes the problem you (and others) are having. The tenth time requires more effort because it involves configuring a device that Windows can't detect and set up automatically. That tenth time's solution is covered in "An older device doesn't work after I install it," on page 112. Here's how to handle those first nine instances.

Tip

Before you can install a device, you might need to have administrator privileges on the computer. You need to be the administrator for a PC or part of the Administrators group. If the computer is at home, you can probably log on as the administrator. If the computer is at an organization, you might need to consult the computer administrator at the organization for help.

How to fix it

1. Click Start, right-click My Computer on the Start menu, and click Properties on the shortcut menu.

2. On the Hardware tab in the System Properties dialog box, click Device Manager.

3. In the Device Manager, see whether the device is visible in the list of devices. If the device isn't visible, click the plus sign next to the category of the device.

   If you still don't see the device, go to "My device isn't listed," on page 118.

4. Right-click the device in the list, and click Uninstall on the shortcut menu. ▶

   If the Confirm Device Removal dialog box opens, click OK.

5. Close the Device Manager, and click OK to close the System Properties dialog box.

6. Click Start, click Shut Down, click Restart in the Shut Down Windows dialog box, and click OK.

Windows will restart the computer, redetect the hardware, and reinstall the driver for the hardware. If Windows can't find and reinstall the driver for the device when it restarts, it usually opens the Add Hardware Wizard. If the Add Hardware Wizard doesn't open, follow these steps:

1. Right-click My Computer on the Start menu, and click Properties on the shortcut menu.

2. On the Hardware tab of the System Properties dialog box, click Add Hardware Wizard.

3. Click Next on the first page of the wizard. ▶

4. In the Add Hardware Wizard, click Yes, I Have Already Connected The Hardware, and click Next.

5. On the next page of the wizard, at the bottom of the list of installed hardware, click Add A New Hardware Device, and click Next.

6. On the next page of the wizard, click Install The Hardware That I Manually Select From A List, and click Next.

7. In the list of hardware categories, select the category that matches your device, and click Next.

 If you don't see the hardware category that matches your device, click Show All Devices. ▶

8. On the next page of the wizard, click the manufacturer and model of the device, and click Next.

9. If the device isn't listed, click Have Disk. Insert the disk or CD that contains the Windows XP driver for the device into the drive, click Browse to browse to the disk, and click Open. If, instead, you downloaded the driver for the device from the manufacturer's Web site, enter the path to the driver or click Browse to browse to the folder containing the driver, and click OK.

If this solution didn't solve your problem, go to the next page.

A new device I've installed doesn't work

(continued from page 117)

Downloading an updated driver from Windows Update

Most hardware manufacturers create updated device drivers to fix problems they've discovered or that have been reported by other users. If you can't get a device to work as expected, follow these steps to check the Windows Update Web site. If you download the driver from a manufacturer's Web site, make a note of the folder where you've placed it, and use the Add Hardware Wizard, as described in the previous procedure, to install the driver.

1. Click Start, and click Control Panel on the Start menu.

2. In Control Panel, click Add Or Remove Programs, click Add New Programs in the Add Or Remove Programs dialog box, and click Windows Update.

3. On the Windows Update Web page, click Pick Updates To Install to expand the list of updates.

4. In the updates list, click Driver Updates. ▶

5. On the Driver Updates page, click the update for the device, and click Install.

My device isn't listed

If you don't see your device listed under the proper category in the Device Manager, the driver for the device isn't installed. If the device is fairly new and it's Plug and Play compatible (the specifications on the box or in the user manual specifically include the words *Plug and Play*), you can have Windows detect the device and install the driver. If Windows doesn't find the driver, and your computer is connected to the Internet, Windows searches for the driver at the Microsoft Web site. (If you're not connected to the Internet, Windows prompts you to do so.) If the device is somewhat older, you might need to follow the manufacturer's step-by-step instructions for installing the device.

These devices usually require configuration by hand as opposed to automatic detection and configuration by Windows. For information about installing non–Plug and Play devices, see "An older device doesn't work after I install it," on page 122.

    To install a Plug and Play device, follow these steps:

Tip

If your computer is connected to a network at an organization, you might be prevented by the system administrator from installing new hardware. If you're having trouble, check with the system administrator to see whether this is the case.

1. Make sure the device is properly plugged into or attached to your computer. Shut down Windows and turn off the computer, and then make sure the device is inserted into a slot or plugged tightly into a port. Then restart the computer.

    If the device is a PC Card that you've inserted into a PC Card slot in a laptop, you don't need to shut down and restart the computer.

2. Click Start, right-click My Computer on the Start menu, and on the Hardware tab of the System Properties dialog box, click Add Hardware Wizard.

3. On the first page of the Add Hardware Wizard, click Next.

4. If the wizard says that it can help you install software for your new device, click Search For And Install The Hardware Automatically, and click Next. ▶

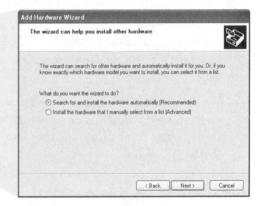

5. When the Wizard asks whether you've already connected the hardware to this computer, click Yes, I Have Already Connected The Hardware, and click Next.

6. If your device isn't in the list of installed hardware, click Install The Hardware From A List Or Specific Location, and click Next.

7. If the Found New Hardware Wizard opens and asks you to choose your search and installation options, leave the Search option selected, and click Next.

8. If you have an installation disk or CD that contains the driver for the device, insert it into the drive, leave Search Removable Media selected, and click Next. If you've downloaded the driver for the device, click Include This Location In The Search, and enter the location of the driver, or click Browse to browse to the folder that contains the driver, and click Next.

9. Click Next, and click Finish to install the driver.

If this solution didn't solve your problem, go to the next page.

A new device I've installed doesn't work

(continued from page 119)

Is the device disabled?

Even if a device is listed, its driver is installed, and it reports no conflicts or problems, the device won't work if it's disabled in the current hardware profile. Hardware profiles let you record different hardware configurations when you use a computer with different devices at different times. For a laptop, for example, you can have one hardware profile to use when the laptop is plugged into a docking station and a second hardware profile to use when it's independent. To make sure a device isn't disabled, follow these steps:

1. Click Start, right-click My Computer on the Start menu, and click Properties on the shortcut menu.

2. On the Hardware tab of the System Properties dialog box, click Device Manager.

3. In the Device Manager window, click the plus sign next to the category of device if the device isn't visible, and then right-click the device. If Enable is available on the shortcut menu, click it. ▶

4. You can also click Properties on the shortcut menu, and on the General tab of the Properties dialog box, click the Device Usage down arrow, and click Use This Device (Enable) in the list.

Installing USB devices

Installing a USB device sometimes requires a different procedure than for most other devices. Before you plug in a USB device, you might have to install a driver by running an installation program from a disk or CD that accompanies the new device. After you install the driver, Windows can recognize and install the USB device when it's plugged into the USB port on your computer. Before you install a USB device, carefully read the installation instructions for the device to determine how it must be installed.

Tip

For Plug and Play to work, both your computer and the devices you install must be Plug and Play capable. Nearly all devices and computers designed for Windows and made since 1995 are Plug and Play capable, but if you're not sure about yours, check the computer's user guide. If the computer is not Plug and Play capable, check the manufacturer's Web site to see whether you can download and run a program that will upgrade the computer's BIOS to Plug and Play capability.

A device doesn't work after I install Windows XP

Source of the problem

Although Windows XP comes with drivers for thousands of hardware devices, it might not come with a driver for your hardware device if the device isn't a common one. Unusual multimedia devices sometimes fit in this category, such as devices that let you watch television or listen to radio while you work

What you need is a Windows XP driver for the device. Where you can get it is either from the Windows Update Web site or from the device manufacturer's Web site. If you're connected to the Internet, Windows searches the Windows Update Web site when it can't find a driver for a new device (and prompts you to connect to the Internet if it's necessary). If neither the Windows Update Web site nor the manufacturer's Web site can provide the driver you need, you won't be able to use the device until a driver becomes available. Here's how to find a new driver, if it exists.

Before you start

Before you waste time tracking down a driver for a completely obscure device, you should check the Hardware Compatibility List at the Microsoft Web site. Use this address: *www.microsoft.com/hcl/default.asp*.

How to fix it

1. Click Start, and click Control Panel on the Start menu.

2. In Control Panel, click Add Or Remove Programs, click Add New Programs in the Add Or Remove Programs dialog box, and click Windows Update.

3. On the Windows Update Web page, click Pick Updates To Install to expand the list of updates.

4. In the updates list, click Driver Updates.

5. On the Driver Updates page, click the update for the device, and click Install.

Checking the manufacturer's Web site

If you couldn't find the driver for a device at the Windows Update Web site, your last option is to check the manufacturer's Web site. The instructions at the manufacturer's Web site should guide you to the driver and give you the option to download it.

An older device doesn't work after I install it

Source of the problem

The Plug and Play feature in Windows assigns an add-in device, such as an internal modem or a network adapter, to any available address, one of two kinds, IRQ and I/O, both of which are limited resources in every computer). But an older device (Microsoft calls these *legacy devices*) requires a fixed address. As a result, the device may squabble with another device that wants the same address, producing a resource conflict. Resource conflicts generate error messages, or the devices involved in the battle just plain grind to a halt.

If you absolutely want to use an older device (your aging but still fully functional high-speed printer, which requires its own add-in card, for example) you have a few options. You can identify a free address and set the older device to use the address, as described below, or you can rearrange the addresses used by other devices to free them up for the older device. You can also remove or disable the older device. That's not a good solution, of course, but you might prefer it when you find out how many steps might be required to find a free resource and set a device to use it.

How to fix it

1. Make sure you have the user manual, which tells you how to set jumpers or switches on the device to change settings like the IRQ, DMA, and I/O address.

   If you don't have this information, you won't be able to complete this procedure. Try the manufacturer's Web site to obtain the information, or look on the device itself. Sometimes the information is printed right on the device.

2. Click Start, right-click My Computer on the Start menu, and click Properties on the shortcut menu.

3. On the Hardware tab of the System Properties dialog box, click Device Manager, and look in the list of devices to see whether the icon for the older device shows a yellow exclamation point or a red check mark. These symbols can indicate that the device has a problem, such as a resource conflict.

> **Tip**
>
> To change resource settings for devices in your computer, you must have administrative privileges. You need to be the administrator for a PC or part of the Administrators group. If the computer is at home, you can probably log on as the administrator. If the computer is at an organization, you might need to consult the computer administrator at the organization for help.

4. Right-click the older device, and click Properties. On the Resources tab, the Conflicting Device List identifies the resource conflict. ▶

5. Clear the Use Automatic Settings check box.
    If the Properties dialog box doesn't have a Resources tab, you can't change its resources, so you need to change other conflicting devices instead.

6. In the Resource Type column on the Resources tab in the device's Properties dialog box, click a resource type, and click Change Setting. If the error message *This resource setting cannot be modified* appears, click a different resource type.

7. In the Edit dialog box, scroll through the settings in the Value box, and click a different setting until the Conflicting Device List box reports No Conflicts.

8. When the Conflicting Device List reports No Conflicts, make a note of the setting, click OK to try the new setting, and then click Yes when the Creating A Forced Configuration message box appears.

9. Shut down the computer, remove the device from the computer, and change the jumper or switch on the device to match the setting you've changed.

10. Restart the computer, and try using the older device again. If it still doesn't work, repeat steps 2 through 9, choosing different settings in steps 6 and 7 until the device works.

11. Click OK, click OK again, click Yes when the Creating A Forced Configuration message box appears, and restart the computer. If the device still doesn't work, continue trying other available settings for the resource until you find one that works.

Tip

Some devices come with installation programs that you can run to change the settings on the device. Check the user manual for the device to determine the procedure you need to follow.

When to give up

Finding resources that don't conflict and getting a device to work with those resources can be a laborious task. Before you waste all that time, see whether you can buy a new, Plug and Play version of the device. Check the manufacturer's Web site for information or go to a computer mail-order company's Web site. You might be surprised to find that the new device is much less expensive than you'd anticipated and that it offers new features that will be well worth the cost.

My IDE device won't work

Source of the problem

The hard disk in most popular computer models connects to an IDE (Integrated Drive Electronics) connection within the computer, the most popular type of connection for disk drives. Some CD-ROM drives and tape backup drives also connect to an IDE connection.

When you buy a computer, its hard disk is usually configured properly. (In fact, Windows is usually installed, so you can turn on the computer and get right to work or play.) But when you need to add or replace a hard disk, you must be careful to use the correct IDE settings when you configure the computer, or the IDE device won't work.

How to fix it

● Make sure to set one hard disk as the *master* and the other hard disk as the *slave* if you connect two hard disks to the same IDE cable in your computer. Usually, you choose the master or slave designation for a hard disk by changing the position of a small electrical connector on the disk called a jumper. Check the hard disk's manual for information about changing the jumper.

● Make sure the secondary IDE connection has not been disabled if you've added the hard disk to the second IDE connection in the computer. You can enable the secondary IDE connection by using the computer's BIOS configuration program. Check your computer's user manual to determine how to start the BIOS configuration or setup program. (In many computers, you start the BIOS configuration program by pressing the Delete key while the computer is starting.)

● Check the user manual for the hard disk to determine the *mode* your hard disk operates in, and then use the computer's BIOS configuration or setup program to choose the correct mode. IDE hard disks operate in one of several numbered modes; these modes determine the speed of the connection.

● Make sure the cable connecting the IDE connection and the hard disk is not connected upside down. Both the IDE connection and the hard disk should have an end labeled *1* or *Pin 1*, which corresponds to the side of the cable that's marked with a stripe.

My SCSI device won't work

Source of the problem

Although most popular computers use IDE hard disks, with the controlling electronics for the disk embedded right in the disk drive, computers designed for sophisticated applications such as video editing and computer graphics often use SCSI (pronounced "scuzzy") hard disks, which connect to a SCSI controller in the computer.

You can trace most glitches with SCSI devices to two problems: an incorrect SCSI ID number assigned to the device (each device requires a unique number), and lack of termination of the SCSI cables (every SCSI circuit needs to be capped off at both ends by a terminator). But you should also ensure that the SCSI controller is properly configured in Windows. Here's how to fix all these problems.

How to fix it

1. Start the configuration program for the SCSI controller card using the instructions in the SCSI controller card's documentation. Usually you start the configuration program by pressing a combination of keys while the computer is starting.

2. In the configuration program, select the option that lists the SCSI ID numbers and the devices that are assigned to numbers to find an available SCSI ID number.

3. Change the device's SCSI ID number to an available SCSI ID number. Consult the device's user manual to learn how. No two devices can be assigned the same ID number.

    Make sure the hard disk is set to SCSI ID 0 if the hard disk is the primary hard disk in your computer and the one the computer uses when it boots.

4. Make sure the connection between the SCSI controller and the hard disk is properly terminated at both ends. To terminate a SCSI cable, you attach a plug called a SCSI terminator. Most SCSI controller cards are terminated automatically without the need for a plug. Check the controller's user manual for instructions about terminating the controller.

5. Right-click My Computer on the Start menu, and click Properties on the shortcut menu. On the Hardware tab in the System Properties dialog box, click Device Manager, and click the plus sign next to SCSI Controllers. Click the SCSI controller card, and click Properties.

6. On the General tab of the Properties dialog box for the card, make sure you see This Device Is Working Properly in the Device Status area. If this doesn't appear, follow the procedure in "A new device I've installed doesn't work," on page 116.

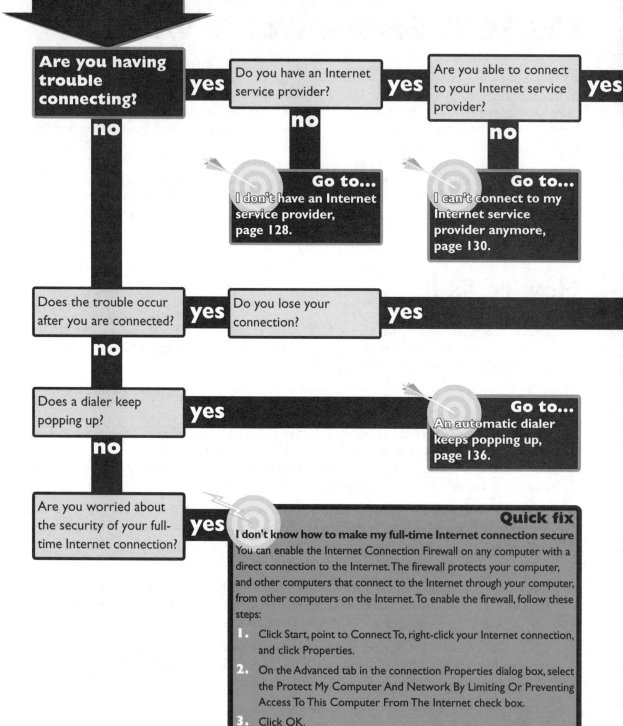

Are you having trouble connecting?

yes → Do you have an Internet service provider?

yes → Are you able to connect to your Internet service provider?

yes →

no ↓

no ↓

Go to...
I don't have an Internet service provider, page 128.

Go to...
I can't connect to my Internet service provider anymore, page 130.

no (from "Are you having trouble connecting?")

Does the trouble occur after you are connected? **yes** → Do you lose your connection? **yes** →

no ↓

Does a dialer keep popping up? **yes** →

Go to...
An automatic dialer keeps popping up, page 136.

no ↓

Are you worried about the security of your full-time Internet connection? **yes** →

Quick fix

I don't know how to make my full-time Internet connection secure
You can enable the Internet Connection Firewall on any computer with a direct connection to the Internet. The firewall protects your computer, and other computers that connect to the Internet through your computer, from other computers on the Internet. To enable the firewall, follow these steps:

1. Click Start, point to Connect To, right-click your Internet connection, and click Properties.

2. On the Advanced tab in the connection Properties dialog box, select the Protect My Computer And Network By Limiting Or Preventing Access To This Computer From The Internet check box.

3. Click OK.

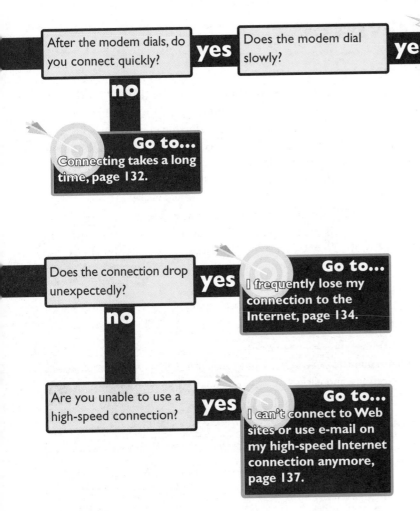

After the modem dials, do you connect quickly? **yes** → Does the modem dial slowly? **yes** →

no ↓

Go to...
Connecting takes a long time, page 132.

Does the connection drop unexpectedly? **yes** →

Go to...
I frequently lose my connection to the Internet, page 134.

no ↓

Are you unable to use a high-speed connection? **yes** →

Go to...
I can't connect to Web sites or use e-mail on my high-speed Internet connection anymore, page 137.

Quick fix
My modem dials too slowly
To save a little time whenever your modem dials, follow these steps, which will make the modem dial faster:

1. Click Start, and click Control Panel on the Start menu.
2. Click Printers And Other Hardware, and click Phone And Modem Options.
3. On the Modems tab of the Phone And Modem Options dialog box, click your modem, and click Properties.
4. On the Advanced tab of the modem Properties dialog box, type s11=50 in the Extra Initialization Commands box, and click OK.
5. Click OK, and close Control Panel.

If your solution isn't here, check these related chapters:

- Connections, page 2
- E-mail, page 58
- Internet Explorer, page 138
- Optimizing, page 212

Or see the general trouble-shooting tips on page xv.

I don't have an Internet service provider

Source of the problem

You can't browse the Web without signing up with an Internet service provider (ISP). An ISP provides phone numbers your modem can dial to connect your computer to the Internet. Once you're connected, you can visit Web sites, send and receive e-mail messages, download files, participate in online communities, and take advantage of other services, like videoconferencing and chatting.

Online services, such as America Online, also act as ISPs. They provide Internet connections in addition to offering services exclusively for their members, including online news and information, chat rooms, message boards, and e-mail addresses.

Finding an ISP is not hard. Lots of ISPs are looking for your business, and a local ISP probably advertises in your hometown newspaper. But if you don't know where to start or how to get connected, you can take advantage of the New Connection Wizard, which helps you choose an ISP and set up a membership.

How to fix it

1. Click Start, point to All Programs, point to Accessories, point to Communications, and click New Connection Wizard.

2. On the first page of the New Connection Wizard, click Next.

3. In the wizard, leave Connect To The Internet selected, and click Next. ▶

4. Leave Choose From A List Of Internet Service Providers selected, and click Next.

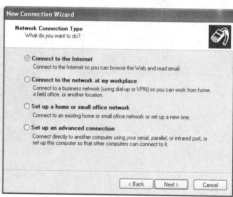

5. On the next page of the wizard, click Get Online With MSN if you'd like to sign up with MSN as your ISP, or click Select From A List Of Other ISPs, and click Finish.

6. If you've chosen to set up an account with MSN, respond to the on-screen prompts, which will guide you through the process of creating a new account.

7. If you've chosen to select from a list of other ISPs, double-click Refer Me To More Internet Service Providers in the Online Services window.

8. The Internet Connection Wizard opens, connects to the Microsoft Internet Referral Service, and downloads information about ISPs in your area. In the Internet Service Providers list, click each ISP to read about its services and rates.

9. Click the ISP you want to use, and click Next.

10. Follow the remaining steps of the wizard, clicking Next after each step.

The wizard will set up an icon on the desktop that you can double-click to sign up for membership, or it will request the information it needs to set up your account at the ISP and then set up an icon that you can double-click to connect to the ISP.

Signing up independently

The Internet Connection Wizard can sign you up with a large, national ISP that offers phone numbers in your area code, but you might prefer to sign up with a local ISP, one that offers a phone number that's a local call. In addition, a local ISP might provide news and services specific to your community and might host your personal or business Web site (although some national ISPs also let you set up home pages).

You can probably find a local ISP by asking friends or by checking the yellow pages or the ads in your local newspaper. Another option is to visit a school, library, or cyber café that offers Internet access and go to a Web site that lists ISPs, such as *www.thelist.com* or *www.isp.com*.

> **Tip**
> Before you sign up with any ISP, make sure their phone number is a local call from your home. Also look for unlimited usage for your monthly fee, and be sure to inquire about a setup or activation fee. If you'd like to create your own home page, find out whether the ISP offers Web space that's either free or available for a small monthly fee.

When you don't need to find an ISP

Companies that offer cable modem or Digital Subscriber Line (DSL) service (see "The wonder of a full-time Internet connection," on page 133) usually act as your ISP. For a monthly fee, they provide unlimited Internet access, and they usually provide an e-mail address too. And if you want to take advantage of the extra benefits of an online service such as America Online or MSN, you can sign up for a membership and connect to the online service through your high-speed cable modem or DSL line.

> **Tip**
> Free ISPs offer free Web access, but you might have to look at advertising in your browser window.

I can't connect to my Internet service provider anymore

Source of the problem

After you sign up for an account with an ISP, the ISP you've chosen should provide you with all the information you need to set up a connection. Some ISPs even send disks or CDs with programs you can run to create and configure a connection in Dial-Up Networking. But if you've had a connection running in the past and you can no longer connect, you should check for an incorrect password or phone number, a modem problem, or a corrupt password list by following these steps.

How to fix it

1. Make sure you're properly logged on to Windows by clicking Start and checking the user name at the top of the Start menu. If the incorrect user name is displayed, click Log Off, and log on using your correct identity.

2. Click Start, point to Connect To, right-click your ISP connection in the list, and click Properties.

3. On the Options tab of the Properties dialog box, make sure the Prompt For Name And Password, Certificate, Etc. and Prompt For Phone Number check boxes are selected, and click OK. ▶

4. Click Start again, point to Connect To, and click your ISP connection in the list.

5. In the Connect dialog box, verify that the entries in the User Name and Password boxes exactly match those you chose when you set up the ISP account or that were given to you by your ISP, including the capitalization of the letters in your user name. Also, retype your password.

   Some ISPs require you to enter a prefix and slash before your user name. If your ISP does, make sure the appropriate prefix precedes your user name in the User Name box.

6. In the Phone Number box, verify the phone number given to you by the ISP.

7. Click Properties, and on the General tab of the Properties dialog box, select the Use Dialing Rules check box, and verify the information in the Area Code and Country/ Region Code boxes.

8. Click Dialing Rules, select your location in the list in the Phone And Modem Options dialog box, and click Edit.

9. Examine and correct the four entries in the Dialing Rules area of the Edit Location dialog box to indicate whether you need to dial a 9 or a 1 before dialing a call, and then click OK to close the Edit Location dialog box, but do not click OK again. ▶

Next check the modem's settings by following these steps:

1. In the Phone And Modem Options dialog box, click the Modems tab.

2. On the Modems tab, select your modem in the list of modems, and click Properties.

3. In the Properties dialog box for your modem, click the Diagnostics tab, and click Query Modem. If an error message reports that the modem failed to respond, verify that the modem is turned on and properly plugged into the computer. If the modem is on and connected properly, or if the modem is internal, right-click My Computer on the Start menu, click Properties on the shortcut menu, click the Hardware tab in the System Properties dialog box, and click Device Manager. Verify that Device Manager is not reporting a problem with the modem driver (indicated by a yellow exclamation point on the modem's icon). If Device Manager reports a problem, click Update Driver to install a new modem driver, or click Roll Back Driver to restore the previously installed driver. For more information about these options, see "A new device I've installed doesn't work," on page 116.

4. On the Advanced tab in the Properties dialog box for your modem, click Change Default Preferences.

5. On the General tab of Default Properties dialog box, make sure Data Protocol is set to Standard EC, Compression is set to Enabled, and Flow Control is set to Hardware.

6. Click OK, and close the remaining dialog boxes.

Connecting takes a long time

Source of the problem

Waiting for your modem to dial and connect takes long enough—you don't have to suffer through an even longer delay while Windows and your ISP negotiate a working Internet connection. By changing a few settings for the connection, you can disable features that are intended only for a network connection and not for the Internet connection you want to make. Because you don't need the network connection features if you're not connected to a network, disabling them reduces the time it takes to connect to the Internet.

How to fix it

1. Click Start, point to Connect To, right-click your ISP connection, and click Properties.

2. In the Properties dialog box for the connection, click the Networking tab.

3. Click Settings, and in the PPP Settings dialog box, clear the Enable Software Compression check box, and click OK. ▶

4. Select Internet Protocol (TCP/IP) in the list of connection items, and click Properties.

5. In the Internet Protocol (TCP/IP) Properties dialog box, click Advanced.

6. In the Advanced TCP/IP Settings dialog box, clear the Use IP Header Compression check box, and click OK. ▶

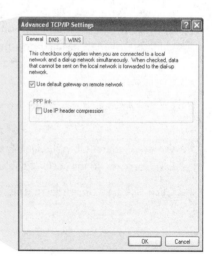

7. Click OK to close the Internet Protocol (TCP/IP) Properties dialog box.

8. Click OK to close the Properties dialog box for the connection.

After you change networking settings, you should also change a few modem settings by following these steps:

1. Click Start, and click Control Panel on the Start menu.

2. In Control Panel, click Printers And Other Hardware, and click Phone And Modem Options.

3. On the Modems tab in the Phone And Modem Options dialog box, select the modem you use to dial your ISP.

4. Click Properties.

5. On the Advanced tab in the Properties dialog box for the modem, click Change Default Preferences.

The wonder of a full-time Internet connection

If you're lucky enough to have cable modem or DSL service (two types of high-speed, full-time Internet connection) in your area, sign up and sign up quick—especially if you're plagued by poor-quality phone connections. Full-time Internet connections cost a bit more per month than regular dial-up connections, but you might be able to disconnect that second phone line that you use only for a modem.

A full-time, high-speed Internet connection will totally transform the way you use the Internet. Not only will you eliminate the twin problems of getting an Internet connection (no more busy signals) and staying connected, but you'll also be able to click through Web sites at high speed, download files quickly, watch videos on the Web, listen to music and other broadcasts, make phone calls over the Internet, and take advantage of every new technology geared toward people with *broadband access* (a fancy term for a high-speed Internet connection).

6. In the Default Preferences dialog box for the modem, make sure the Flow Control option is set to Hardware. ▶

7. Click OK.

8. Click OK again twice to close the open dialog boxes.

9. Close Control Panel.

10. Try establishing a new Internet connection with your modem.

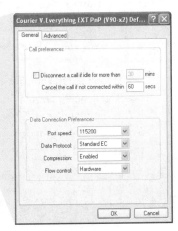

I frequently lose my connection to the Internet

Source of the problem

From time to time, everyone gets disconnected from the Internet without warning. Imperfect phone line connections are just part of the challenge of going on line. But if you find that you're disconnected frequently, you can take a number of steps to make your connections more stable and reliable, such as checking your phone line, checking your time-out period at your ISP, disabling call waiting, and others. You should try all of these procedures.

How to fix it

1. Make sure the connection between your modem and the computer is tight. Also check the line from the modem to the wall jack.

2. Do a quick check of your phone line by picking up the handset, listening to the line, and pressing any number other than 0. Listen for snaps, crackles, or pops on the line—not to mention buzzes, clicks, or hisses. Report any of those problems to your local phone company and request a repair to clean up your phone line and remove static and other noises that can interfere with connections.

If everything seems okay with your phone line and connection, see whether an ISP time-out or call waiting is disconnecting you by following these steps:

1. Check with your ISP to see whether you're automatically disconnected after a period of inactivity.

    Your ISP might offer unlimited time each month, but it can still disconnect you after a predetermined interval if you don't use the connection for a while. If you find this *time-out* period is too short and your ISP won't increase the interval for your account, you can download utilities from many file download sites on the Web, such as *www.download.com*, that will periodically use the connection to keep it active.

2. Click Start, and click Control Panel on the Start menu.

3. In Control Panel, click Printers And Other Hardware, and then click Phone And Modem Options.

4. If you don't have call waiting installed on your phone line, skip to step 6. Otherwise, in the Phone And Modem Options dialog box, select your current location in the list of locations, and click Edit.

5. On the General tab of the Edit Location dialog box, select the To Disable Call Waiting, Dial check box, click the down arrow, click the sequence of keypad presses that will disable call waiting on your line (such as *70), and click OK. ▶

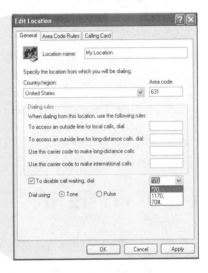

You might have to check with your phone company or consult your local phone book to determine which key sequence will temporarily disable call waiting.

6. On the Modems tab of the Phone And Modem Options dialog box, click the modem you use to dial your ISP.

7. Click Properties.

8. On the Modem tab in the Properties dialog box for the modem, click the Maximum Port Speed down arrow, and click a speed value that is half the current speed. For example, if the current speed is 115200, click 57600.

9. On the Advanced tab, click Change Default Preferences.

10. In the Default Preferences dialog box, clear the Disconnect A Call If Idle For More Than check box, if necessary.

11. In the Data Connection Preferences area of the dialog box, click the Compression down arrow, and click Disabled. ▶

12. Click OK.

13. Check your modem's user manual to see whether it has a setting that forces the modem to stay connected for a short period even without a carrier. If you find such a setting, type it in the Extra Initialization Commands box on the Advanced tab in the modem Properties dialog box.

14. Click OK twice.

15. Close Control Panel.

An automatic dialer keeps popping up

Source of the problem

It can be great to set Windows so it will dial your ISP whenever an Internet program, such as your
e-mail software, needs to go on line, but you'd never know it with all the people who curse this
feature every time the Internet dialer pops up unexpectedly. Fortunately, you can stop the dialer in
its tracks and prevent it from trying to make an Internet connection when you're not ready. You'll
regain manual control of your Internet connection so you can prepare all your e-mail messages
before going on line to send them. Here's how to take back control from the dialer.

How to fix it

1. Click Start, and click Control Panel on the Start menu.

2. In Control Panel, click Network And Internet
   Connections, and then click Set Up Or Change Your
   Internet Connection.

3. On the Connections tab in the Internet Properties
   dialog box, click Never Dial A Connection. ▶

4. Click OK, and close Control Panel.

> ### Tip
>
> Before you can repair a
> connection, you might need
> to have administrator privi-
> leges on the computer. You
> need to be the administra-
> tor for a PC or part of the
> Administrators group. If the
> computer is at home, you
> can probably log on as the
> administrator. If the com-
> puter is at an organization,
> you might need to consult
> the computer administrator
> at the organization for help.

I can't connect to Web sites or use e-mail on my high-speed Internet connection anymore

Source of the problem

If your Internet connection stops working and you have a cable or DSL modem or you connect to the Internet through another computer on a home or office network, you can have Windows attempt to repair the connection. Repairing a connection involves renewing the lease on an IP address and other similar highly technical internal adjustments. Fortunately, having Windows make the repair itself is a simple task, as described here.

How to fix it

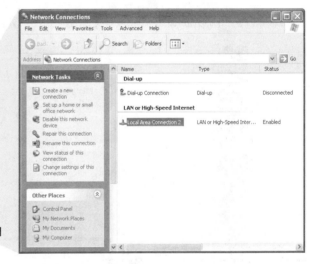

1. Click Start, point to Connect To, and click Show All Connections.

2. In the Network Connections window, click the connection that you use to reach the Internet in the LAN Or High-Speed Internet list.

3. Click Repair This Connection in the Network Tasks list. ▶
    You can also right-click the high-speed Internet or LAN connection and click Repair on the shortcut menu.

Other connection tasks

In the Network Connections window, the Network Tasks list offers a handful of tasks to help you manage connections, and two can be particularly helpful: Rename This Connection and View Status Of This Connection.

If you have network adapters in your computer, one connected to your network and one connected to a cable or DSL modem, you'll see two connections listed under LAN Or High-Speed Internet. You can rename each connection to clearly identify it by selecting the connection, clicking Rename This Connection in the tasks list, typing a new name, and pressing Enter. You can also click View Status Of This Connection to obtain more detailed technical information about your connection, which you can provide to someone helping you troubleshoot a connection problem.

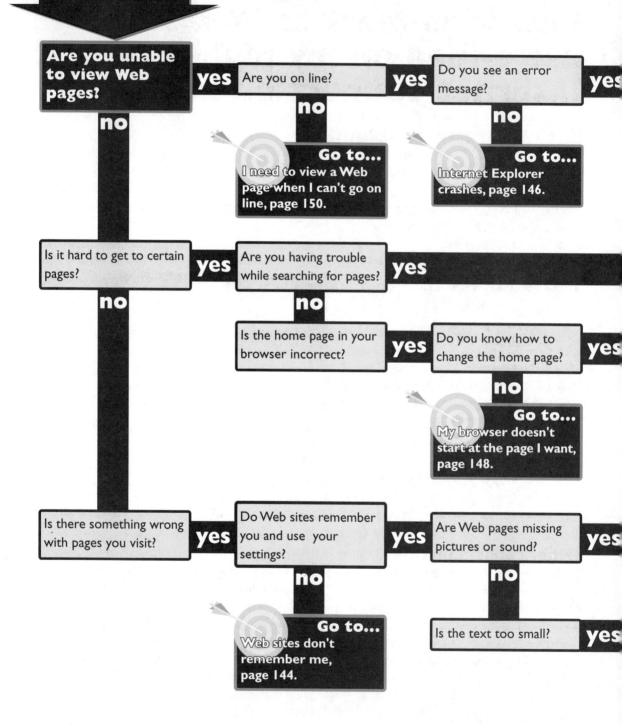

Are you unable to view Web pages?

yes → Are you on line? **yes** → Do you see an error message? **yes**

no ↓

no → Go to... I need to view a Web page when I can't go on line, page 150.

no → Go to... Internet Explorer crashes, page 146.

Is it hard to get to certain pages? **yes** → Are you having trouble while searching for pages? **yes**

no ↓

no ↓

Is the home page in your browser incorrect? **yes** → Do you know how to change the home page? **yes**

no → Go to... My browser doesn't start at the page I want, page 148.

Is there something wrong with pages you visit? **yes** → Do Web sites remember you and use your settings? **yes** → Are Web pages missing pictures or sound? **yes**

no → Go to... Web sites don't remember me, page 144.

no → Is the text too small? **yes**

Internet Explorer

Does the error report that the page cannot be displayed?

yes

Go to...
I get a message saying *The page cannot be displayed*, page 140.

no

Go to...
I get a message saying *You are not authorized to view this page*, page 149.

Quick fix

When I search for a site, Internet Explorer goes directly to a site without showing me alternatives If Internet Explorer goes to the most likely site when you enter a question mark and a search term, such as "? sailing," rather than displaying a list of possible sites, follow these steps:

1. In Internet Explorer, click Internet Options on the Tools menu.
2. In the Internet Options dialog box, click the Advanced tab.
3. In the Settings list, select the Just Display The Results In The Main Window check box under Search From The Address Bar and click OK.

Quick fix

I can't change the home page on my office computer Your system administrator might have prevented you and others from changing the home page. Lobby your system administrator to change your home page or allow you to do it.

Go to...
Web pages don't show pictures or play sound, page 143.

If your solution isn't here, check these related chapters:
- Connections, page 2
- Downloading files, page 50
- Internet connections, page 126
- Programs, page 234

Or see the general troubleshooting tips on page xv.

Quick fix

The text on Web pages is too small to read easily To make text on Web pages appear larger, follow these steps:

1. In Internet Explorer, point to Text Size on the View menu. A dot appears next to the current size.
2. Click the next largest size.

I get a message saying
The page cannot be displayed

Source of the problem

Whenever Internet Explorer can't display a Web page, it shows a page that reads *The page cannot be displayed*. Either Internet Explorer can't reach the Web page you've requested, or it found the Web site but the browser's configuration is keeping it from showing the page. To find the culprit and fix the problem, you need to first rule out a number of possible causes, such as the connection, the Web page address, and proxy settings.

How to fix it

1. Connect to the Internet.

    If your computer dials an Internet connection only when you start Internet Explorer or your e-mail program, go ahead and start that program. If you receive a *The page cannot be displayed* message immediately, your Internet connection is faulty. Continue with the next step to trouble-shoot the connection. If your home page appears, and the error message appears only when you go to a particular page, the problem is most likely at the Web site's server. Try visiting the site again later.

2. Click Start, point to All Programs, point to Accessories, and click Command Prompt.

3. In the Command Prompt window, type **ipconfig /all** and press Enter.

4. Make a note of the first address shown for the DNS Servers (four numbers separated by periods—such as 192.168.254.23). ▶

5. Type **ping** followed by a space followed by the exact address you recorded in step 4, such as **ping 192.168.254.23**, and then press Enter. ▶

    The Ping command tells you how many packets of information it sent to the address you specified, how many were received back, and how many were lost. If you received back four packets, your Internet connection is fine. If all four packets were lost, your Internet connection is not working. If you received back only two or three of the four packets, your Internet connection is working, but not reliably. To learn how to troubleshoot your Internet connection, see "I can't connect to my Internet service provider anymore," on page 130.

6. Close the Command Prompt window.

If your computer connects to the Internet through a network, you might need to enter *proxy settings*, because your computer must be communicating with the Internet through a *proxy server*. Proxy servers protect your computer from being exposed on the Internet. If your ISP or your network administrator hasn't told you to use proxy settings, skip to "More sleuthing," below. Here's how to enter proxy settings:

1. Click Start, click Control Panel, click Network And Internet Connections, and click Internet Options.

2. On the Connections tab of the Internet Properties dialog box, click the connection in the Dial-Up And Virtual Private Network Settings list that you use to access the Internet, and then click Settings.

> If you're connected to a home or office network that provides Internet access, click LAN Settings.

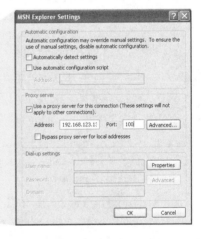

3. Select the Use A Proxy Server For This Connection check box or the Use A Proxy Server For This LAN check box if you are connected to a home or office network that provides Internet access, and in the Address and Port boxes, type the information given to you by your ISP or network administrator. ▶

4. Click OK.

More sleuthing

If your connection isn't the problem, perhaps it's the Web page address, the temporary Internet files, or the version of the Winsock file you're using. Here's how to check these possibilities:

1. Carefully check the address you typed in Internet Explorer's Address bar for typos. An extra space, an incorrect letter, or an extra or missing period might be the problem.

> If you clicked a link rather than typed an address, the link could be wrong. Click another link to jump to another Web page. If that works, you might be able to reach your destination by going to the home page of the Web site (type only the address portion, ending in .com, .net, or .org, without anything following) and then navigating to the page from there.

> *If this solution didn't solve your problem, go to the next page.*

I get a message saying *The page cannot be displayed*

(continued from page 141)

2. On the Tools menu in Internet Explorer, click Internet Options.

3. On the General tab of the Internet Options dialog box, click Delete Files.

4. In the Delete Files dialog box, select the Delete All Offline Content check box, and click OK. Click OK again to close the Internet Properties dialog box. ▶
     If this step fixes the problem, click Internet Options on the Tools menu again, and on the General tab of the Internet Options dialog box, click Settings. Under Amount Of Disk Space To Use, drag the slider slightly to the right so that Internet Explorer won't run short of temporary file space again, click OK, and click OK again.

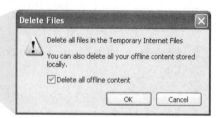

5. Click Start, and click Search on the Start menu.

6. In the Search Results window, click All Files And Folders, type **Winsock.dll** in the All Or Part Of The File Name box, and click Search.

7. In the list of found files, right-click each Winsock.dll file that is *not* located in the Windows or Windows\System folder, click Rename, and rename the file Winsock.tmp to make sure it won't be used by Windows.

8. Repeat steps 6 and 7, but search for copies of Winsock32.dll, Wsock.vxd, and Wsock32.vxd that are not located in the Windows or Windows\System folder. Rename each of these using .tmp as the new file extension.

If deleting duplicate Winsock files fixes the problem but one of your Internet programs no longer functions properly, check the manufacturer of the malfunctioning program's Web site for assistance.

If all else fails, try again a little while later. The Web site might be overloaded with other users or temporarily unable to send the Web page.

Web pages don't show pictures or play sound

Source of the problem

To speed up Web browsing, particularly when you're using a slow modem line, you can turn off graphics, multimedia, videos, and sounds and view only the text on Web pages. Text comes in across a slow modem line quickly—everything else takes much longer. But if you don't see pictures when you want them and you can't hear sounds or play multimedia files, you need to enable multimedia and graphics again.

How to fix it

1. Click Start, and click Internet on the Start menu.

2. On the Tools menu in Internet Explorer, click Internet Options.

3. In the Internet Options dialog box, click the Advanced tab.

4. In the Settings list on the Advanced tab, under Multimedia select the Play Animations In Web Pages, Play Sounds In Web Pages, Play Videos In Web Pages, and Show Pictures check boxes. ▶

5. Click OK.

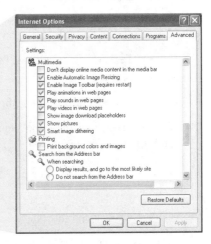

Showing one picture

If you've intentionally turned off graphics because your modem connection is slow but you've just got to see a particular picture on a page because the text that appears in its place is so tantalizing, right-click the placeholder text, and click Show Picture on the shortcut menu.

Web sites don't remember me

Source of the problem

Many Web sites send your computer very small files called *cookies* so that they can identify you the next time you visit. When you return to a site that has sent a cookie, the site retrieves the cookie, identifies you, and personalizes the Web pages you see. But if you have Internet Explorer set to refuse cookies because you're worried about privacy, Web sites can't tell that you're a returnee, so they can't display your personalized information. An online shopping site, for example, can't greet you by name and display products that fit the interests you identified on an earlier visit. If it bothers you that Web sites that once greeted you warmly have now forgotten you, restore Internet Explorer's ability to accept cookies by following this procedure.

How to fix it

1. Click Start, and click Internet on the Start menu.

2. On the Tools menu in Internet Explorer, click Internet Options.

3. In the Internet Options dialog box, click the Privacy tab.

4. On the Privacy tab, drag the slider to Medium, and click OK. ▶

If the Security Level is already at Medium or lower, follow these steps:

1. Click the Advanced button.

2. In the Advanced Privacy Settings dialog box, select Override Automatic Cookie Handling.

3. Click Accept under both First-Party Cookies and Third-Party Cookies, and click OK. ▶

4. Click OK again to close the Internet Options dialog box.

Choosing your cookies

Rather than reject all cookies outright or accept every cookie a Web site sends your way, you can review each cookie when it arrives and decide whether you want to accept or reject it. This gives you the ultimate in control, but it can also make browsing annoying, as endless Privacy Alert windows open about incoming cookies. ▶

To try this option, follow these steps:

1. Click Start, and click Internet on the Start menu.

2. On the Tools menu in Internet Explorer, click Internet Options.

3. In the Internet Options dialog box, click the Privacy tab.

4. On the Privacy tab, click Advanced.

5. In the Advanced Privacy Settings dialog box, select Override Automatic Cooking Handling.

6. Select Prompt for both first-party and third-party cookies. ▶

7. Click OK.

When you see how many cookies arrive, you'll almost certainly want to avoid being prompted about each one.

Worried about your privacy?

Cookies give Web site operators the ability to store information on your hard disk about you and your visit. The cookies record your personal preferences, selections you've made, or any other personal information that you've entered in forms. Cookies were established as a convenience, enabling you to return to a Web site, receive a personalized greeting, and find all your preferences instituted. The Web site reads your cookie and puts all your customized settings in place. But cookies can also be used to track you on line, and they allow those who create Web sites to create a profile about you without your realizing it.

Whether you choose to accept cookies or universally reject them is up to you. But if you reject cookies, you'll be trading convenience for privacy on the odd chance that a Web site has malicious intent. Remember, cookies can store only the information that you've entered about yourself at a Web site, so you might want to focus your efforts on being cautious about the information you choose to reveal.

Internet Explorer crashes

If you get an error message when you try to open a Web page, if Internet Explorer stops responding as you scroll through a page, or if Internet Explorer won't display a full page, you should systematically eliminate a number of possible causes, including clearing the Internet Explorer cache and history folders, which might contain a bad file; giving Internet Explorer more Windows resources; updating the display drivers for your video adapter; and removing old cookies, which keep a record of visits to each Web site. Any one of these items could cause Internet Explorer to crash. In addition, there could be a problem with the TCP/IP protocol that your computer uses to communicate with Web pages.

How to fix it

1. Click Start, click Control Panel on the Start menu, click Network And Internet Connections, and click Internet Options.

2. On the General tab of the Internet Options dialog box, click Delete Files, click OK, click Clear History, and click Yes. ▶

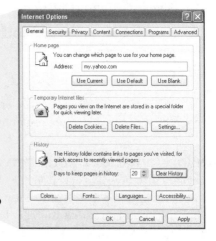

3. Click OK to close the Internet Options dialog box, and close Control Panel.

    In addition to these changes, you should make sure you've installed the latest driver for your display adapter because Internet Explorer uses the drivers to display Web page graphics.

4. Check the manufacturer's Web site for an updated driver, and if a new driver is available, download and install it..

    If an updated driver is not available, click Internet Options on the Tools menu, click the Advanced tab in the Internet Options dialog box, and clear the Use Smooth Scrolling check box in the Settings list and click OK.

Next, check the functioning of TCP/IP by following these steps:

1. Click Start, point to All Programs, point to Accessories, and click Command Prompt.

2. In the Command Prompt window, type **ping 127.0.0.1** at the prompt.

3. Press Enter.

Finally, if Internet Explorer still crashes, check to see whether a cookie is causing a problem by following these steps:

1. Click Start, and click My Computer on the Start menu.

2. In the My Computer window, double-click the disk drive that contains the Windows folder.

3. Double-click the Documents And Settings folder to open it.

4. Double-click the folder inside the Documents And Settings folder whose name matches your logon name, and then double-click the Cookies folder.

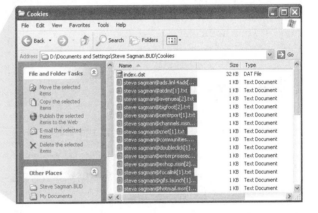

5. Select all the files in the Cookies window except index.dat.

6. Press Ctrl+X to cut them, and close the Cookies window.

7. Right-click the desktop, point to New, and click Folder.

8. Type **Cookies** to name the folder, press Enter, double-click the folder, and press Ctrl+V to paste the cookies in the new folder.

If Internet Explorer now works without crashing, copy a few of the cookies back to the Cookies folder and try browsing again. Continue to copy cookies back to the original Cookies folder until you get an error message. When this happens, cut the last few cookies you copied, and copy them back one by one until you get an error message. Delete the last cookie you copied—it's the one causing the problem.

9. Delete the Cookies folder on the desktop.

My browser doesn't start at the page I want

Source of the problem

Unless you specify a different home page, each time you start your Web browser you'll see the default home page. In Internet Explorer, the initial default home page is *www.msn.com*, but other browsers have their own initial default home pages that can be changed.

MSN is a great starting place for your exploration of the Web, but you might want to change your home page to another Internet portal that offers similarly helpful information like news, stock market updates, movie reviews, and television schedules, or you might want to start at a Web page devoted to your hobby or special interest. Of course, if you've created your own Web site, you can make it your home page.

How to fix it

1. Click Start, and click Internet on the Start menu.

2. In the Address bar, type the address of the Web page that you'd like to make your new home page, and press Enter.

3. On the Tools menu in Internet Explorer, click Internet Options.

4. On the General tab in the Internet Options dialog box, click Use Current in the Home Page area. ▶

5. Click OK.

Going home

Clicking the Home button on the Internet Explorer toolbar always takes you back to the home page you've chosen.

Internet Explorer

I get a message saying *You are not authorized to view this page*

Source of the problem

Most public Web sites are open to everyone—in fact, the more, the merrier. Companies work hard to attract people to their Web sites. But some sites are reserved for private use. They provide information for the customers of the company, or they provide services to employees. You're most likely to encounter a private site if you work in a company that lets departments set up internal Web sites. If you're not a member of the department, you're politely rebuffed with a *You are not authorized to view this page* message.

Webmasters, the people who create and control Web sites, can selectively provide permission to access their sites on the Internet by requiring a user name and password. In a corporate network, Webmasters have more control and can grant admission to people based on their network logon names or the departments to which they belong.

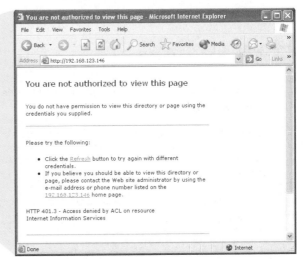

How to fix it

- Contact the Webmaster for the site or your network administrator to obtain a user name and password for the site.

- If you're supposed to have access to the site with your existing user name and password, make sure you log on to Windows with your proper user name and password.

I need to view a Web page when I can't go on line

Source of the problem

Internet Explorer has perfected the fine art of making Web pages available even when you can't connect to the Internet. Of course, when you're not connected, you can't visit new Web sites or update the information on a page.

But when you are connected, you can save a page for viewing later by making it available off line. Then when you need to refer to the information on a page, you can view it in Internet Explorer almost as if you were still connected to the Internet.

How to fix it

1. Connect to the Internet, and in Internet Explorer, open the Web page you want to view when you're off line.

2. On the Favorites menu, click Add To Favorites.

3. In the Add Favorite dialog box, select the Make Available Offline check box. ▶

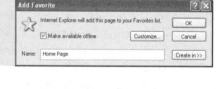

4. Enter a more memorable name in the Name box if you want.

5. Click Customize.

6. On the first page of the Offline Favorite Wizard, click Next.

7. On the next page of the wizard, click No if the current Web page is the only page you want to view off line, or click Yes if you'll also want to view the pages that are linked to the current page. ▶

   If you click Yes, you can then change the number in the Download Pages box to download additional pages that are linked to the page you're making available off line.

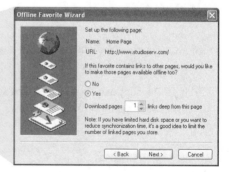

8. Click Next.

9. If you want the page updated (synchronized) on a regular schedule, click I Would Like To Create A New Schedule, and click Next.

If you'd rather update the page only when you want (by clicking Synchronize on the Tools menu), just click Next and skip to step 11.

10. On the next page of the wizard, type an interval and a time for the page to be synchronized, type a more recognizable name for the schedule if you want, and click Next. ▶

You can also select the check box on this page of the wizard if you want Windows to connect to the Internet at the designated times.

11. If the site requires a password, click the Yes option on the next page of the wizard, enter your user name, and enter the password twice.

12. Click Finish, and click OK.

Viewing an offline page

Later you can view the offline page that you've synchronized.

1. Click Internet on the Start menu, and on the File menu in Internet Explorer, click Work Offline.

2. On the toolbar, click the Favorites button.

3. In the Favorites list, click the link for the Web page.

Changing the synchronization schedule

To modify the schedule of links you download, right-click the link to the synchronized Web page in the Favorites list, and click Properties on the shortcut menu. The options on the Schedule and Download tabs of the Properties dialog box let you define how much information you'll download at each synchronization and modify when the synchronizations will occur.

Tip

To remove a page you've downloaded for viewing off line, right-click the link in the Favorites list, and clear the Make Available Offline check box. Then, in the Confirm Offline Item Delete dialog box, click Yes.

Tip

Before you save a page for offline viewing, it's best to navigate to the main Web page on the Web site, which contains links to this and other pages you might be interested in viewing off line.

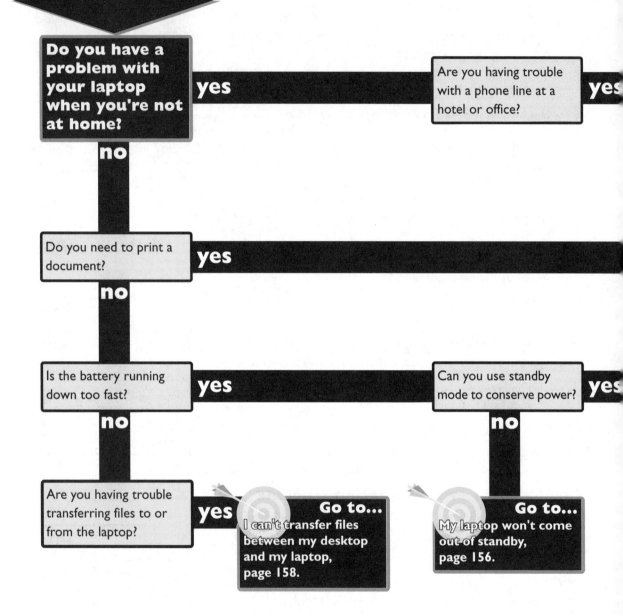

Do you have a problem with your laptop when you're not at home?

yes → Are you having trouble with a phone line at a hotel or office? **yes**

no

Do you need to print a document? **yes**

no

Is the battery running down too fast? **yes** → Can you use standby mode to conserve power? **yes**

no

no

Are you having trouble transferring files to or from the laptop? **yes**

Go to...
I can't transfer files between my desktop and my laptop, page 158.

Go to...
My laptop won't come out of standby, page 156.

Go to...
A hotel room phone line or an office phone line won't work with my laptop, page 160.

Quick fix

I don't want to forget to print a document when I return home or to my office You can send a document to a printer even if you're traveling with a laptop and not connected to the printer. When you reconnect to the printer, back at your office or at home, the document will be printed.

1. Click Start, and click Printers And Faxes on the Start menu.

2. Right-click the printer you want to use, and click Use Printer Offline on the shortcut menu.

   When you return home or to the office and reconnect to the printer, click Use Printer Offline again to clear the check mark on the shortcut menu and begin printing.

Go to...
The battery runs down too fast, page 154.

If your solution isn't here, check these related chapters:

- Connections, page 2
- E-mail, page 58
- Hardware, page 114
- Optimizing, page 212

Or see the general troubleshooting tips on page xv.

The battery runs down too fast

Source of the problem

It's the law of laptops. Laptop batteries always run out before you can finish what you're doing. So to squeeze every ounce of juice from your battery, you need to employ power management in Windows, which works with the power management features that are built into your laptop to extend the length of time your battery lasts.

The Advanced Configuration and Power Interface (ACPI) power management system in newer laptops gives you greater control over power management than Advanced Power Management (APM) in older laptops, but Windows works with both power management systems. To determine whether your laptop uses APM or ACPI, see "Checking your laptop's power management support," on the facing page. If your laptop provides only APM power management, be sure to also refer to "Turning off the laptop's built-in power management," on the facing page.

How to fix it

1. Click Start, and click Control Panel on the Start menu.

2. In Control Panel, click Performance And Maintenance, and then click Power Options.

3. On the Power Schemes tab in the Power Options Properties dialog box, click the Power Schemes down arrow, and click Portable/Laptop in the list. ▶

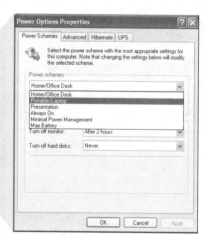

4. In the Running On Batteries column, click the System Standby, Turn Off Monitor, and Turn Off Hard Disks down arrows, and reduce the number of minutes after which each power-saving action will occur.

5. Click the Advanced tab, and select the Always Show Icon On The Taskbar check box, so that you can right-click the power management icon on the taskbar to change power management properties.

6. Click OK.

Turning off the laptop's built-in power management

If your laptop provides APM rather than ACPI, the power management built into your laptop and the power management in Windows might vie for control. If the laptop uses APM, you should change how power management works in your laptop and let Windows win this particular battle. Leave power management running in your laptop so that Windows can use it to control your laptop's devices, but you should disable the laptop's ability to turn off or dim its screen, slow the processor, stop the hard disk from spinning, and take other power-saving actions. Windows will take care of those.

Each laptop provides a different way to control its built-in power management. You should check the laptop's documentation or check with the laptop's manufacturer, but the usual method involves restarting the laptop and pressing a key while the laptop is starting up. This starts a configuration program that you can use to disable timings and power management actions, such as putting the computer on standby, turning off the screen, and turning off the hard disk. After you save the configuration settings and restart Windows, you can use power management in Windows instead to control the laptop's systems.

Checking your laptop's power management support

The specifications in your laptop's user manual can tell you the level of power management provided in the laptop, but if you don't have the manual, you can still check by following these steps:

1. Click Start, right-click My Computer on the Start menu, and click Properties on the shortcut menu.

2. On the Hardware tab in the System Properties dialog box, click Device Manager.

3. Click the plus sign next to System Devices.
   If you see a reference to a Microsoft ACPI-Compliant System, and other ACPI BIOS entries in the list, your computer supports ACPI. If you see a reference to Advanced Power Management Support, click it, and click Properties to check the APM version, which should be listed on the Settings tab in the Advanced Power Management Support Properties dialog box. ▶

4. Close Device Manager, and click OK to close any dialog boxes that are open.

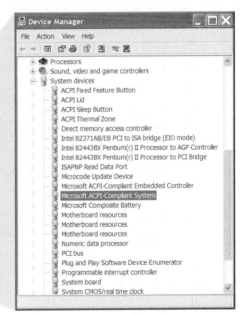

APM 1.1 can put your laptop on standby and turn off the screen. APM 1.2 can also stop the hard disk. If your laptop has APM support rather than ACPI, these are the only power-saving features you can control with Windows power management.

My laptop won't come out of standby

Source of the problem

Putting your laptop on standby turns off the screen, stops the hard disk, and puts the laptop in a power-saving mode from which it can emerge quickly—or at least that's the plan. But if Windows is unable to resume operation successfully after entering standby mode a few times, it assumes that your computer is incompatible with standby mode and disables standby. You can probably fix standby mode and thereby restore it by following these steps.

How to fix it

1. Go to the laptop manufacturer's Web site and check the support area to determine whether you can download and run a file that will update the laptop's BIOS, the program inside the laptop that controls many of the computer's basic functions. Updating the BIOS is the most likely solution for fixing the computer's incompatibility with standby mode.

   If that didn't solve the problem, your next action is to determine whether a device driver is interfering with standby mode.

2. Click Start, right-click My Computer on the Start menu, and click Properties on the shortcut menu.

3. On the Hardware tab in the System Properties dialog box, click Device Manager.

4. In Device Manager, click the plus sign next to a category of device installed in your computer that your computer can safely run without, such as a network adapter or scanner.

5. Right-click the device in the list, and click Disable. ▶

6. Click Yes to confirm that you want the device disabled.

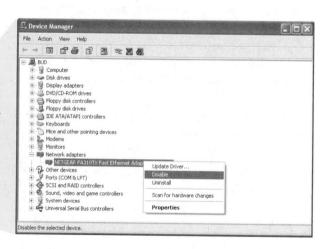

7. Close Device Manager, click OK to close the System Properties dialog box, and then restart the computer.

8. After the laptop restarts, try putting it on standby by clicking Start, clicking Shut Down, and selecting Stand By. ▶

9. Click OK.

10. Press any key or move the mouse to exit standby mode.

If your laptop doesn't come out of standby successfully, follow these steps:

1. Click Start, right-click My Computer on the Start menu, and click Properties on the shortcut menu.

2. On the Hardware tab in the System Properties dialog box, click Device Manager.

3. In Device Manager, click the plus sign next to the device you disabled, right-click the device, and click Enable. ▶

4. Right-click a different device, and click Disable on the shortcut menu.

5. Close Device Manager.

6. Click OK to close the System Properties dialog box, and then restart the computer.

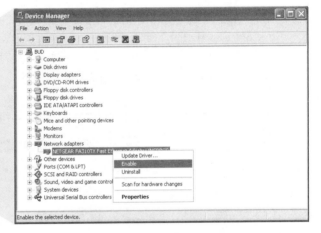

7. After the laptop restarts, try putting it on standby by clicking Start, clicking Shut Down, and selecting Stand By.

8. Click OK.

9. If your laptop comes out of standby successfully, repeat the steps above until the computer is unable to return from standby, and then either remove the device you discovered was causing the problem, or obtain an updated driver for the device that won't conflict with standby mode.

> **Tip**
>
> Because Windows simply turns off the screen and the hard disk without saving your files, you should always save your work before putting a laptop on standby. That way an unforeseen problem won't cause you to lose your work.

I can't transfer files between my desktop and my laptop

Source of the problem

If you need to continue the work you've started on a desktop computer while you're traveling with a laptop—or vice versa—but you don't have a system for transferring files between the two computers, you have several options. A number of products make desktop-to-laptop connections easy to establish, and Windows provides built-in support for synchronizing files between computers.

How to fix it

- If the laptop has a network adapter, ask to have an additional network connection installed in your office so that you can connect your laptop as well as your desktop. When both computers are on the network, you can copy files from one to the other.

- Set up a simple home network with a crossover network cable and two network adapters, or use a home networking product that provides a network over your home phone lines or through USB cables. For more information about setting up a home network, see "I don't know how to set up a home network," on page 186.

- Upload the files you need from one computer to an online file storage Web site, such as MSN Online File Cabinets (*communities. msn.com/filecabinets*), and then download the files using the other computer. ▶

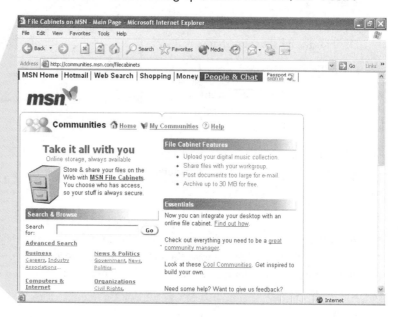

- If the laptop has an infrared port, obtain an infrared adapter for the desktop that plugs into the desktop's serial port or one of its USB ports. Many infrared adapters come with file transfer applications, so you can beam files from one computer to another.

- If the desktop computer is at home, set up the computer to use Remote Desktop so you can dial in to the desktop and transfer files over the phone as though you were connected by a network cable. For more information about using Remote Desktop, see "I can't connect to my desktop remotely," on page 210.

- Connect a DirectParallel cable between the parallel ports on the desktop and laptop, and make a direct network connection on both machines. For more information about obtaining a cable and creating a connection, see *www.lpt.com*.

- Ask your company's network administrator whether you can sign on to your company's network through Virtual Private Networking (VPN), which would allow you to use your laptop to communicate with your desktop computer through the Internet.

- Use a file synchronization program, such as Symantec's pcAnywhere or LapLink.com's LapLink, to transfer files between your desktop and laptop.

- Use a removable drive, such as a Zip drive, that you can connect to the parallel port of each computer.

Setting up programs for easy file transfer

The key to making files easy to transfer between computers is to locate your data files in an easy-to-find folder. In the My Documents folder on the desktop, for example, you can create a folder named My Laptop and then copy the files you want to take with you into this folder. Among these files would be the documents you want to take along and your data files, such as your Microsoft Outlook data file.

In Outlook, all your contacts, calendar information, e-mail messages, and other personal information are stored in a single .pst file. You can right-click Outlook Today, click Properties on the shortcut menu, and click Advanced in the Personal Folders Properties dialog box to determine the location of the .pst file.

After you close Outlook and then copy this .pst file to the My Laptop folder, where you can easily retrieve it along with the rest of your files, you can open the file in Outlook by pointing to Open on the File menu, clicking Outlook Data File, and then selecting the .pst file in the Open Outlook Data File dialog box.

A hotel room phone line or an office phone line won't work with my laptop

Source of the problem

Unlike the analog phone lines in your home, many office and hotel phone systems are digital, so they won't work with standard laptop modems. More critical is that many digital phone systems carry a higher electric current than standard phone lines, so you could damage the modem or the laptop by innocently plugging into one of these lines. You don't have to worry about plugging a modem into a jack labeled *data port* in your hotel room, but check with the front desk before you plug a modem into a wall jack. If you're not sure whether a hotel or an office phone line is digital or analog and no one can tell you for certain, here are a few workarounds.

How to fix it

1. Before you plug your modem into a hotel or an office phone line, plug in a phone line tester such as the IBM Modem Saver, which tests for dangerous conditions.

These small and inexpensive devices give a readout, usually as small status lights on the device, telling you whether the line is safe and ready for use. Search for *modem saver* on the Internet to find companies that sell these products.

2. Use an adapter that can convert a digital line to an analog line suitable for your laptop's modem. These devices are available from the same companies that sell modem savers.

3. If you have the flexibility to choose your own hotel, stay at a hotel that lists data ports in its rooms as one of its accommodations for travelers. In many cities, you can even stay at a hotel that offers a high-speed Internet connection in the room, but to connect you'll need to bring along a network adapter for your laptop and follow the instructions given to you by the front desk personnel.

> **Tip**
>
> If you're traveling outside North America, you'll need to bring along not only an adapter for the power line, but also an adapter for the phone system. You should also clear the Wait For Dial Tone Before Dialing check box on the Modem tab in the Modem Properties dialog box, because many foreign dial tones are not recognized by domestic modems.

Laptops

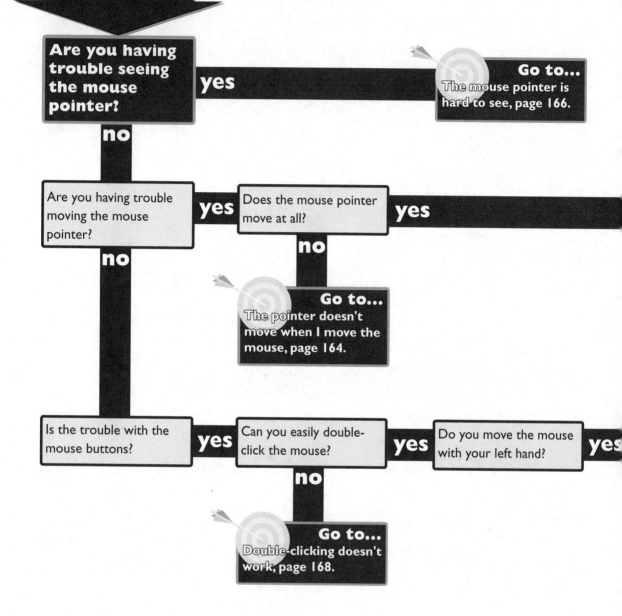

Are you having trouble seeing the mouse pointer?

yes → **Go to...** The mouse pointer is hard to see, page 166.

no

Are you having trouble moving the mouse pointer?

yes → **Does the mouse pointer move at all?**

yes →

no

Go to... The pointer doesn't move when I move the mouse, page 164.

no

Is the trouble with the mouse buttons?

yes → **Can you easily double-click the mouse?**

yes → **Do you move the mouse with your left hand?**

yes

no

Go to... Double-clicking doesn't work, page 168.

Does the mouse pointer move too fast or slow? **yes**

Quick fix

The mouse is too sensitive You can adjust the sensitivity of the mouse so you don't have to move it so delicately, or pick it up and set it back down to traverse the entire screen. Follow these steps:

1. Click Start, and click Control Panel on the Start menu.

2. In Control Panel, click Printers And Other Hardware, and then click Mouse.

3. On the Pointer Options tab in the Mouse Properties dialog box, drag the Select A Pointer Speed slider toward Slow or Fast, click Apply, and test the new mouse sensitivity.

4. When you're happy with the sensitivity, click OK.

Go to...

The buttons are backwards because I'm left-handed, page 167.

If your solution isn't here, check these related chapters:

- The desktop, page 12
- The display, page 40
- Hardware, page 114

Or see the general trouble-shooting tips on page xv.

The pointer doesn't move when I move the mouse

Source of the problem

Small children whose fingers barely reach the mouse buttons maneuver the mouse with pinpoint control. But if your mouse pointer won't move where you want it to or simply won't move at all, you need to follow the steps below (using the keyboard) to make sure the driver for the mouse is installed and the mouse is enabled. After all, without the mouse (or trackball, or track pad, or pointing stick), you can't take full advantage of pointing and clicking in Windows, and you'll never know the many secrets revealed by clicking that *other* mouse button.

How to fix it

1. Press Ctrl+Esc to open the Start menu.

2. Press the Up Arrow key a few times to move the highlight to Control Panel, and then press Enter.

3. Press the Tab key repeatedly to move the highlight (an outline) to Performance And Maintenance, press Enter, press the Tab key repeatedly to move the highlight to System, and press Enter.

4. In the System Properties dialog box, press the Right Arrow key until the Hardware tab comes to the front.

5. Press Tab a few times to move the highlight to Device Manager, and press Enter.

6. Press Tab, press the Down Arrow key repeatedly to move the highlight to Mice And Other Pointing Devices, and then press the plus sign key (on the numeric keypad).

    If you're using a laptop that doesn't have a numeric keypad, look on the keyboard for the key combination that functions as the numeric keypad plus sign key.

7. Press the Down Arrow key to move the highlight to your mouse model, and then press Enter to open the Properties dialog box for the mouse. ▶

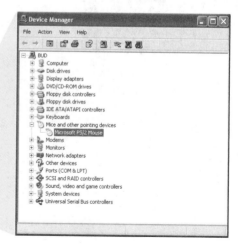

8. On the General tab in the Mouse Properties dialog box, verify that Use This Device is selected in the Device Usage box. If it isn't, press Tab to move the highlight to the Device Usage box, press the Up Arrow key to select Use This Device, press Enter, and check to see whether your mouse is working. If it isn't, repeat steps 1 through 7 above, and then continue with the next step.

9. Press the Right Arrow key twice to move the highlight to the Driver tab.

10. Press Alt+P to open the Hardware Update Wizard. ▶

11. Press Enter.

12. If your mouse or your computer came with a disk or CD containing drivers, insert the disk or CD into the drive.

13. When the wizard shows a list of compatible drivers, move the highlight to the driver that matches your mouse, and press Enter.

If the wizard doesn't show a list, press Tab to move the highlight to the check boxes for the locations you want to search for a driver, press the Spacebar to select the check boxes, and press Enter. Move the highlight to the driver that is compatible with your mouse, and press Enter.

14. If you're asked whether to restart your computer, press Tab to move the highlight to Yes, and press Enter.

The mouse moves erratically

Nearly all mice require periodic cleaning. If your mouse uses a mouse ball, open the mouse ball compartment on the bottom of the mouse, remove the mouse ball, and wipe it clean. Also wipe off the gunk that might have accumulated on the rollers in the mouse ball compartment. Check your desktop for accumulated gunk too. (Don't be embarrassed. We all get gunk.)

If you use a mouse with a red-light sensor underneath and your mouse moves erratically, the surface of your desk or work area might be too smooth for the sensor to work. Or if your mouse seems to be slipping on the desk surface instead, you're a perfect candidate for a mouse pad. Several companies make flat mouse pads that stick to the desk and provide a hard, nonskid surface. Some people find that the softer, spongier variety of mouse pad can make the mouse slightly more difficult to maneuver.

The mouse pointer is too hard to see

Source of the problem

Windows comes with a variety of mouse pointers you can use, some of which are larger and easier to see, especially when you're using a dim laptop screen or when the mouse pointer gets lost on a large monitor with lots of screen area. If you're using a desktop theme (a collection of icons, a background graphic, sounds, and mouse pointers) to enliven your desktop, you might be disappointed to find that your bigger mouse pointer no longer looks like a rocket ship or a ballpoint pen, but that's a small price to pay if you're struggling to use your computer. Here's how to choose a larger and more suitable mouse pointer.

How to fix it

1. Click Start, and click Control Panel on the Start menu.

2. In Control Panel, click Printers And Other Hardware, and then click Mouse.

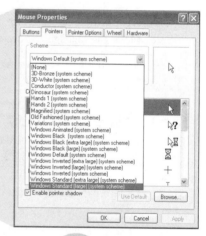

3. On the Pointers tab in the Mouse Properties dialog box, click the Scheme down arrow, and then click Windows Standard (Large). ▶

4. Click Apply, and take a look at the resulting mouse pointer. If it's still not large enough, click the Scheme down arrow again, and click Windows Standard (Extra Large).

   For an extra-visible set of mouse pointers, click Magnified in the Schemes list.

5. Click OK to close the Mouse Properties dialog box.

> **Tip**
> You might be able to press the Ctrl key to have Windows help you find the pointer if it's lost. If not, select the Show Location Of Point When I Press The CTRL Key check box on the Pointer Options tab of the Mouse Properties dialog box.

The buttons are backwards because I'm left-handed

Source of the problem

Lefties, you don't have to put up with a mouse that's backwards. By simply changing the button configuration, you can swap the functions of the left and right mouse buttons to make the mouse more suitable for you.

All models of mouse can be switched, even if one of the buttons is slightly larger than the other. Some models of mouse come with a disk that provides setup software for the mouse. The setup software often includes an option to switch the left and right mouse buttons. But you can always use the option that is built right into Windows in the Mouse Properties dialog box.

How to fix it

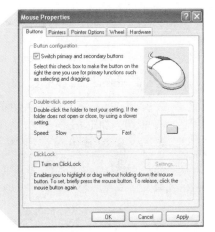

1. Click Start, and click Control Panel on the Start menu.

2. In Control Panel, click Printers And Other Hardware, and then click Mouse.

3. On the Buttons tab in the Mouse Properties dialog box, select the Switch Primary And Secondary Buttons check box in the Button Configuration area. ▶

4. Click OK to close the Mouse Properties dialog box.

Mouse options for lefties and righties

If you've recently bought a new mouse for your computer, you can probably just plug it in, start Windows, and begin using the mouse without installing any special software. But if your mouse came with an installation disk, you should install the software it provides. The software might very well add more tabs that offer additional options in the Mouse Properties dialog box. Or it might allow you to start a special mouse settings program with options for customizing the mouse, such as assigning commands to its buttons.

Double-clicking doesn't work

Source of the problem

Double-clicking is a skill that some of us never master. Even if we usually double-click without thinking twice, we sometimes end up pushing icons around the desktop rather than starting programs with them. Whether double-clicking is always a challenge or sometimes a nuisance, you can make a few adjustments that will reduce the need to double-click and also make double-clicking easier and more reliable.

To reduce the need to double-click, you can make Windows act like Web pages, with links you can single-click rather than icons you must double-click. That will take away some of the difficulty of having to double-click. But because you can't entirely eliminate double-clicking, you can make it easier by reducing the double-click speed, which gives you a little more time between clicks. Here's how to accomplish both of these tasks.

How to fix it
(by switching to single-click style)

1. Click Start, and click My Computer on the Start menu.

2. On the Tools menu, click Folder Options.

3. On the General tab in the Folder Options dialog box, click Single-Click To Open An Item (Point To Select), and click OK. ▶

Now you can just single-click icons on the desktop and in folders.

> ## Tip
> After you choose to single-click to open an item, you can have icon titles underlined only when you point to them on the screen by clicking Underline Icon Titles Only When I Point At Them before clicking OK in step 3.

How to fix it
(by adjusting double-clicking)

1. Click Start, and click Control Panel on the Start menu.

2. In Control Panel, click Printers And Other Hardware, and then click Mouse. ▶

3. On the Buttons tab in the Mouse Properties dialog box, drag the Double-Click Speed slider to the left to increase the time allowed between the two mouse clicks. ▶

Double-click the folder image in the test area. If the folder opens, you've double-clicked successfully.

4. Click OK to close the Mouse Properties dialog box.

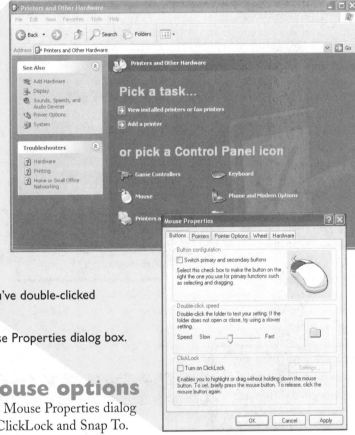

Other helpful mouse options

Two other helpful options in the Mouse Properties dialog box you should know about are ClickLock and Snap To.

Selecting Turn On ClickLock, on the Buttons tab in the Mouse Properties dialog box, allows you to highlight text or drag objects without having to hold down the mouse button while moving the mouse. You single-click and hold down the mouse button a moment until ClickLock engages. Then you can release the mouse button and move the mouse to highlight text or drag an object, such as a window. To release ClickLock, just click again.

Selecting Snap To, on the Pointer Options tab of the Mouse Properties dialog box, moves the mouse pointer to the default button in dialog boxes, such as OK or Apply, after you select an option in the dialog box.

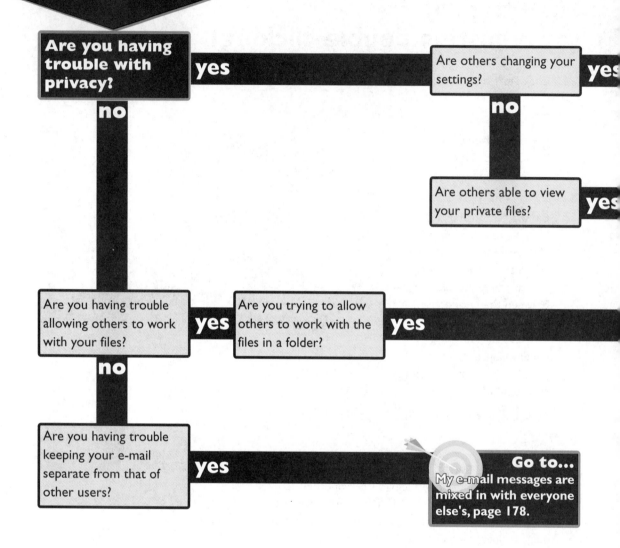

Are you having trouble with privacy?

yes → **Are others changing your settings?** **yes**

no ↓   **no** ↓

Are others able to view your private files? **yes**

Are you having trouble allowing others to work with your files?

yes → **Are you trying to allow others to work with the files in a folder?** **yes**

no ↓

Are you having trouble keeping your e-mail separate from that of other users?

yes →

Go to...
My e-mail messages are mixed in with everyone else's, page 178.

Multiple users

Go to...
Others in my home or office keep changing my settings, page 172.

Go to...
Others can view the files I want to keep private, page 176.

Are you able to set permissions for the folder?

yes

Is someone else who uses your computer unable access the files you want to share?

yes

Go to...
Another user can't access the files on my computer, page 174.

no

Quick fix

A folder I want to make secure doesn't have a Security tab in its Properties dialog box Only folders located on hard disks that use the NTFS file system have a Security tab. If you need to assign permissions for a folder, allowing only certain users to open the folder or work with its contents, move the folder to a hard disk that's formatted with NTFS. To determine which disks in your computer use NTFS, follow these steps:

1. Click Start, and click My Computer on the Start menu.
2. On the View menu, click Choose Details.
3. In the Choose Details dialog box, select the File System check box, and click OK.
4. Examine the File System column in My Computer, which describes the file system for each hard disk.

If your solution isn't here, check these related chapters:

- E-mail, page 58
- Files, page 72
- Folders, page 82
- Networks, home, page 180

Or see the general trouble-shooting tips on page xv.

Others in my home or office keep changing my settings

Source of the problem

Unless you take steps to prevent it, others who use your computer might change your settings every time they add a desktop icon, change a Start menu item, or create a Web favorite.

With Windows XP, you can easily set up one computer to serve the needs of several people. Each person who logs on with a different user name and password gets a personalized desktop, Start menu, My Documents folder, and favorites. The key to creating unique identities for people in your role as the administrator of your computer is to create user accounts, assign capabilities to them, and establish how others will be able to log on. Here's how to do it.

How to fix it

1. Log on to Windows with your administrator account.

   The user name and password you create when you install Windows XP is the Computer Administrator identity, with the power to create and delete other accounts.

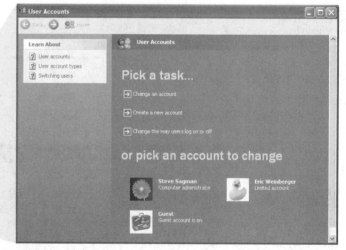

2. Click Start, click Control Panel on the Start menu, and in Control Panel, click User Accounts. ▶

   The User Accounts window shows at least two accounts: your computer administrator account and a guest account, a generic account that anyone can use to log on and perform basic tasks, such as browsing the Web. If a User Accounts dialog box opens rather than the User Accounts window, your computer is part of a domain rather than a workgroup, so your computer administrator should handle the task of managing accounts.

3. In the User Accounts window, click Create A New Account.

4. On the Name The New Account page, enter a name for the new account.

   You can use any name, including a single name or a first and last name separated by a space.

5. Click Next, and on the Pick An
   Account Type page, click
   Limited. ▶

   Someone with a limited
   account can't delete essential
   files, install new programs in
   Windows, or change the accounts
   of others who use the computer.
   Only computer administrator
   accounts have these capabilities.

6. Click Create Account.

   The account appears in the
   User Accounts window.

7. If you want to create additional
   accounts, click Create A New
   Account again, and repeat steps 4 through 6.

8. In the User Accounts window, click Change The Way Users Log On Or Off.

9. In the Select Logon And Logoff Options
   screen, select Use The Welcome Screen
   only if you want others to be able to
   select a user name from a list when
   Windows starts. ▶

   Allowing others to log on by
   clicking their name on the Welcome
   screen is a convenience to users, but it
   doesn't enforce security. Anyone can click
   any user name to masquerade as someone else and log on to the computer.
   To require each user to enter a user
   name and password, leave the Use The
   Welcome Screen option cleared.

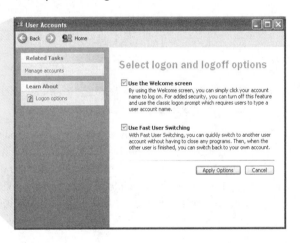

10. If you selected Use The Welcome Screen in step 9, you can also select Use Fast User Switching,
    which lets others switch to their user accounts without logging you off your account.

    To switch user accounts, anyone can click Start, click Log Off on the Start menu, and then
click Switch User in the Log Off Windows dialog box.

Another user can't access the files on my computer

Source of the problem

Your desktop, settings, and favorites are all protected when you set up multiple accounts on a single computer, so others can log on and change their settings, and not yours. Your files are also protected from viewing by others—a benefit if you want to maintain some privacy, but a hindrance if you want to share the information in a file with others, such as a family calendar, or a workgroup itinerary.

If the other users are on other computers on the network, you can share the contents of a disk or folder, which requires specifically designating the disk or folder as a shared resource. But if the people you'd like to share files with are other users on your own computer, there's a much easier way to share files—by placing them in your Shared Documents folder, which makes them available to everyone who can connect to your computer.

Here's how to share disks and folders with other users on a network and how to share files with other users on your own computer.

How to fix it

1. Click Start, and click My Computer on the Start menu.

2. In My Computer, right-click a disk or folder that you want to give others access to, and click Sharing And Security on the shortcut menu.

3. If the item you selected is a disk, click New Share on the Sharing tab in the Properties dialog box. If the item you selected is a folder, click Share This Folder on the Sharing tab.

   If you have Simple File Sharing turned on, the Sharing tab looks different. In the Network Sharing And Security section, select Share This Folder On The Network, click OK, and skip step 4.

4. If the item you selected is a disk, enter a name in the New Share dialog box, and click OK. If the item you selected is a folder, change the name in the Share Name box if you'd like, and click OK. ▶

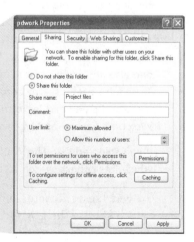

Multiple users

When you share a disk or folder, you grant access to the disk or folder to everyone on the network. When you have Simple File Sharing turned on, all network users can access its contents. But to be more selective about who can access the disk or folder, follow these steps:

1. Click Start, and click My Computer on the Start menu.

2. On the Tools menu in My Computer, click Folder Options, and then, on the View tab, make sure the Use Simple File Sharing check box is not selected in the Advanced Settings list and click OK.

3. In My Computer, right-click the disk or folder you've shared, and click Sharing And Security on the shortcut menu.

4. In the Properties dialog box for the disk or folder, click Permissions. ▶

5. In the Permissions dialog box, click Add.

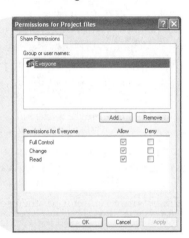

6. In the Enter The Object Names To Select box in the Select Users, Computers, Or Groups dialog box, type the user names or group names of the people to whom you want to give access to the resource, separating them with semicolons, and click OK.

7. In the Group Or User Names list in the Permissions dialog box, select Everyone, and click Remove.

8. Click OK to close each open dialog box.

Using the Shared Documents folder

1. Click Start, and click My Computer on the Start menu.

2. In My Computer, open the folder containing the document you want to share with others who use this computer.

3. Click Start, and click My Computer on the Start menu.

4. In My Computer, open the Shared Documents folder. ▶

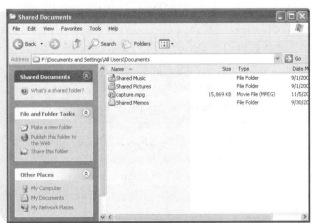

5. Drag the documents you want to share from the folder window to the Shared Documents folder.
   Now other users of this computer can open the Shared Documents folder to view and work with those files.

Others can view the files I want to keep private

Source of the problem

Just because you've agreed to share your computer with others in your household or office doesn't mean you need to share all your private files, too. Unless you take steps to protect your files, they can be open territory to anyone who uses your computer.

Windows XP provides the capability to protect your My Documents folder, making it impervious to others. Once you protect your My Documents folder, you can use it to store files and folders that only you can open.

The easiest way to protect a folder is to turn on Simple File Sharing. Then, you must store your My Documents folder on a disk drive that uses the NTFS file system, which could be your main hard disk, one of the other drive letters on your hard disk, or a second hard disk in your computer. Finally, you must ensure that everyone who logs on to your computer is required to enter a user name and password, so Windows can tell who's using the computer.

Here's how to protect your My Documents folder, place it on an NTFS disk drive if it's not already there, and enforce the use of user names and passwords.

How to fix it

1. Click Start, click My Computer on the Start menu, and click Folder Options on the Tools menu of My Computer.

2. On the View tab of the Folder Options dialog box, select the Use Simple File Sharing check box, and click OK.

3. Click Start, and right-click My Documents on the Start menu.

4. Click Properties on the shortcut menu, and click the Sharing tab in the My Documents Properties dialog box.

5. In the Local Sharing And Security area of the Sharing tab, select the Make This Folder Private check box. ▶

   If the Make This Folder Private check box isn't available, the disk drive that contains the My Documents folder is not formatted with the Windows XP file system, NTFS. You can either convert the disk drive to NTFS or move the folder to a disk drive that you've formatted with NTFS.

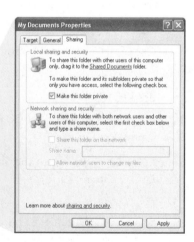

To convert a disk drive to NTFS, follow these steps:

1. Click Start, click Run, in the Run dialog box type **command** in the Open box, and click OK.

2. In the Command Prompt window, type **convert driveletter /fs:ntfs**, replacing *driveletter* with the letter of the drive that contains your private files. ▶

3. Press Enter.

4. Follow the steps on screen to convert the hard disk to NTFS.

If you already have a disk drive that uses NTFS, follow these steps to move the My Documents folder to the NTFS disk drive:

1. Click Start, right-click My Documents on the Start menu, and click Properties on the shortcut menu.

2. On the Target tab in the My Documents Properties dialog box, click Move.

3. In the Select A Destination dialog box, click the disk drive that you want to hold the My Documents folder, and click Make New Folder.

4. Type **My Documents**, and press Enter.

5. With the My Documents folder still selected, click OK in the Select A Destination dialog box.

6. In the My Documents Properties dialog box, click OK, and in the Move Documents message box, click Yes.

> ### Warning
> When you finish using the computer or leave it unattended, you must be sure to log off Windows by clicking Start and clicking Log Off on the Start menu.

Next, you need to turn off the Welcome screen so everyone who logs on at your computer must enter a user name and password rather than select a user name from a list.

1. Click Start, click Control Panel on the Start menu, and click User Accounts.

2. In the User Accounts window, click Change The Way Users Log On Or Off, and clear the Use The Welcome Screen check box. ▶

  The Use Fast User Switching check box is now cleared and unavailable.

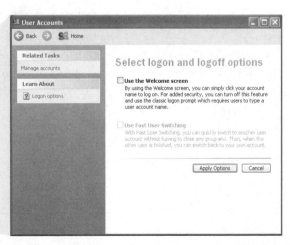

My e-mail messages are mixed in with everyone else's

Source of the problem

If other people in your family or office use your computer, you might find that their e-mail messages in Outlook Express are mixed in with yours. Mixing together everyone's e-mail provides two disadvantages: It's a nuisance to locate your own e-mail messages among those of others, and you can read everyone else's e-mail messages while they can read yours. That doesn't exactly assure you of much privacy.

If you use Outlook Express, you can solve this problem by setting up a separate identity for each person who uses the computer. After you open Outlook Express, you can select your identity to see and work with only your own e-mail messages.

How to fix it

1. On the File menu of Outlook Express, point to Identities, and click Add New Identity.

2. In the Identity section of the New Identity dialog box, type your name. ▶

3. If you want your e-mail to be password-protected, select the Require A Password check box, type a password twice in the Enter Password dialog box, and click OK.

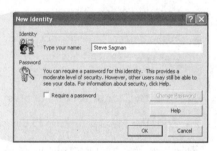

4. Click OK in the New Identity dialog box.

5. Click Yes when you're asked whether you want to switch to the new identity.

6. When the Internet Connection Wizard opens, click Create A New Account if it appears as an option on your screen and you don't already have an account in an existing e-mail program, such as Microsoft Outlook.

    If you want to use an account you already have in Microsoft Outlook or Exchange, click Use Existing Account.

> ### Tip
> It's your computer, so your identity should be the one Outlook Express uses when it starts. To set your identity as the default, click File, point to Identities, and click Manage Identities. Click the Use This Identity When Starting A Program down arrow, click your identity in the list, and click Close.

7. If you're creating a new account, follow the steps of the wizard to enter your user name, mail servers, and other information necessary to set up the account. If you're using an existing account, confirm the settings detected by the wizard by clicking Accept Settings, and click Next.

If the settings are incorrect, click Change Settings, click Next, and follow the steps of the wizard to enter revised information.

8. Click Finish to close the wizard.

9. If the Outlook Express Import dialog box opens because you have existing Outlook or Exchange messages and an existing address book, click Do Not Import At This Time, and then click Finish.

Switching identities

As long as you switch to your own identity when you start Outlook Express, you'll be working with your own e-mail messages and settings.

1. On the File menu in Outlook Express, click Switch Identity.

2. In the Switch Identities dialog box, click the identity you want to use.

3. Enter a password if necessary, and click OK. ▶

Managing identities

You can add more identities, remove an identity, or change the properties of an identity by following these steps:

1. On the File menu in Outlook Express, point to Identities, and click Manage Identities. ▶

2. In the Manage Identities dialog box, you can do all of the following:

- Add an identity by clicking New.

- Remove an identity by clicking an identity in the Identities list and clicking Remove.

- Change the name of an identity or give an identity a password by selecting an identity and clicking Properties.

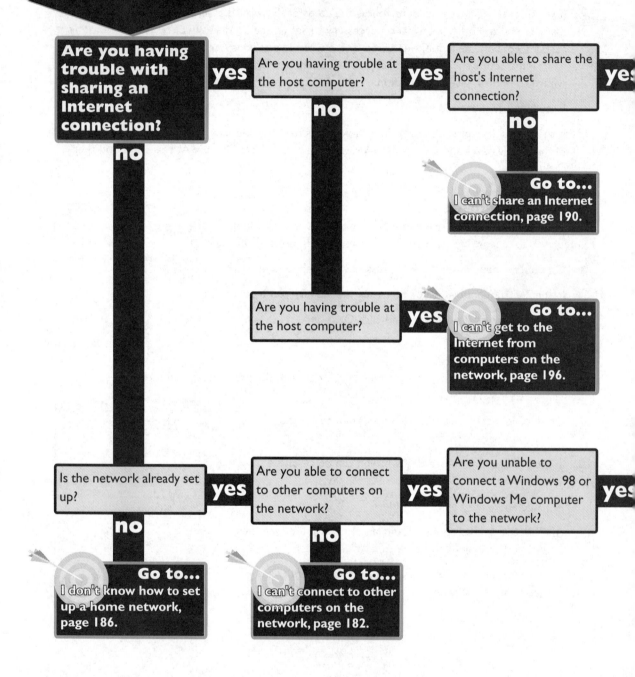

Are you having trouble with sharing an Internet connection? — **yes** → Are you having trouble at the host computer? — **yes** → Are you able to share the host's Internet connection? — **yes**

Are you able to share the host's Internet connection? — **no** →
Go to...
I can't share an Internet connection, page 190.

Are you having trouble at the host computer? — **no** → Are you having trouble at the host computer? — **yes** →
Go to...
I can't get to the Internet from computers on the network, page 196.

Are you having trouble with sharing an Internet connection? — **no** → Is the network already set up? — **yes** → Are you able to connect to other computers on the network? — **yes** → Are you unable to connect a Windows 98 or Windows Me computer to the network? — **yes**

Is the network already set up? — **no** →
Go to...
I don't know how to set up a home network, page 186.

Are you able to connect to other computers on the network? — **no** →
Go to...
I can't connect to other computers on the network, page 182.

Does the host dial the ISP when necessary?

yes

Does the host computer not disconnect from the ISP when necessary?

yes

no

Quick fix

The host computer won't hang up an Internet connection when a client computer is done with it When you quit Internet Explorer on one of the computers on a home network that has Internet Connection Sharing running, the computer that has the Internet connection doesn't disconnect from you Internet service provider. (ISP). The only way to end the Internet session is to end the connection on the host computer.

Go to...
The Internet Connection Sharing host computer won't dial the ISP when a client computer needs an Internet connection, page 194.

Go to...
I don't know how to set up a Windows 98 or Windows Me computer to connect with a Windows XP computer, page 195.

If your solution isn't here, check these related chapters:

- Connections, page 2
- E-mail, page 58
- Internet Explorer, page 138
- Optimizing, page 212

Or see the general trouble-shooting tips on page xv .

I can't connect to other computers on the network

Source of the problem

After you've installed the network adapters, connected the cables, and configured the network in Windows or simply run the Network Setup Wizard, the computers in your home should begin talking to one another. You won't exactly hear the buzz of conversation, but you should be able to click My Network Places on the Start menu, click View Workgroup Computers in the Network Tasks list, and find other computers listed. If not, you need to check your network settings by following these steps.

Before you start

This solution consists of a number of procedures to try. After each procedure, follow these steps to check your network connection:

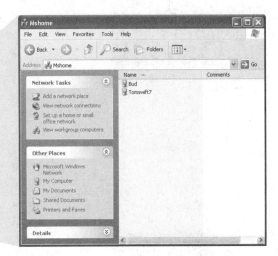

1. Click Start, and click My Network Places on the Start menu.

2. In the Network Tasks list, click View Workgroup Computers.

3. If the My Network Places window displays the computers on your network, your connection is working. ▶

    If no computers appear, continue to the next procedure in this solution.

How to fix it

1. First make sure you've logged on with your correct user name and password by clicking Start and checking the user name at the top of the Start menu. If you need to log off and log back on with the correct user name, make sure any open documents are saved, click Start, click Log Off, and then click Log Off in the Log Off Windows dialog box.

2. When Windows restarts, select your user name on the Welcome screen or enter your user name and password in the Log On To Windows dialog box, and click OK.

Next, check your computer name and workgroup name by following these steps:

1. Click Start, right-click My Computer on the Start menu, and click Properties on the shortcut menu.

2. On the Computer Name tab in the System Properties dialog box, make sure the Full Computer Name listed is a unique name on the network and that the workgroup name in the Workgroup box is the same as the name used by the other computers on your network. ▶

3. If you need to change either of these entries, click Change, enter the changes in the Computer Name Changes dialog box, and click OK.

4. Click OK when you see a message saying *You must restart this computer for the changes to take effect.*

5. Click OK to close the dialog box, and click Yes when you're asked whether you want to restart your computer.

Make sure your LAN connection is enabled by following these steps:

1. Click Start, right-click My Network Places on the Start menu, and click Properties on the shortcut menu.

2. In the Network Connections window, examine the entry for your LAN connection. If the entry is Disabled, select the LAN connection and click Enable This Network Device in the Network Tasks list. ▶

If this solution didn't solve your problem, go to the next page.

I can't connect to other computers on the network

(continued from page 183)

Make sure File and Printer Sharing for Microsoft Networks is installed by following these steps:

1. Click Start, right-click My Network Places on the Start menu, and click Properties on the shortcut menu.

2. In the Network Connections window, right-click your LAN connection, and click Properties on the shortcut menu.

3. In the Properties dialog box, look for File And Printer Sharing For Microsoft Networks in the list of items, and make sure its check box is selected. ▶

If File And Printer Sharing For Microsoft Networks isn't selected, select its check box, and close the dialog box. If it's not present, continue with this procedure.

1. Click Install, and in the Select Network Component Type dialog box, click Service, and click Add.

2. In the Select Network Service dialog box, click File And Printer Sharing For Microsoft Networks, click OK, and click Close to close the Properties dialog box.

If File and Printer Sharing for Microsoft Networks is installed but you still can't see other computers on the network, verify that the network protocol you need is installed. The network protocol is the language that computers speak on the network. For a home network, you'll need TCP/IP on all computers for accessing the Internet. TCP/IP alone should be enough to provide communication among the computers on a network, but if you just can't get your computers to communicate with TCP/IP alone, you can also install the NetBEUI protocol to ensure file transfers and resource sharing.

1. Click Start, right-click My Network Places on the Start menu, and click Properties on the shortcut menu.

2. In the Network Connections dialog box, right-click your network connection, and click Properties on the shortcut menu.

3. If Internet Protocol (TCP/IP) isn't selected in the items list, select its check box, and click OK.

Networks, home

If you still can't view other computers on the network, you can try adding the NetBEUI network protocol. The NetBEUI protocol allows the computers on a network to easily communicate with one another. You'll still need TCP/IP installed on any computer that you'd like to be able to connect to the Internet, even if it's through Internet connection sharing, but unlike TCP/IP, NetBEUI requires no configuration and it's easy to use. To install NetBEUI, follow these steps:

1. Click Start, right-click My Network Places on the Start menu, and click Properties on the shortcut menu.

2. In the Network Connections dialog box, right-click your network connection.

3. Click Properties on the shortcut menu.

4. Click Install.

5. In the Select Network Component Type dialog box, click Protocol, and click Add. ▶

6. In the Select Network Protocol dialog box, click Have Disk.

7. Insert the Microsoft Windows XP CD in the CD-ROM drive.

8. In the Install From Disk dialog box, click Browse.

9. In the Locate File dialog box, click the Look In down arrow, and select the CD-ROM drive.

10. In the folder window, double-click these folders in order: valueadd, msft, net, and netbeui.

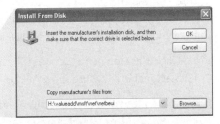

11. Select netnbf.inf, and click Open.

12. In the Install From Disk dialog box, click OK. ▶

13. In the Select Network Protocol dialog box, click NetBEUI Protocol, and click OK. ▶

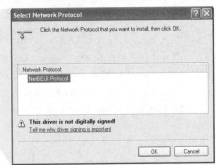

14. Click Yes when you're asked whether you want to restart your computer.

I don't know how to set up a home network

Source of the problem

When you have two or more computers in a single home, you should certainly link them and gain the benefits and cost savings of a home network. In no time, you'll be swapping files and sharing resources such as an Internet connection. You'll pay a little bit for the hardware you need to connect the computers in a network, but you'll probably save money in the long run by sharing items on the network, such as printers, an Internet connection and other devices attached to computers on the network.

To set up a home network with two computers, you'll need three hardware devices and some cable, all of which you can buy in a single kit. All the software you need to create the network is built into Windows XP, including the Network Setup Wizard, which completely configures the network. The Network Setup Wizard can even set up Internet connection sharing, and set up an Internet connection firewall to protect your network from hackers and snoops.

When you're ready to set up a home network, follow the steps in this solution.

Before you start

Before you use the Network Setup Wizard to create a home network, decide whether you want to share a single Internet connection among all the computers on your network. If you do decide to share a connection, you'll need to say so when you follow these steps:

1. Click Start, point to Connect To on the Start menu, and click Show All Connections.

2. In the Network Connections window, click Create A New Connection in the Network Tasks list.

3. Follow the steps of the New Connection Wizard to create an Internet connection. For more information about creating an Internet connection, see "I don't have an Internet service provider" on page 128.

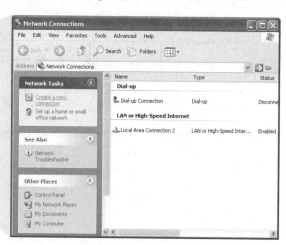

How to fix it

1. Get a home network kit.

   A typical home network kit contains a pair of Plug and Play network adapters (one for each computer), a hub (into which both network adapters plug), and matching cables. Inexpensive home network kits are available at computer stores and from online computer merchants.

   The network adapters in the kit plug into your computers, the hub (a small junction box) sits somewhere between the two computers, and the cables connect each computer to the hub.

   You can buy home network kits that contain two network adapter cards for connecting a pair of desktop computers, or you can obtain kits that contain one regular network adapter card for your desktop computer and one PC card or USB network adapter for connecting your laptop to the network. And you can always buy additional network adapters and cables to add more computers to the hub, as a typical hub contains four or more ports into which you can plug computers.

   You can also buy kits that use your existing phone lines rather than network cables. These have the advantage of letting you avoid running cables through your house. Another option that avoids cables is a wireless network. But the hardware required to create a wireless network (a wireless router and wireless network adapters) is considerably more expensive.

2. Turn off each computer and install the network adapter.

3. Position the hub between the two computers.

4. Connect a cable from each computer to the hub.

   The hub can be located anywhere between the two computers. If the computers are in adjacent rooms, you'll need to run the cable through the wall. If both computers are on the ground floor of your home but in different rooms, consider running the cable through the floor to a hub located in the basement. If the computers are located on different floors, you can use a phone line network kit rather than run cables between floors to take advantage of the existing phone wiring in your home.

5. Turn on each computer and wait as Windows recognizes the network adapters and installs the software for the network.

6. Click Yes if you're asked whether you want to restart each computer.

7. Now that you've installed the hardware and let Windows install the underlying software for the network, you need to configure the network. Some home network kits come with setup software that configures the network for you, but in Windows you should use the Network Setup Wizard to configure the network.

> If this solution didn't solve your problem, go to the next page.

I don't know how to set up a home network

(continued from page 187)

Using the Network Setup Wizard

Home networking is so popular and beneficial that Windows XP includes a special wizard devoted to setting up and configuring a home network. To run the Network Setup Wizard on each computer on the home network and set up its network connection, follow these steps:

1. Click Start, click Control Panel on the Start menu, and click Network And Internet Connections in Control Panel.

2. In the Network And Internet Connections window, click Set Up Or Change Your Home Or Small Office Network.

3. On the first page of the Network Setup Wizard, click Next, and click Next again on the next page of the wizard. ▶

4. If this computer will be used to connect directly to the Internet (with a dial-up or full-time connection to an Internet service provider), click This Computer Connects Directly To The Internet.

   If this computer will connect to the Internet through another computer on the network, click This Computer Connects To The Internet Through Another Computer On My Network Or Through A Residential Gateway.

   If no computers on the network will connect to the Internet, click Other.

5. Click Next.

6. If you clicked This Computer Connects Directly To The Internet in the Network Setup Wizard, select your Internet connection in the list shown on the next page of the wizard. ▶

7. Click Next.

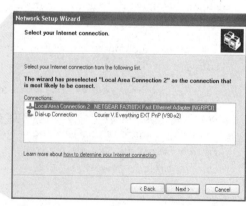

8. On the Give This Computer A Description And Name page of the wizard, enter a description for the computer and change the computer name to something more memorable, if you want, and click Next.

    Some Internet service providers require that you use a particular computer name. If your ISP has set a name for your computer, do not change it.

9. On the Name Your Network page of the wizard, enter a name for the network, and click Next.

    You can use any name, such as homenetwork. Make a note of this network name because you'll need to use the same network name when you run the Network Setup Wizard on all other computers on the network. ▶

10. On the next page of the wizard, click Next to have the wizard set up the connection.

11. On the You're Almost Done page, which advises you to run the Network Setup Wizard on the other computers on the network, click Create A Network Setup Disk, which you can use to set up the network on other computers that are running a previous version of Windows, such as Windows 98 or Windows Me.

    It's not necessary to create a Network Setup Disk if you have the Windows XP CD handy, because you can use the CD to set up the network on other computers. If you prefer to use the CD, click the Use My Windows XP CD option on the final page of the wizard. For more information about setting up the network on computers that are running a previous version of Windows, see "I don't know how to set up a Windows 98 or Windows Me computer to connect with a Windows XP computer," on page 195.

    If you don't need to run the wizard to set up other computers on the network, click Just Finish The Wizard; I Don't Need To Run The Wizard On Other Computers.

12. Click Next and follow the instructions provided by the wizard. Click Finish when you reach the last page of the wizard.

Tip

If you need to run the Network Setup Wizard on a Windows 98 or Windows Me computer, see "I don't know how to set up a Windows 98 or Windows Me computer to connect with a Windows XP computer," on page 195.

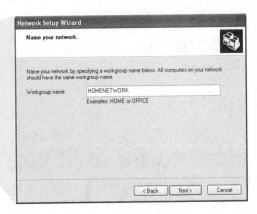

I can't share an Internet connection

Source of the problem

Internet Connection Sharing could be the very best reason to set up a home network. One Internet connection—one Internet service provider (ISP) account, one phone line, one monthly bill—can serve your entire household. Internet Connection Sharing works particularly well if you have an always-on Internet connection, such as a cable modem, which provides enough speed for everyone to use simultaneously. But if you don't know how to get Internet Connection Sharing up and running, follow these steps.

Before you start

Make sure that the Windows XP computer with the Internet connection can connect to the Internet. Other computers on the home network can be running Windows 98, Windows Me, or Windows 95.

How to fix it (if you haven't yet set up the network)

1. On the computer that's directly connected to the Internet, click Start, click Control Panel on the Start menu, and click Network And Internet Connections in Control Panel.

2. In the Network And Internet Connections window, click Set Up Or Change Your Home Or Small Office Network.

3. On the first page of the Network Setup Wizard, click Next, and click Next again on the next page of the wizard.

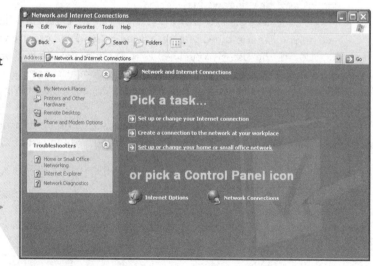

4. Click This Computer Connects Directly To The Internet.

5. Click Next.

6. Select your Internet connection in the list shown on the next page of the wizard, and click Next

7. On the Give This Computer A Description And Name page of the wizard, enter a description for the computer and change the computer name to something more memorable, if you want, and click Next.

   Some Internet service providers require that you use a particular computer name. If your ISP has set a name for your computer, do not change it.

8. On the Name Your Network page of the wizard, enter a name for the network.

   You can use any name, such as homenetwork. Make a note of this network name because you'll need to use the same network name when you run the Network Setup Wizard on all other computers on the network.

9. On the last page of the wizard, click Next to have the wizard set up the connection.

On each of the other computers on the network, follow these steps:

1. Click Start, click Control Panel on the Start menu, and click Network And Internet Connections in Control Panel.

2. In the Network And Internet Connections window, click Set Up Or Change Your Home Or Small Office Network.

3. On the first page of the Network Setup Wizard, click Next, and click Next again on the next page of the wizard.

4. Click This Computer Connects To The Internet Through Another Computer On My Network Or Through A Residential Gateway. ▶

5. Click Next.

6. On the Give This Computer A Description And Name page of the wizard, enter a description for the computer and change the computer name to something more memorable, if you want, and click Next.

   Some Internet service providers require that you use a particular computer name. If your ISP has set a name for your computer, do not change it.

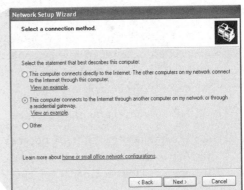

If this solution didn't solve your problem, go to the next page.

I can't share an Internet connection

(continued from page 191)

7. On the Name Your Network page of the wizard, enter a name for the network.
   Use the same name as you used on the computer that connects directly to the Internet, such as homenetwork.

8. On the next page of the wizard, click Next to have the wizard set up the connection.

9. On the You're Almost Done page, which advises you to run the Network Setup Wizard on the other computers on the network, click Just Finish The Wizard; I Don't Need To Run The Wizard On Other Computers, and click Next.

10. Click Finish at the last page of the wizard.

How to fix it (if you've already got the network running)

1. On the host computer (the one with the Internet connection), click Start, and click Control Panel on the Start menu.

2. In Control Panel, click Network And Internet Connections.

3. In the Network And Internet Connections window, click Network Connections.

4. In the Network Connections window, right-click the Internet connection, either your dial-up connection or a high-speed Internet connection, such as the network adapter that's connected to your cable modem.

5. Click Properties on the shortcut menu.

6. On the Advanced tab of the Properties dialog box, select the Allow Other Network Users To Connect Through This Computer's Internet Connection check box. ▶

7. If you want others on the network to be able to control the Internet connection, also select the Allow Other Network Users To Control Or Disable The Shared Internet Connection check box.

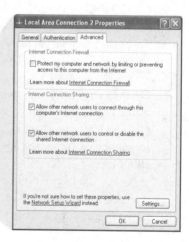

8. Select the Protect My Computer And Network By Limiting Or Preventing Access To This Computer From The Internet check box.

9. Click OK.

10. Close the Network Connections window.

When the client is running Windows Me or Windows 98

1. Insert the Windows XP CD in the CD-ROM drive.

2. In the Welcome To Microsoft Windows XP window, click Perform Additional Tasks. ▶

3. On the next page, click Set Up A Home Or Small Office Network. ▶

4. In the Network Setup Wizard dialog box, click Yes to run the wizard.

5. Follow the steps of the wizard to install the Network Setup Wizard.

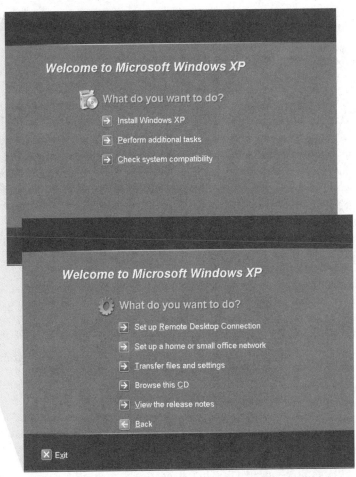

Welcome to Microsoft Windows XP

What do you want to do?

→ Install Windows XP

→ Perform additional tasks

→ Check system compatibility

Welcome to Microsoft Windows XP

What do you want to do?

→ Set up Remote Desktop Connection

→ Set up a home or small office network

→ Transfer files and settings

→ Browse this CD

→ View the release notes

← Back

X Exit

The Internet Connection Sharing host computer won't dial the ISP when a client computer needs an Internet connection

Source of the problem

When one of the computers that isn't directly connected to the Internet (a *client computer*) needs an Internet connection, the computer with the connection (the *host computer*) should automatically dial in to the ISP and establish the connection. This is more than just courtesy. If the host computer won't establish an Internet connection when a client computer needs it, the client computers won't be able to reach the Internet at all. When the host computer won't dial when a client needs it to, follow these steps.

How to fix it

1. On the host computer, click Start, and click Control Panel on the Start menu.

2. In Control Panel, click Network And Internet Connections, and then click Internet Options.

3. On the Connections tab in the Internet Properties dialog box, click Always Dial My Default Connection.

4. In the Dial-Up And Virtual Private Network Settings list, make sure the connection you want to use is selected and designated as the default. If it isn't, click it, and click Set Default.

5. Select the connection in the Dial-Up Settings list, click Settings, and then in the Dial-Up Connection Settings dialog box, click Properties.

6. On the Advanced tab, make sure the Establish A Dial-Up Connection Whenever A Computer On My Network Attempts To Access The Internet and the Allow Other Users To Control Or Disable The Shared Internet Connection check boxes are selected. ▶

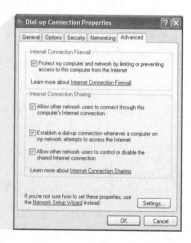

7. Click OK, and then close Control Panel.

I don't know how to set up a Windows 98 or Windows Me computer to connect with a Windows XP computer

Source of the problem

On every Windows XP computer, you can easily run the Network Setup Wizard to connect the computer to the network. But the Network Setup Wizard is not a part of Windows 98 or Windows Me.

Fortunately, it's easy to set up the Network Setup Wizard on a Windows 98 or Windows Me computer by installing it from your Windows XP CD. To do so, follow these steps:

How to fix it

1. Make sure you've run the Network Setup Wizard on the Windows XP computer that will be connected directly to the Internet on your home network.

2. Insert the Windows XP Home Edition or Professional CD into the CD-ROM drive of the Windows 98 or Windows Me computer.

3. In the Welcome To Microsoft Windows XP window, click Perform Additional Tasks. ▶

4. On the next page, click Set Up A Home Or Small Office Network. ▶

5. In the Network Setup Wizard dialog box, click Yes to run the wizard.

6. Follow the steps of the wizard to install the Network Setup Wizard.

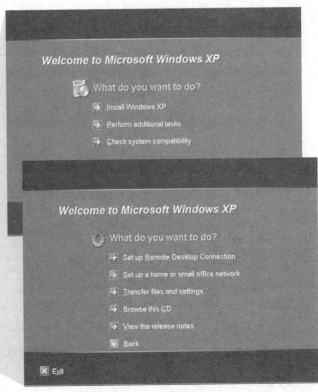

I can't get to the Internet from computers on the network

Source of the problem

After you've installed Internet Connection Sharing, all the computers on the network should have simultaneous access to the Internet. But if you can connect to the Internet from the host computer, and connect to the host computer from one of the computers on the network that's not directly connected to the Internet (a *client computer*), but you can't browse the Web, there's a problem with the way Internet Connection Sharing is installed. To fix the problem, follow these steps.

How to fix it

1. First, make sure the computer that has the connection to the Internet is turned on and connected to the Internet. Also make sure you can browse the Web from this computer.

> If the host computer can't browse the Web, see "I can't connect to my Internet service provider anymore," on page 130.

2. Try to browse the Web from another client computer on the home network.

> If this works, Internet Connection Sharing is operational, but the network connection between the inoperable computer and the host computer isn't. See "I can't connect to other computers on the network," on page 182. If you can't browse the Web from any other computer, go on to the next step.

Run the Network Setup Wizard on the client computer by following these steps:

1. Click Start, click Control Panel on the Start menu, and click Network And Internet Connections in Control Panel.

2. In the Network And Internet Connections window, click Set Up Or Change Your Home Or Small Office Network. ▶

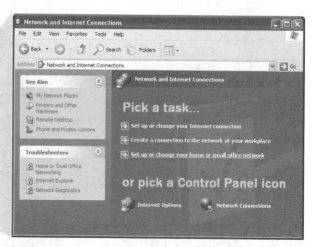

3. On the first page of the Network Setup Wizard, click Next, and click Next again on the next page of the wizard.

4. Click This Computer Connects To The Internet Through Another Computer On My Network Or Through A Residential Gateway. ▶

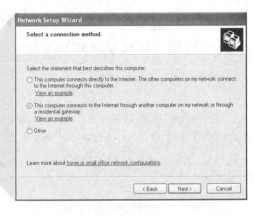

5. Click Next.

6. On the Give This Computer A Description And Name page of the wizard, enter a description for the computer and change the computer name to something more memorable, if you want, and click Next.

   Some Internet service providers require that you use a particular computer name. If your ISP has set a name for your computer, do not change it.

7. On the Name Your Network page of the wizard, enter a name for the network.

   Use the same name as you used on the computer that connects directly to the Internet, such as homenetwork.

8. On the next page of the wizard, click Next to have the wizard set up the connection.

9. On the remaining pages of the wizard, click Just Finish The Wizard; I Don't Need To Run The Wizard On Other Computers, and click Finish to close the wizard.

If you still can't connect to the Internet from a client computer, follow these steps to correct the IP address of the client computer.

1. Click Start, and then click Run on the Start menu.

2. In the Run dialog box, type **cmd** in the Open box, and click OK.

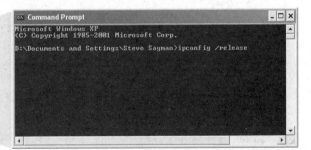

3. Type **ipconfig /release**, and press Enter. ▶

4. Type **ipconfig /renew**, and press Enter.

5. Type **exit** and press Enter to close the command prompt window.

If this solution didn't solve your problem, go to the next page.

I can't get to the Internet from computers on the network

(continued from page 197)

If you still can't connect to the Internet from a client computer, make sure the default gateway IP address is correct by following these steps:

1. Click Start, and then click Run on the Start menu.

2. In the Run dialog box, type **cmd** in the Open box, and click OK.

3. Type **ipconfig**, and press Enter. ▶

4. Make a note of the default gateway, and then type **exit** and press Enter to close the command prompt window.

5. If the default gateway is not listed as 192.168.0.1, click Start, and click Control Panel on the Start menu.

6. In Control Panel, click Network And Internet Connections, and then click Network Connections.

7. Right-click the Local Area Network connection that you use to connect to your network, and then click Properties on the shortcut menu.

8. On the General tab of the Properties dialog box, click Internet Protocol (TCP/IP), and then click Properties.

9. On the General tab of the Internet Protocol (TCP/IP) Properties dialog box, click Obtain An IP Address Automatically.

10. Click Advanced.

11. In the Default Gateways area of the Advanced TCP/IP Settings dialog box, click Add.

12. In the Gateway box in the TCP/IP Gateway Address dialog box, type **192.168.0.1**. ▶

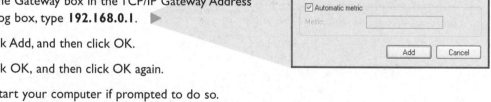

13. Click Add, and then click OK.

14. Click OK, and then click OK again.

15. Restart your computer if prompted to do so.

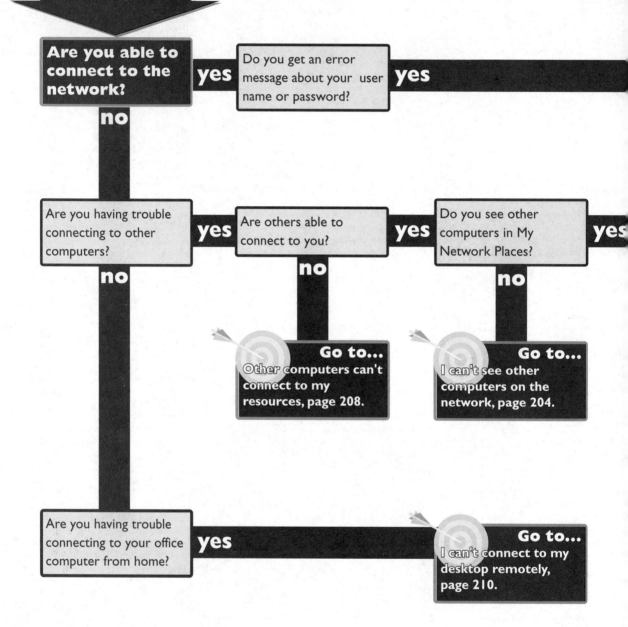

Are you able to connect to the network?

yes → Do you get an error message about your user name or password? **yes** →

no ↓

Are you having trouble connecting to other computers?

yes → Are others able to connect to you? **yes** → Do you see other computers in My Network Places? **yes** →

no ↓

no ↓

no ↓

Go to... Other computers can't connect to my resources, page 208.

Go to... I can't see other computers on the network, page 204.

Are you having trouble connecting to your office computer from home? **yes** →

Go to... I can't connect to my desktop remotely, page 210.

Networks, office

Go to...
I can't log on to the network, page 202.

Are you having trouble finding a particular computer or printer on the network?

yes

Quick fix

I can't find a computer in My Network Places If the computer you need to connect to isn't visible in My Network Places and you know its name, you can search for it by follow these steps:

1. Click Start, and click Search on the Start menu.

2. In the Search Companion pane of the Search Results window, click Computers Or People.

3. In the Search Companion pane, click A Computer On The Network.

4. In the Computer Name box, type the name of the computer, and click Search.

If your solution isn't here, check these related chapters:

- Connections, page 2
- The desktop, page 12
- Networks, home, page 180
- Startup, page 276

Or see the general trouble-shooting tips on page xv.

I can't log on to the network

Source of the problem

Before you can exchange files, send e-mail messages on the network, or print using a network printer, you need to log on to the network so that the network can register your presence and set up your connection. You normally log on to the network when you log on to Windows. But if you can't log on because you get an error message about your password, or logging on simply doesn't work, your first step should be to check with your network administrator to make sure your network account is valid. The network administrator might also be able to help resolve other issues that could be keeping you off the network. If you work in a small office without a network administrator or if there's nothing wrong with your account, begin troubleshooting by trying to log on again using the following steps.

How to fix it

1. Click Start, and then click Log Off.

2. Click Log Off when you're asked whether you are sure you want to log off.

3. Click your user name on the Welcome screen. ▶
    Or if the Log On To Windows dialog box opens, carefully enter your user name and password. Be sure to use the proper combination of uppercase and lowercase characters in your user name.

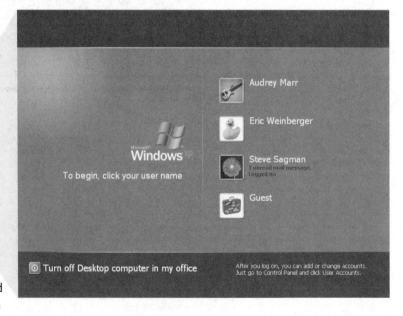

4. If you also usually enter a domain name, enter the domain name in the Domain box.

5. Click OK.
    If you still can't log on, go on to the next steps.

Check your computer name and domain or workgroup name by following these steps:

1. Click Start, right-click My Computer on the Start menu, and click Properties on the shortcut menu.

2. On the Computer Name tab in the System Properties dialog box, make sure there's a name for your computer next to Full Computer Name, and also make sure either the Workgroup or Domain name shown is correct. ▶

   The computer name must be unique on the network, the workgroup name must be the same as the workgroup name used by the other computers you need to communicate with, or the domain name must be the name assigned by the computer administrator.

If any of these entries are incorrect, follow these steps:

1. Click Change on the Computer Name tab in the System Properties dialog box.

   If the Change button isn't available, you're not logged on to the computer as an administrator. You need to log off and log back on using an administrator account.

2. In the Computer Name Changes dialog box, enter a revised name in the Computer Name box.

3. In the Member Of area of the Computer Name Changes dialog box, click Domain or Workgroup, enter the correct domain or workgroup name, and click OK.

4. Click Yes if you're asked whether you want to restart the computer.

   Make sure the correct network client is installed. For a Windows network, the client is Client For Microsoft Networks. Large organizations with a Novell network may require Client Service For NetWare. If you're part of a large organization, check with the network administrator to determine the proper client.

To check and install the client, if necessary, follow these steps:

1. Click Start, right-click My Network Places on the Start menu, and click Properties on the shortcut menu.

2. In the Network Connections dialog box, right-click your LAN connection, and click Properties on the shortcut menu.

3. On the General tab in the connection Properties dialog box, look for either Client For Microsoft Networks or Client Service For Netware in the list of items, and make sure the client's check box is selected.

   If neither client is installed, click Install, double-click Client in the Select Network Component Type dialog box, click the client you need to install in the Select Network Client dialog box, and click OK.

I can't see other computers on the network

Source of the problem

Using My Network Places on the Start menu, you should be able to browse through the network finding other computers you can access, shared folders you can open, and other resources you can use. To find all these resources, you click View Workgroup Computers in the Network Tasks list in the My Network Places window. But if all you see is a blank window that lists no computers, you need to make sure you're logged on to the network with the correct user name and password, and you need to ensure that all the network components are working properly. To begin, follow these steps.

How to fix it

Make sure you've logged on with the correct user name and password.

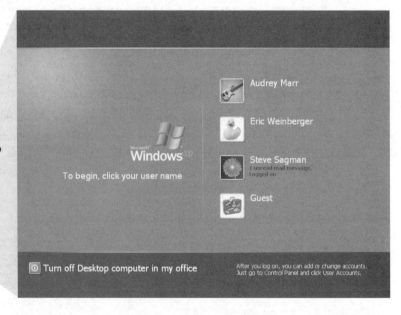

1. Click Start, and then click Log Off.

2. Click Log Off when you're asked whether you're sure you want to log off.

3. Click your user name on the Welcome screen. ▶

    If the Log On To Windows dialog box opens, carefully enter your user name and password. Be sure to use the proper combination of uppercase and lowercase characters in your user name.

4. If you also usually enter a domain name, enter the domain name in the Domain box.

5. Click OK.

Check your computer name and domain or workgroup name by following these steps:

1. Click Start, right-click My Computer on the Start menu, and click Properties on the shortcut menu.

2. On the Computer Name tab in the System Properties dialog box, make sure there's a name for your computer next to Full Computer Name and also make sure either the Workgroup or Domain name shown is correct. ▶

The computer name must be unique on the network, the workgroup name must be the same as the workgroup name used by the other computers with which you need to communicate, or the domain name must be the name assigned by the computer administrator.

If any of these entries are incorrect, follow these steps:

1. Click Change on the Computer Name tab in the System Properties dialog box.

If the Change button isn't available, you're not logged on to the computer as an administrator. You must log off and log back on using an administrator account.

2. In the Computer Name Changes dialog box, enter a revised name in the Computer Name box. ▶

3. In the Member Of area of the Computer Name Changes dialog box, click Domain or Workgroup, enter the correct domain or workgroup name, and click OK.

4. Click Yes if you're asked whether you want to restart the computer.

Check your network adapter and cables by following these steps:

1. Click Start, right-click My Computer on the Start menu, and click Properties on the shortcut menu.

2. On the Hardware tab in the System Properties dialog box, click Device Manager.

3. In the Device Manager window, look in the list of devices to see whether your network adapter appears with an exclamation point, a question mark, or a red X on its icon.

> If this solution didn't solve your problem, go to the next page.

I can't see other computers on the network

(continued from page 205)

An exclamation point or a question mark on the icon of a network adapter indicates either a hardware problem with the adapter or a software conflict. For information about solving these problems, see "A new device I've installed doesn't work," on page 116. A red *X* indicates that the network adapter is disabled. To enable the adapter, right-click it, and click Enable on the shortcut menu.

4. Close the Device Manager window, and click OK to close the System Properties dialog box.

5. Make sure the network cable is firmly plugged into the network card. (The cable probably looks like the cable used for cable TV.) If you can easily see the back of your computer, make sure the green light near the network cable jack is on, indicating that the network adapter is connected to the network. If the light isn't on, recheck your cable connections.

6. Check the network adapter manufacturer's Web site for an updated driver for the adapter, and download and install any update that's available.

Use the Repair option to correct problems with your network configuration by following these steps:

1. Click Start, click Control Panel on the Start menu, click Network And Internet Connections in the Control Panel window, and then click Network Connections.

2. In the LAN Or High-Speed Internet connections list, right-click your network connection, and click Repair on the shortcut menu.

3. After the repair is complete, click OK, and close the Network Connections window.

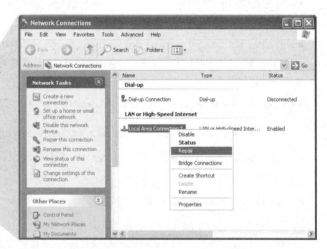

Run Network Diagnostics to gather any information it can provide about possible problems with your hardware or software configuration by following these steps:

1. Click Start, click Control Panel on the Start menu, and click Network And Internet Connections in the Control Panel window.

2. In the list of Troubleshooters, click Network Diagnostics. ▶

3. In the Help And Support Center window, click Scan Your System. Network Diagnostics scans your system. ▶

After Network Diagnostics finishes scanning your system, examine the list shown in the Help And Support Center window. If an item on the list reports Failed, click the plus sign next to the item to expand the list, and examine the item in more detail. ▶

4. Close the Help And Support Center window, and close Control Panel.

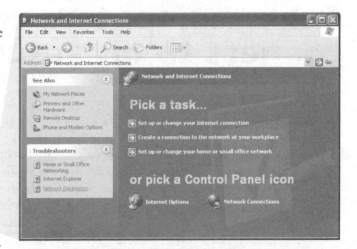

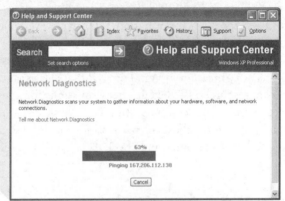

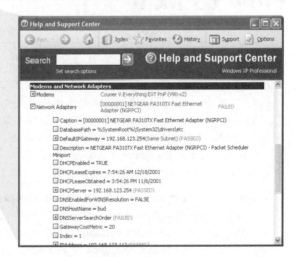

Other computers can't connect to my resources

Source of the problem

Each computer attached to a network is able to share its resources with other computers on the network. But unless you specifically allow sharing of particular disk drives, folders, or printers, these resources won't be available to other people working at other computers.

Everything you learned about sharing in elementary school applies here. Sharing is letting others use your resources, and you should be magnanimous in sharing, particularly in a small office network where, for example, you might be the only one who's connected to the color printer that everyone wants to use. But while it's good to share, you should also use discretion in sharing your computer's resources. Rather than share an entire disk drive, for example, which would also share all the folders and subfolders on the disk drive, you should share only those folders that you've designated for public information. Otherwise, everyone will be able to see everything that's on your computer.

Permissions also might prevent others from accessing a resource on your computer. Permissions are a security measure in Windows XP that allows you to permit or deny others, by user name, access to resources. By default, the permissions for a resource are set so that everyone can access the resource in your computer. But if you've shared a resource and someone still can't access it, you might need to adjust the permissions for the resource.

To share a resource and check its permissions, follow these steps.

How to fix it

1. Click Start, and click My Computer on the Start menu.

2. In the My Computer window, navigate to the disk drive, folder, or device you want to share.

    If the resource is already shared, you'll see a cradling hand on its icon in My Computer. ▶

    If a disk is shared, the folders on the disk are shared, too. If a folder is shared, the subfolders inside the folder are shared.

    C (C:)
    D (D:)
    E (E:)
    F (F:)

3. Right-click the resource, click Sharing And Security on the shortcut menu, and on the Sharing tab in the Properties dialog box for the folder, click Share This Folder. ▶

    If the device is a disk, click New Share.

4. In the Share Name box, enter a descriptive name for the shared resource, and click OK.

In the Comment box, you can optionally type a brief description of the shared resource.

The icon for the shared resource now shows a cradling hand to indicate that the resource is shared.

If someone still can't access a resource on your computer, check the permissions for the resource by following these steps:

1. Click Start, click My Computer on the Start menu, and in the My Computer window, navigate to the resource whose permissions you want to change.

2. Right-click the resource, and click Properties on the shortcut menu.

3. In the Properties dialog box for the resource, click Permissions.

If the Permissions button isn't available, look for a separate tab in the Properties dialog box labeled Security and click it. If the dialog box contains no Security tab and the Permissions button isn't available, the disk that contains the resource is not formatted with the NTFS file system. You must either move the folder to a disk that's formatted with NTFS, or convert the drive to NTFS. For information about NTFS, see "I can't compress the contents of a hard disk," on page 108.

4. Click Add, and in the Select Users Or Groups dialog box, type a user name or group name in the Enter The Object Names To Select box, and then click Check Names. ▶

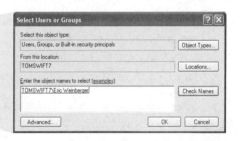

If the user name or group name is valid on the network, the name will become underlined. If the user name or group name is not valid, the Name Not Found dialog box will allow you to make a correction.

5. When the user name or group name becomes underlined, click OK. Click OK again to close the Permissions dialog box, and click OK to close the Properties dialog box.

> **Tip**
>
> When you share resources on a network, you can add a dollar sign ($) to the end of the name of a shared resource to make the resource available but not visible in someone else's Network Neighborhood or My Network Places window. Because others can't view your shared resources by browsing, only those to whom you've given the share name will know that they can connect to the resource.

> **Tip**
>
> To make a resource available to everyone on the network, enter the group name Everyone when you assign permissions to the resource.

I can't connect to my desktop remotely

Source of the problem

Remote Desktop Connection is designed to make it easy to connect to your computer in the office and work with its programs and files from home, just as if you were still sitting in the office. And while it's not difficult to set up a remote desktop connection, it's not always easy to get a connection up and running. Before you can use Remote Desktop Connection, your office network must be set up so that it allows you to dial in to connect to the network or connect to it through the Internet. The administrator of your office network can let you know whether this is possible. Here's how to use Remote Desktop Connection the correct way.

Before you start

To enable Remote Desktop, you must be logged on as the computer administrator or as a member of the Administrators group.

How to fix it

Make sure Remote Desktop is activated by following these steps:

1. On the computer whose desktop you want to work with remotely, click Start, right-click My Computer on the Start menu, and click Properties on the shortcut menu.

2. In the System Properties dialog box, click the Remote tab.

3. Select the Allow Users To Connect Remotely To This Computer check box. ▶

4. Click OK to close the Remote Sessions message box, and click OK to close the System Properties dialog box.

If the remote computer is running Windows 95, Windows 98, Windows NT 4.0, or Windows 2000, follow these steps to install Remote Desktop Connection:

1. Insert the Windows XP Professional CD in the CD-ROM drive.

2. On the Welcome page, click Perform Additional Tasks, and then click Set Up Remote Desktop Connection and follow the steps on the screen.

Run Remote Desktop Connection and establish a connection by following these steps:

1. Click Start, point to Programs in Windows 95, Windows 98, Windows NT 4.0 or Windows 2000 (point to All Programs in Windows XP) and point to Accessories.

2. Point to Communications, and click Remote Desktop Connection.

3. In the Remote Desktop Connection dialog box, type the computer name or the IP address of the computer, and click Connect. ▶

4. In the Log On To Windows dialog box, type your user name and password, and domain if necessary, just as you do when you're sitting at your office computer, and then click OK.

To end a remote desktop connection, follow these steps:

1. In the Remote Desktop Connection window, click Start, and then click Shut Down.

2. Select Log Off *username*, and click OK.

Changing Remote Desktop Connection options

1. Click Start, and point to Programs in Windows 95, Windows 98, Windows NT 4.0 or Windows 2000 (point to All Programs in Windows XP) and point to Accessories.

2. Point to Communications, and click Remote Desktop Connection.

3. In the Remote Desktop Connection dialog box, click Options to expand the window.

4. Modify settings on the Display, Local Resources, Programs, and Experience tabs of the Remote Desktop Connection dialog box to fine-tune the connection. ▶

5. On the General tab, click Save As to save the options in a file.

6. In the Save As dialog box, enter a name for the file in the File Name box, and then click Save.

   Later, you can return to the General tab in the Remote Desktop Connection dialog box, click Open, and select the saved file to reinstitute all your current settings.

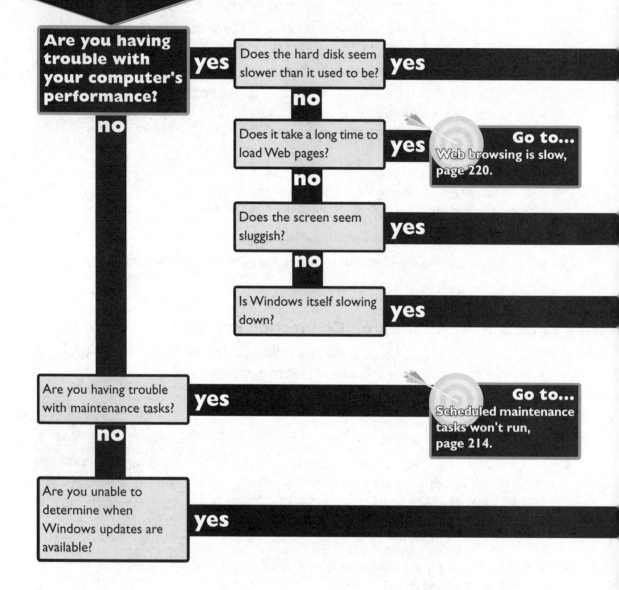

Are you having trouble with your computer's performance?

yes → Does the hard disk seem slower than it used to be?

    yes →

    no ↓

Does it take a long time to load Web pages?

    yes → **Go to...** Web browsing is slow, page 220.

    no ↓

Does the screen seem sluggish?

    yes →

    no ↓

Is Windows itself slowing down?

    yes →

no ↓

Are you having trouble with maintenance tasks?

    yes → **Go to...** Scheduled maintenance tasks won't run, page 214.

no ↓

Are you unable to determine when Windows updates are available?

    yes →

Optimizing

Go to...
My hard disk has slowed down, page 216.

Go to...
Windows is becoming sluggish, page 218.

Quick fix

My computer seems slow at drawing graphics If items on the screen seem to take a long time to draw, try these steps to speed them up:

1. Click Start, right-click My Computer on the Start menu, and click Properties on the shortcut menu.

2. On the Advanced tab of the System Properties dialog box, click Settings in the Performance area.

3. On the Visual Effects tab of the Performance Options dialog box, click Adjust For Best Performance, and click OK to close the open dialog boxes.

4. Right-click an empty area of the desktop, and click Properties on the shortcut menu.

5. On the Settings tab of the Display Properties dialog box, click the Color Quality down arrow, and if the current setting is Highest, click Medium, and click OK.

Quick fix

I never know when an update is available from Windows Update To keep informed about updates as they become available on Windows Update, turn on Automatic Updates by following these steps:

1. Click Start, right-click My Computer on the Start menu, and click Properties on the shortcut menu.

2. On the Automatic Updates tab of the System Properties dialog box, click Download The Updates Automatically And Notify Me When They Are Ready To Be Installed, and click OK.

   You can also select Notify Me Before Downloading Any Updates And Notify Me Again Before Installing Them On My Computer if you'd rather not have the updates downloaded automatically.

If your solution isn't here, check these related chapters:

- The display, page 40
- Hard disks, page 102
- Hardware, page 114
- Programs, page 234

Or see the general trouble-shooting tips on page xv.

Scheduled maintenance tasks won't run

Source of the problem

The Task Scheduler lets you schedule routine tasks, such as defragmenting the hard disk to keep your files quickly accessible, running ScanDisk to circumvent disk errors before they threaten your files, and running Disk Cleanup, which eliminates excess files that can clog your disks. But if the Task Scheduler won't run the tasks you've scheduled, investigate the causes by following these steps.

How to fix it

1. Verify that your computer's clock is set to the correct time. The Task Scheduler depends on the clock to determine when to start tasks.

   To change your computer's clock, right-click the clock on the taskbar, click Adjust Date/Time on the shortcut menu, enter the correct time in the Date And Time Properties dialog box, and click OK. ▶

   To get the exact time from the Time Service Department at the U.S. Naval Observatory, go to *tycho.usno.navy.mil/what.html*.

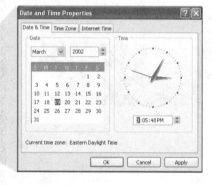

2. Click Start, and click Control Panel on the Start menu.

3. In Control Panel, click Performance And Maintenance, and then click Scheduled Tasks.

4. On the Advanced menu in the Scheduled Tasks window, click either Start Using Task Scheduler or Continue Task Scheduler, if either command is available. ▶

   If one of these commands is available, the Task Scheduler was either stopped or paused.

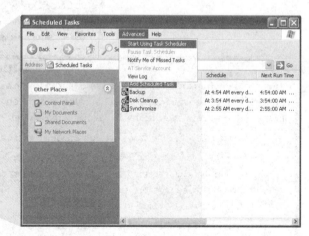

5. Close the Scheduled Tasks window.

6. Make sure your computer is not turned off when the maintenance tasks are scheduled to run.

If you've set the Task Scheduler to run maintenance tasks overnight, be sure to leave the computer on overnight, at least on the night the maintenance tasks are scheduled to run.

7. If you're using a computer without Advanced Configuration and Power Interface (ACPI) power management or with Advanced Power Management (APM) earlier than version 1.2, make sure your computer is not in standby mode when the Task Scheduler is scheduled to run maintenance tasks. Windows won't be able to pull your computer out of standby mode to run scheduled tasks.

If your computer provides ACPI power management or APM version 1.2 (rather than APM version 1.1 or earlier), the Task Scheduler can wake the computer from standby mode to run its scheduled tasks. The computer's documentation or manufacturer can tell you the level of power management built into your computer.

8. Click Start, and click Control Panel on the Start menu.

9. In Control Panel, click Performance And Maintenance, and then click Scheduled Tasks.

10. Each maintenance task that you've scheduled should have an icon in the Scheduled Tasks list. ▶

If you don't see an icon for a task, double-click Add Scheduled Task, and reschedule the task.

11. Close the Scheduled Tasks window.

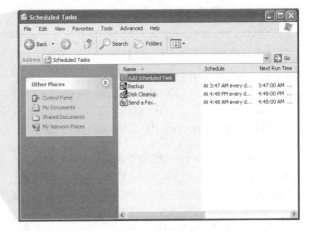

> **Tip**
>
> To be notified if the Task Scheduler misses any tasks because the computer was turned off or the Task Scheduler was stopped or paused, click Start, point to All Programs on the Start menu, point to Accessories, and point to Scheduled Tasks. Click the Advanced menu in the Scheduled Tasks window, and click Notify Me Of Missed Tasks.

My hard disk has slowed down

Source of the problem

If your hard disk seems to be dawdling when it used to be snappy, it's probably slowing down as it fills up with files. Nothing affects the perceived performance of your computer more than the real speed at which your hard disk is working, but the more you use a hard disk, the more its files become fragmented, and the more it seems to slow down. To restore a hard disk to its full speed, you must regularly defragment the hard disk—every week, every month, or at an interval that makes sense for you. For more about fragmentation, see "Why defragment?" on the facing page.

In addition to defragmenting your hard disk, here are several other procedures you can use not only to restore the speed of your hard disk, but also perhaps to make it run even better than new.

How to fix it

1. Before you defragment a hard disk, see "The disk defragmenter keeps starting over," on page 112, to learn the steps you should take in advance.

2. Click Start, click My Computer on the Start menu, right-click the hard disk you want to defragment, and click Properties on the shortcut menu.

3. On the Tools tab in the Properties dialog box, click Defragment Now. ▶

4. In the Disk Defragmenter window, click Defragment.
   When the defragmentation is complete, click Yes to quit Disk Defragmenter, click OK to close the Properties dialog box, and close the My Computer window.

In addition to defragmenting the hard disk, you can enable write caching for the hard disk. Write caching speeds up the process of saving information to your hard disk, but it presents one important risk: if the computer loses power unexpectedly, a file you were saving might become corrupted. Be sure your power source is reliable before enabling write caching by following these steps:

1. Click Start, and click My Computer on the Start menu.

2. In My Computer, right-click your hard disk, and click Properties.

3. On the Hardware tab of the Properties dialog box, select the hard disk, and click Properties.

4. On the Policies tab in the second Properties dialog box, make sure the Enable Write Caching On The Disk is selected. ▶

5. Click OK, and click OK again to close the first Properties dialog box.

6. Close the My Computer window.

Why defragment?

Every time you save a file, Windows stores bits and pieces of it in the spaces that were created when you deleted other files. A large file can be scattered in dozens of small fragments on a hard disk. When you open the file, the hard disk must gather all those fragments, reassemble them into a single unit, and then deliver the reconstituted file to Windows.

By routinely defragmenting the hard disk (weekly or monthly, depending on how much you use your computer), you move the bits and pieces of files into contiguous chunks, doing the reassembly work before you need to open the file.

Defragmenting a hard disk will make it noticeably faster, so be sure to include it as a task that the Task Scheduler performs regularly. See "Scheduled maintenance tasks won't run," on page 214, for more information about properly scheduling disk defragmenting.

Other ways to speed up the hard disk

Adding more memory to your computer, as well as shutting down programs you aren't using, also helps speed up a hard disk because it allows Windows to create a larger cache in the computer's memory. As Windows reads files, it grabs a few more files from the hard disk and stores them in the cache. The next time Windows needs the same files or files stored nearby on the hard disk, it can get them quickly from the cache rather than retrieve them from the hard disk, which takes longer.

Windows also uses the cache to temporarily hold some components of the programs you're running. For example, it might store in the cache the part of the program that saves your documents. As you work, Windows finds the components it needs in the cache, so that it doesn't have to tie up your hard disk with retrieving them.

Windows is becoming sluggish

Source of the problem

The longer you use Windows, the more encumbered it becomes by all the software and hardware you've installed. Windows must give each program and device you've added a little time and attention, and it eventually becomes noticeably bogged down and loses its crisp responsiveness to your mouse clicks and menu commands.

Some computer enthusiasts periodically start fresh with a clean, new installation of Windows. That's probably taking things a bit too far. If you're not ready for that level of hassle, you can take several less drastic steps to restore a good deal of the old bounce to Windows.

How to fix it

1. Click Start, and click Control Panel on the Start menu.

2. In Control Panel, click Add Or Remove Programs.

3. In the Add Or Remove Programs dialog box, click a program in the list that you rarely or never use, and click Remove or Change/Remove to remove the program.

   Follow the steps required by the program that uninstalls the software, clicking Yes if you're asked whether you want to restart the computer.

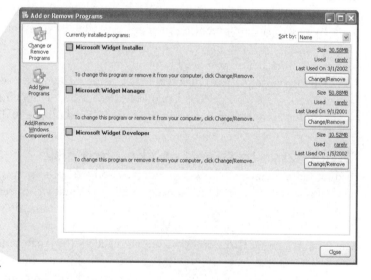

4. Repeat steps 1 through 3, continuing to remove programs until you've pared down the program list to only those programs you actually use.

5. In the same dialog box, click Add/Remove Windows Components.

6. In the Windows Components Wizard, clear the check boxes next to Windows components that you rarely or never use, and click Next.

7. Click OK, and then click Yes if you're prompted to restart the computer.

Because the speed of the hard disk is so critical to the speed of Windows, follow these steps to make sure your hard disk is performing optimally:

1. Defragment the hard disk and follow the other procedures described in "My hard disk has slowed down," on page 216, to optimize the speed of your hard disk.

2. Free up as much space as possible on your hard disk (at least 100 MB) to provide more space for virtual memory. For information about freeing up space, see "My hard disk is getting full," on page 104.

Although the special effects in the Windows XP user interface, such as menus that fade into view and taskbar buttons that slide across the taskbar, make working in Windows more fun, they take their toll on your computer's performance. To adjust them to provide for maximum performance, follow these steps:

1. Click Start, right-click My Computer on the Start menu, and click Properties on the shortcut menu.

2. On the Advanced tab in the System Properties dialog box, click Settings in the Performance area.

3. On the Visual Effects tab of the Performance Options dialog box, click Adjust For Best Performance.
   If you really can't live without a visual effect, you can select its check box to reenable it.

While you have the Performance Options dialog box open, you can make a few more changes to obtain the best performance in Windows:

1. On the Advanced tab in the Performance Options dialog box, click Programs in both the Processor Scheduling and Memory Usage areas.

2. Click OK, and click OK to close the System Properties dialog box. Click Close to close the Add Or Remove Programs dialog box.

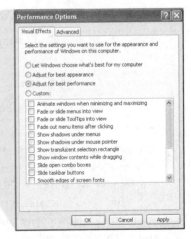

> **Tip**
>
> The best way to make Windows run faster is to improve the hardware on which it's running. Adding more memory, replacing your hard disk or video adapter with a newer model, or even going so far as to replace the motherboard and processor with faster versions can have huge payoffs in your productivity. Your local computer store might be able to perform one or more of these upgrades. You should seek a minimum of 128 MB of memory, but increasing memory to 256 MB will have a noticeable difference in performance.

Web browsing is slow

Source of the problem

Web browsing is never rapid enough, no matter how fast your connection to the Internet. Even if you've got a high-speed Internet connection, such as a Digital Subscriber Line (DSL) or a cable modem, you can encounter Internet slowdowns, technical glitches at your Internet service provider (ISP), and busy Web servers that can't send out Web pages quickly enough. But if your regular dial-up connection seems slower than usual, or if you're plagued by chronically slow browsing, you can check a few things and change a few settings to make sure you're getting the most out of your modem and your browser.

How to fix it

1. Connect to your ISP as you normally do, and then verify the speed at which you're connected by double-clicking the connection icon, in the notification area near the clock on the taskbar.

2. If you're familiar with your typical connection speed, and the current connection speed is substantially slower than usual (a connection speed of 19,200 bps rather than your usual 36,400 bps, for example), click Disconnect and dial the connection again; otherwise, click OK to close the dialog box.

   If you still can't get a connection that's as fast as usual, disconnect and restart Windows, which resets your networking connections.

Turn off the display of pictures, so that your browser downloads only the text on Web pages, as follows:

1. Click Start, and click Internet on the Start menu.

2. On the Tools menu in Internet Explorer, click Internet Options.

3. On the Advanced tab in the Internet Options dialog box, clear the Show Pictures check box under Multimedia in the Settings list, and click OK. ▶

   Turning off pictures is particularly helpful when you're using a slow connection in an office or a hotel room, but it can disable navigational features on Web pages, such as areas that you can click to move through a Web site. To view an individual picture on a page, right-click the placeholder frame that appears at the picture's position, and click Show Picture on the shortcut menu.

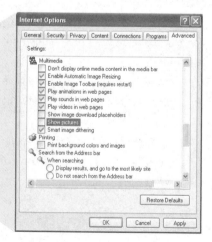

Disable the Content Advisor, which helps you control the Internet content that can be viewed on the computer, by following these steps:

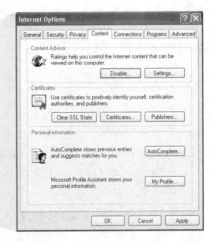

1. In Internet Explorer, click Internet Options on the Tools menu.

2. On the Content tab in the Internet Options dialog box, click Disable in the Content Advisor area, and click OK. ▶

If an Enable button is visible in the Content Advisor area, the Content Advisor is not running.

Disable page transitions, which fade Web pages in and out, by following these steps:

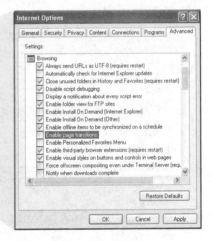

1. In Internet Explorer, click Internet Options on the Tools menu.

2. On the Advanced tab in the Internet Options dialog box, clear the Enable Page Transitions check box under Browsing, and click OK. ▶

Follow these steps to check your modem and its connection:

1. Visit the modem manufacturer's Web site, and look for an updated driver or software that you can download and install to update the modem's BIOS (also called *firmware*). The BIOS controls the operation of the modem, and updating it might enhance the modem's speed, especially if the BIOS update upgrades your modem from a V.34 model (28.8 or 33.6 Kbps) to V.90 (also referred to as 56K).

2. Connect a regular phone to the modem line and listen for line noise. If you hear noise, ask your local phone company to clear the phone line. Be persistent with the phone company if you live in a community where your phone connections are strong and clear, but the modem on a separate modem line is unable to connect at anything close to its typical speed.

3. Verify that the cords connecting your modem to the computer and to the wall jack are tightly plugged in. If the cord connections are tight and you're still having trouble, replace the cords with new ones.

> If this solution didn't solve your problem, go to the next page.

Web browsing is slow

(continued from page 221)

Follow these steps to check your modem settings:

1. Click Start, right-click My Computer on the Start menu, and click Properties on the shortcut menu.

2. On the Hardware tab in the System Properties dialog box, click Device Manager.

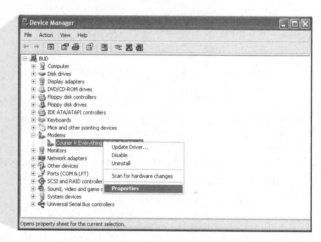

3. In Device Manager, click the plus sign next to Modems.

4. Right-click your modem, and click Properties on the shortcut menu. ▶

5. On the Advanced tab in the Properties dialog box for the modem, click Advanced Port Settings.

6. In the Advanced Port Settings dialog box, drag the Receive Buffer and Transmit Buffer sliders all the way to the right, to High. ▶

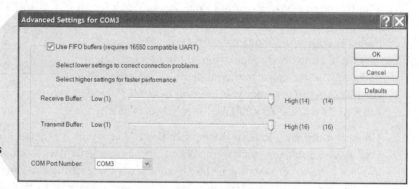

7. Click OK.

8. Click OK again to close the Properties dialog box for the modem.

If you're using an external modem, follow these steps to check your port settings. (If your modem is internal, skip these steps.)

1. In Device Manager, click the plus sign next to Ports.

2. Right-click the port your modem uses, and click Properties on the shortcut menu.

3. On the Port Settings tab in the Communications Port Properties dialog box, click the Bits Per Second down arrow, and click 115200. ▶

4. Click the Flow Control down arrow, and click Hardware.

5. Click Advanced, and in the Advanced Port Settings dialog box, drag the Receive Buffer and Transmit Buffer sliders all the way to the right, to High.

6. Click OK to close the dialog boxes, and close Device Manager.

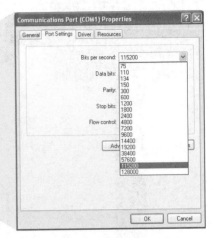

Here's another step to take to obtain maximum browsing speed:

● Make sure that you've closed all other programs that use your Internet connection, such as ICQ, AOL Instant Messenger, and MSN Messenger Service.

And finally, turn off the Active Desktop by following these steps:

1. Right-click anywhere on the desktop, and click Properties on the shortcut menu.

2. On the Desktop tab of the Display Properties dialog box, click Customize Desktop.

3. On the Web tab of the Desktop Items dialog box, clear the check boxes for any and all Web pages in the Web Pages list. ▶

4. Click OK twice to close the dialog boxes.

5. Click OK to close the Desktop Items dialog box.

6. Click OK to close the Display Properties dialog box.

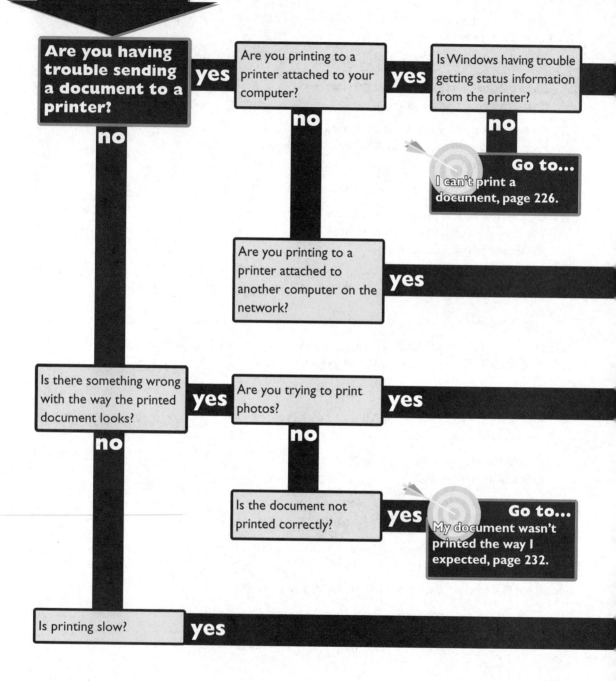

Are you having trouble sending a document to a printer?

yes → Are you printing to a printer attached to your computer?

yes → Is Windows having trouble getting status information from the printer?

no →

Go to...
I can't print a document, page 226.

Are you printing to a printer attached to another computer on the network? **yes**

no (from "Are you printing to a printer attached to your computer?")

Is there something wrong with the way the printed document looks? **yes** → Are you trying to print photos? **yes**

no (from "Is there something wrong with the way the printed document looks?")

no (from "Are you trying to print photos?") → Is the document not printed correctly? **yes**

Go to...
My document wasn't printed the way I expected, page 232.

Is printing slow? **yes**

Quick fix

Windows doesn't get status information from my printer When your computer seems unable to get status information from the printer, such as a notification that it's out of paper or that the paper path is jammed, the most likely cause is that you're not using a bidirectional printer cable. (Note that very old printers might not be able to send status information at all.)

1. You should replace your current printer cable with an IEEE-1284 cable, which provides bidirectional communications (both to and from the printer).

2. In the computer's configuration program, you need to set the printer port as bidirectional, EPP, or ECP.

Go to...
I can't print using a network printer, page 230.

Go to...
The photos I print aren't clear, page 228.

Go to...
It takes a long time to print a document, page 232.

If your solution isn't here, check these related chapters:

- Hardware, page 114
- Networks, home, page 180
- Networks, office, page 200
- Optimizing, page 212

Or see the general trouble-shooting tips on page xv.

I can't print a document

Source of the problem

A few moments after you click Print, your printer should respond, coming out of its slumber and cranking out pages in living color or in black and white. But if your printer goes on resting when it should be hard at work, the cause could be anything, from a printer that's still hung up from the last job you sent its way to a configuration problem in the part of Windows that handles printing. To investigate these possibilities and others one by one, go through this series of steps. You'll check out the most common problems and then move on to other possibilities.

How to fix it

● Make sure the printer is ready and supplied with paper and toner or ink. Most printers have a message display that reads *Ready* or *Online*, or a light that is illuminated when the printer is prepared to begin printing.

   If the printer appears to be ready but the document isn't printed, you might have sent the document to the wrong printer. To see whether this is your problem, follow these steps:

1. Click Start, and click Printers And Faxes on the Start menu.

2. On the View menu in the Printers And Faxes window, click Details.

3. Examine the Documents column to determine whether the printer you wanted to send the document to has a document waiting (indicated by a number other than 0 in the Documents column). ▶

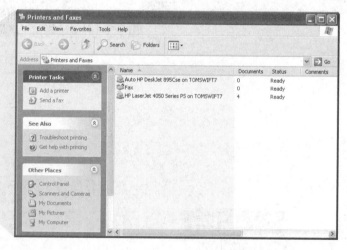

   If there's a document waiting, you sent the document to the correct printer, but if you sent the document to the wrong printer, and that printer hasn't finished printing, you can cancel the document by double-clicking the printer, right-clicking the document in the print queue window, and clicking Cancel on the shortcut menu. Then, in the Print dialog box in the program you were working in, select the correct printer, and print the document again.

If the document is waiting to be printed by the correct printer, you might be able to determine the printer problem by examining the printer queue. Follow these steps:

1. In the Printers And Faxes window, double-click the printer that has the document waiting in its queue, and look in the Status column for information about the printer problem.

2. Correct the problem if you can. Fix a paper jam, turn the printer off and back on, reconnect the printer cable, or press the printer's Online button to put the printer in a ready state. Or put the printer back on line by clicking Use Printer Offline on the Printer menu in the printer window.

    The print queue keeps trying to resend the document, so the document will be printed when the printer problem is resolved.

If no documents are waiting in the print queue, the document was sent through to the printer, but the printer didn't print it. Try these troubleshooting steps:

1. Right-click the printer you want to use, and click Properties on the shortcut menu.

2. On the General tab in the Properties dialog box for the printer, click Print Test Page.

    In the message box that appears, asking whether the test page was printed correctly, click Troubleshoot to open the Printing Troubleshooter. ▶

You should also try to print a different document or print using a different program:

1. Try printing a different document. If you can print another document, the original document you tried to print might be damaged. Try reopening the original document or opening a backup copy and then printing it again.

2. Try printing to the same printer from a different program. If another program is able to print successfully, you need to troubleshoot a printing problem within the program. Check the software manufacturer's Web site for support or a possible update that you can download and install to fix the problem.

If you still can't print, try reinstalling the printer driver. Make sure you have any disks that came with your printer, and follow these steps:

1. Click Start, click Printers And Faxes on the Start menu, and in the Printers And Faxes window, right-click the printer, and click Delete on the shortcut menu. Click Yes when you're asked to confirm the deletion.

2. In the Printer Tasks list in the Printers And Faxes window, click Add A Printer, and follow the steps of the Add Printer Wizard to add the same printer again.

The photos I print aren't clear

Source of the problem

Even a relatively inexpensive recent-model color printer can do a remarkably good job printing pictures you've scanned or photos you've taken with a digital camera. You need to use the correct printer settings though, either in the program you use to edit photos or in the Photo Printing Wizard, and you need to use paper that's been designed specifically for photo printing. Paper for printing digital photos is smoother and often brighter than normal paper (regular paper for photocopying and laser printing), and it provides a dramatic improvement in the quality of photo printouts.

Two other factors can lessen print quality: an incorrect quality setting when you print a photo and misalignment of the printer heads or ink nozzles. To fix these problems, follow these steps.

How to fix it

● Obtain paper that's made specifically for printing photos. Check your printer's documentation or the printer manufacturer's Web site for information about the brands of photo paper that are recommended for use with your printer.

Be sure to specify the correct paper type in the program's Print dialog box by following these steps:

1. On the File menu in the program you're using to view and print photos, click Print, and in the Print dialog box, click Properties. Or on the Printing Options page of the Photo Printing Wizard, click Printing Preferences. ▶

2. On the Paper or Paper/Quality tab in the Properties dialog box for the printer, click the Media down arrow, and click Glossy or Photo Paper in the list. ▶

Depending on the printer, you might need to click Advanced to get to the option that lets you specify the type of paper you're using.

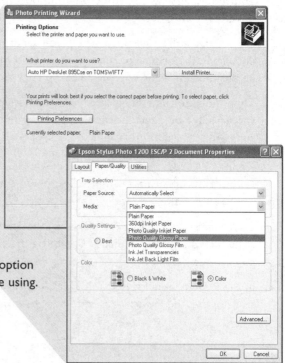

3. In the Quality Settings area of the Paper/Quality tab, click Best to provide the highest quality. ▶

4. Click OK.

For some printers, quality is listed as Best, Normal, or Draft. Other printers use different terminology, such as Presentation for high quality and Normal for medium quality.

Usually there's a trade-off between print speed and print quality, so if the Properties dialog box lists print speeds rather than print quality, choose the slowest print speed.

Check the printer heads or ink nozzles:

● Check the printer's documentation for information about how to run maintenance procedures on the printer, such as cleaning the printer heads and aligning the print cartridges or ink nozzles. Often, you can run these services from one of the tabs in the Properties dialog box for the printer.

Web graphics are printed poorly no matter what I do

A photo on a Web site is intended for quick downloading and viewing on the screen rather than printing, so its *resolution* (the number of dots per inch, or dpi, in the photo) is low. The lower the resolution of an image, the fewer the number of dots overall. The fewer the dots, the smaller the file size. And the smaller the file size, the faster its downloading time is.

> **Tip**
>
> The lack of resolution inherent in Web page images is most noticeable when you print them out at large sizes. Printing them at small sizes can make them look better.

The reason Web designers can get away with low-resolution photos on Web pages is that most displays have a resolution of only 72 dots per inch (actually pixels per inch). It doesn't make sense for a photo on a Web page to be any higher resolution because the screen on which it will be viewed has only a limited number of pixels, so it won't be capable of showing the higher resolution.

In contrast, even inexpensive color printers can produce pictures that have a resolution of 300 dpi or better. But if you print an image from a Web page using a high-resolution printer, the picture will still have only 72 dots per inch, so the image will be indistinct, even on your top-notch printer. You might notice jagged edges, particularly on diagonal or curved lines.

There's really nothing you can do to fix this problem with Web graphics, because the problem is in the image itself—it has nothing to do with the way you're printing it.

I can't print using a network printer

If a printer that's connected to another computer on the network doesn't show up in the Print dialog box in your favorite program, you can have Windows find the printer. You can also have it automatically search for any shared printer on the network that you have access to. From then on, you'll see the network printer listed in the Printers And Faxes window. To find a network printer when you're ready to print, and to turn on the automatic search for network printers, follow these steps.

How to fix it

1. Start the program you want to use to print a document.

2. On the File menu, click Print.

3. In the program's Print dialog box, look for a Find Printer button, and click it if it's available.
   If a Find Printer button is not available, you'll need to use the procedures in either "Searching for a printer automatically" or "Searching for a printer manually," on the opposite page.

4. In the Find Printers dialog box, enter the printer name.

5. Click the printer that's found and click OK to return to the Print dialog box.

6. In the Print dialog box, make the selections you want, and click Print.

Printing

Searching for a printer automatically

1. Click Start, and click Printers And Faxes on the Start menu.

2. On the Tools menu in the Printers And Faxes window, click Folder Options.

3. On the View tab in the Folder Options dialog box, select the Automatically Search For Network Folders And Printers check box, and click OK. ▶

   Windows will find printers that are available to you on the network and list them in the Printers And Faxes window.

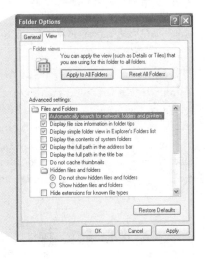

Searching for a printer manually

1. Click Start, and click Printers And Faxes on the Start menu.

2. In the Printer Tasks list, click Add A Printer.

3. On the first page of the Add Printer Wizard, click Next.

4. On the Local Or Network Printer page of the wizard, click A Network Printer, Or A Printer Attached To Another Computer, and click Next. ▶

5. On the Specify A Printer page of the wizard, click Browse For A Printer, and click Next.

6. In the Shared Printers list, select the printer you want to print to, and click Next.

   Printers that are available to you are listed in the Shared Printers list under the computer to which they're connected.

7. On the Default Printer page of the wizard, click No if you have a local printer that is your default printer.

8. Click Next.

9. Click Finish to close the Add Printer Wizard, and close the Printers And Faxes window.

It takes a long time to print a document

Source of the problem

When you use a printer that's connected directly to your computer, you can tell when the printer is busy just by looking at it. But when the printer is connected to another computer on the network and a document isn't being printed as quickly as you expect, you need to check the printer's print queue to determine whether other documents are lined up to be printed ahead of yours—in which case, there's nothing you can do. Here's how to check the print queue and, if the printer is connected directly to your computer, how to take steps to speed up printing.

How to fix it

1. Click Start, and click Printers And Faxes on the Start menu.

2. In the Printers And Faxes window, double-click the printer you're using.

    The printer window shows the print queue, which lists any documents that are waiting to be printed. If no documents are ahead of yours, close the printer window, and move on to the next set of steps to continue troubleshooting.

Follow these steps to delete extraneous files and speed up printing on any printer, including your own:

1. Click Start, click My Computer on the Start menu, right-click your hard disk, and click Properties on the shortcut menu.

2. On the General tab in the Properties dialog box, click Disk Cleanup.

3. On the Disk Cleanup tab in the Disk Cleanup dialog box, select any of these check boxes that are available in the Files To Delete list: Temporary Internet Files, Temporary Files, Temporary Offline Files, Office Files, Recycle Bin, and WebClient/Publisher Temporary Files, and then click OK. ►

4. Click Yes when you're asked whether you're sure you want to delete files, and click OK to close the Properties dialog box for the hard disk.

My document wasn't printed the way I expected

Source of the problem

Unless you adjust settings in the Print dialog box when you choose to print a document, the document is printed with the default settings for the printer, which might not be what you expect.

Any changes you make in the Print dialog box override the default settings for the printer, so you can have finely detailed control of how the printed document will look. Some programs also have Page Setup or Print Setup options on the File menu, which give you even more control over how the document will fit the printed page.

If you'd rather avoid changing the settings in the Print dialog box each time you print, you can change the default settings for the printer in Windows. You'll be able to choose Print on the File menu of any program or click the Print button on the program's toolbar to quickly print the document. Here's how to change the default settings.

How to fix it

1. Click Start, and click Printers And Faxes on the Start menu.

2. In the Printers And Faxes window, right-click the printer you want to use as the default printer, and click Set As Default Printer, if it's available on the shortcut menu.

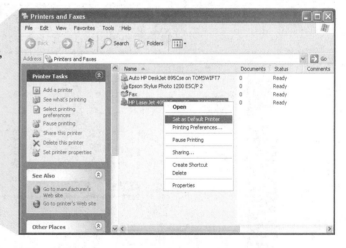

3. Right-click the printer again, and click Properties on the shortcut menu.

4. In the Properties dialog box for the printer, change the settings on the tabs to fit your needs.

5. Click OK.

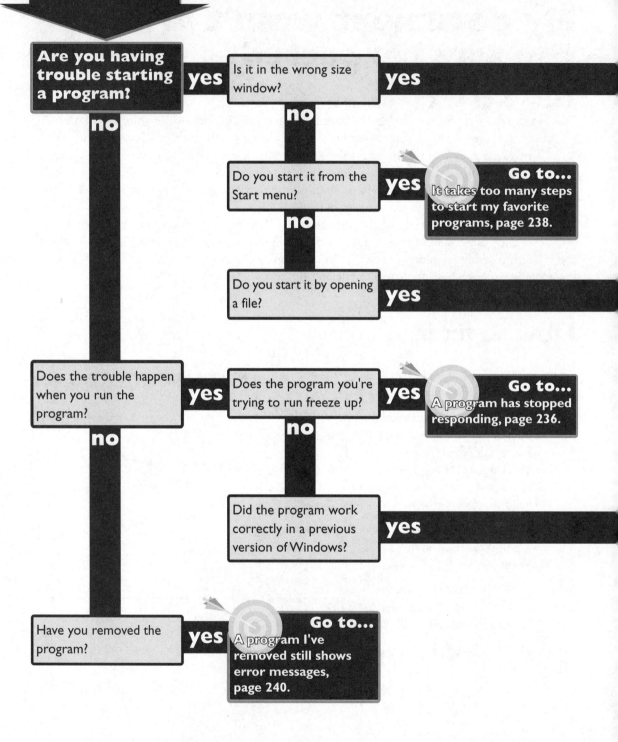

Are you having trouble starting a program?

yes → **Is it in the wrong size window?**

no ↓

yes →

Is it in the wrong size window?

no ↓

Do you start it from the Start menu?

yes → **Go to...** It takes too many steps to start my favorite programs, page 238.

no ↓

Do you start it by opening a file?

yes →

Does the trouble happen when you run the program?

yes → **Does the program you're trying to run freeze up?**

no ↓

yes → **Go to...** A program has stopped responding, page 236.

no ↓

Did the program work correctly in a previous version of Windows?

yes →

Have you removed the program?

yes → **Go to...** A program I've removed still shows error messages, page 240.

Quick fix

A program starts in a window that's the wrong size By changing the properties for a program's shortcut on the Start menu, you can specify whether a program should start in a regular window, minimized as a button on the taskbar, or in a full-screen window.

1. Right-click a program's shortcut on the Start menu or on one of the submenus.
2. On the shortcut menu, click Properties.
3. In the Run list, click Normal Windows, Minimized, or Maximized, and click OK.

Go to...

The wrong program opens when I double-click a file, page 242.

Quick fix

A program used to work correctly but now it doesn't in Windows XP If a program worked correctly in a previous version of Windows, such as Windows Me or Windows 2000, but it doesn't work properly in Windows XP, you can run the program in compatibility mode.

1. Click Start, point to All Programs, point to Accessories, and click Program Compatibility Wizard.
2. Click Next, and follow the steps of the wizard to test the program and adjust compatibility mode settings.

If your solution isn't here, check these related chapters:

- Files, page 72
- Folders, page 82
- The Start menu, page 266
- The taskbar, page 292

Or see the general trouble-shooting tips on page xv.

A program has stopped responding

Source of the problem

When a program stops responding, your first thought might be "Now what have I done?" But when a program just stops working, it's never your fault—programs are just not supposed to do that.

If you're wondering why programs sometimes crash, consider this: The typical computer has a library of programs on its hard disk, a handful of hardware devices installed inside and hanging off its ports (like printers, scanners, and digital cameras), and a marching parade of utility programs running in the background (such as virus checkers, Internet audio programs, and controls for speakers). All those programs and devices should interact gracefully, but they can conflict—for example, by trying to use the same resources in the computer or by giving the computer contradictory instructions. If this happens, a program that has your unfinished task might simply stare back at you without responding to any of your mouse clicks or keyboard presses, no matter how urgent they become.

Fortunately, Windows XP is particularly good at protecting itself from programs that freeze up. In almost every case, you'll be able to end the program that's not responding and continue your work in Windows. Here's how.

How to fix it

1. Press Ctrl+Alt+Del.

2. In the Windows Security dialog box, click Task Manager.

3. On the Applications tab of Windows Task Manager, inspect the list of tasks to see whether any of the programs listed show the text *[Not responding]* in the Status column. ▶

4. Click the program that's not responding, and then click End Task.

5. Wait for at least 30 seconds. Windows might take time to work behind the scenes, and if you wait, you might be able to shut down only the errant program without having to restart the computer.

6. If a message box appears, telling you that you can click End Task to close the program, go ahead and do it.

7. After you've shut down the frozen program, press Ctrl+Alt+Del again, click Task Manager, and verify in Windows Task Manager that the program is no longer in the list. If it's still listed, repeat steps 4 through 6.

8. If you now find any unusual behavior in Windows or the programs you're using, such as slow responses or features that don't work, shut down and restart Windows.

In most cases, you'll be able to click Shut Down on the Start menu and click either Restart or Shut Down in the Shut Down Windows dialog box before clicking OK, but if this doesn't restart Windows, you'll need to turn off your computer using the power switch and then turn it back on. In the process, you might lose the information you haven't saved in some running programs, but others, like Microsoft Outlook, save each change as you make it, so you won't lose any work.

Avoiding program hang-ups in the future

You've probably noticed that hang-ups get more frequent over time. The more programs you install, the more utilities you run, and the more devices you attach, the greater the demands on Windows, which is the underlying software. Periodically, you should clean house:

● Remove programs you rarely use.

● Prevent programs from starting automatically. (See "Programs start automatically, without my approval" on page 278.)

● Run maintenance programs built into Windows, like Disk Cleanup and the disk defragmenter.

Why won't it stop that?

Think you're busy? Windows is just as busy in its own right. It's an environment for running programs like Microsoft Word and Microsoft Excel. It's a window on the Internet. It manages every program in your computer, all your utilities, and all your fonts. It's even contending with the printers, scanners, speakers, and a few accessories—new and cooperative or old and cantankerous—that you've plugged in to soup up your computer. At the same time, it's pretending to be a plain MS-DOS computer so that decade-old, "mission critical" programs still used by some companies won't balk. Because the demands on Windows are great, and because it must accommodate everything from state-of-the-art games to rusty old MS-DOS software, we need to tolerate its occasional mishaps. The best way to protect yourself might still be by following the old adage, "Save early, and save often."

It takes too many steps to start my favorite programs

Source of the problem

There's a command somewhere on the Start menu for just about every program you've installed, but it might be buried several menu levels deep. To start a favorite program, you sometimes have to point to menu option after menu option until you finally find the program's shortcut. What's more, some setup programs for software fill the submenus for programs on the Start menu with so many utilities, accessories, uninstallers, registration programs, and readme files that you can hardly find the command that starts your program.

Windows XP helps you start programs you use frequently by making their shortcuts visible on the left side of the two-column Start menu. If you routinely use three or four programs, you'll find them easily at hand. But you can also take advantage of a few other Windows capabilities to make starting programs easier.

Here are two solutions: one for copying icons for your three or four most used programs to the Quick Launch toolbar, and one for excavating to find the Start menu entries you need and moving them to menus that are easy to reach.

How to fix it (using the Quick Launch toolbar)

1. Make sure you see the Quick Launch toolbar just to the right of the Start button. The Quick Launch toolbar is located on the taskbar and contains icons that you can click to start the programs you use most often. ▶

    If the Quick Launch toolbar isn't visible, see "I don't have a Quick Launch toolbar," on the facing page.

2. Click Start, and point to All Programs.

3. Point to the correct menu and then the correct submenus, until you've found the program you want to start more easily.

4. Hold down the Ctrl key while you drag the icon for the program from the Start menu to the Quick Launch toolbar.

5. Continue to hold down the Ctrl key while you position the mouse pointer where you want to put the icon. (A black vertical line shows where the entry will drop.)

6. Release the Ctrl key, and then release the mouse button to drop the entry into place.

Programs

How to fix it (using the Start menu)

1. Click Start, and point to All Programs.

2. Point to the entry for the program you want on one of the Start menu's submenus.

3. Hold down the Ctrl key and drag the shortcut for the program from the submenu to a higher-level menu on the Start menu. ▶

4. Release the Ctrl key.
   The shortcut appears where you dropped it. To reposition the shortcut, you can move it up or down on the menu simply by dragging it.

I don't have a Quick Launch toolbar

The Quick Launch toolbar might not be visible when you first install Windows XP. And it can be easily turned off at any time. So if you don't find a Quick Launch toolbar with a set of icons right next to the Start button, here's how to summon it.

1. Right-click the taskbar.

2. Point to Toolbars on the shortcut menu.

3. Click Quick Launch on the submenu. ▶

Tip

You can rearrange the icons on the Quick Launch toolbar. You can also make the tool-bar wider to accommodate more icons by making sure the taskbar is not locked (right-click the taskbar and clear the Lock The Taskbar option), and dragging the handle (the vertical bar) on the right side of the toolbar farther to the right.

Tip

For easy management of the taskbar, right-click the Quick Launch toolbar, and click Open Folder to view its icons as shortcuts in a window. You can then manage the Quick Launch toolbar by deleting the shortcuts, dragging in new shortcuts from other windows, or dragging shortcuts to other windows.

A program I've removed still shows error messages

Source of the problem

If you see error messages that appear to emanate from the netherworld beyond the Recycle Bin, programs that you thought you'd removed might still be speaking to you. The reason for this is that you circumvented the correct method for removing programs and, in the process, left parts of the software clinging to your system.

You can't just remove a program by deleting the folder for the program from your hard disk. Instead, you need to use Add Or Remove Programs to remove software properly. If you find yourself in this situation, you can still try using Add Or Remove Programs, but it might be too late. If Add Or Remove Programs doesn't work, you'll need to reinstall the program and then remove it the correct way, as described in the following procedure.

How to fix it

1. Have the program's installation CD handy, or find the downloaded setup program you used to install the program in the first place.

2. Install the program just as you did originally. Be sure to put it in the same folder you used before. If you accepted the recommended installation folder, accept the same recommendation again.

3. Restart the computer, or follow any steps the setup program asks of you until you have a working program. Now you're ready to uninstall the program the correct way.

4. Click Start, and click Control Panel on the Start menu.

5. In Control Panel, click Add Or Remove Programs.

6. In the Currently Installed Programs list in the Add Or Remove Programs dialog box, select the program you want to remove, and click Remove or Change/Remove. ▶

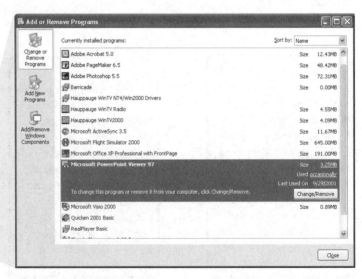

7. Follow the program removal process, responding to whatever messages appear in message boxes, and restart your computer only if you're prompted to do so.

Tip

Some programs add an uninstall shortcut to their menus on the Start menu. Choosing this shortcut is the equivalent of selecting the program in the Add Or Remove Programs dialog box.

If you want to know more

During setup, many Windows programs knit themselves tightly into the fabric of your Windows installation. They copy the files they need into their own folder and the main Windows folder, and they create their own entries in the central Windows configuration file, called the registry. These changes are often all that are needed to produce error messages when you don't go through the proper uninstall process. In addition, many programs also install and run little utility programs, helpers, and monitors that you'll need to remove too. For example, a program that plays streaming audio from the Internet might install a monitor that watches for sound or music coming in on your Internet connection so that it can automatically launch its player. These modules sometimes appear as small icons in the system tray next to the clock. Other times, they run stealthily, without any visible sign.

The only way to properly untangle most programs from Windows is to run their uninstall programs. All programs designed for Windows are supposed to list themselves in the Add Or Remove Programs list and provide uninstall utilities that can properly extract every bit and piece from your system. In fact, for software manufacturers to put the *Designed for Windows* logo on their package, they must include a proper uninstall program in their software.

Tip

You can try selecting the program in Add Or Remove Programs without reinstalling the program first, but by removing the program's folder, you might also have deleted its uninstall program, so this approach might not work.

A message says that not all of the program could be removed

Some uninstall programs finish their business but then display a message saying that they could not remove all files or folders. When you see such a message, you know that the program has been properly extracted from Windows, but not all of its files or folders have been deleted from your hard disk. This happens when the uninstall program can't tell which files and folders to delete. These folders on your hard disk won't interfere with other programs, but they take up valuable hard disk space.

When you see such a message, you can safely delete the program's installation and data folders, which are often subfolders within the Program Files folder. If you don't find these subfolders, look for them on your hard disk by viewing the list of folders in My Computer or by using Search and entering the name of the program in the Search Results window. Obviously, you shouldn't delete any folder on your hard disk unless you're sure it belongs to the program you've deleted. You can often find a list of program-related folders in the software's documentation or on the manufacturer's Web site.

The wrong program starts when I double-click a file

Source of the problem

If you want a particular program to start when you double-click a file in My Computer, Windows Explorer, or on the desktop, but another program starts instead, you need to associate a different program with that file type. Windows checks the file extension at the end of the file name (.doc, .txt, .xls, .jpg, .bmp, .htm, .ppt, .gif, and so on) to determine the file's type, and then it runs the program in its list that's associated with that type. For example, if you double-click a .jpg picture file, Windows will start either Internet Explorer or a photo editing program, depending on which program is associated with .jpg files.

Most of the time, you don't need to worry about the list of associations between file extensions and programs, because the programs you install stake their claim to one or more file types during setup. Microsoft Excel claims .xls (spreadsheets), Internet Explorer claims .htm (Web pages), and so on. But some programs fight with each other for a file type, and you need to step in as referee.

How to fix it

1. Click Start, and click My Computer on the Start menu.

2. On the Tools menu in My Computer, click Folder Options.

3. In the Folder Options dialog box, click the File Types tab, and then scroll through the Registered File Types list and click the file type you want to change, such as Wave Sound. ▶

4. In the Details area on the File Types tab, click Change.

> ### Tip
> Windows hides the file extensions at the end of file names. You can view them by clicking Folder Options on the Tools menu in My Computer and clearing the Hide Extensions For Known File Types in the Advanced Settings list on the View tab.

5. In the list of programs in the Open With dialog box, click the program you'd like to use to open the file, and click OK. ▶

6. Click Close to close the Folder Options dialog box, and close Control Panel.

The association happens immediately, so the program you want will now start when you double-click a file.

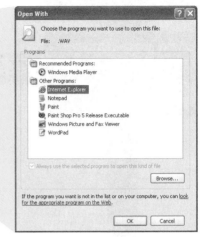

Handling feuding programs

Usually, you need to change the program associated with a file type only after you install a new program that tries to grab the file type. That's when you need to restore the previous file association. But some programs feud and try to take over each other's file extensions each time they start up. Internet Explorer and Netscape, for example, both want to associate themselves with the file extension for a Web page (.htm), but they ask permission before usurping file types whenever they start. Programs that grab without asking aren't well mannered enough for your PC. You don't need to tolerate such nonsense. Don't hesitate to remove those programs and replace them with others that are more considerate.

Associating picture files

One association that seems to go against the settings in the File Types list is the one between picture files (.jpg files in particular) and Windows Picture and Fax Viewer. Even if you've associated .jpg files with your favorite image editor, you might find that double-clicking a picture file opens it in Windows Picture and Fax Viewer.

But once a file is open in Windows Picture and Fax Viewer, you can click the second button from the right in the viewer (just to the left of the Help button, which displays a question mark). When you click this button, the viewer closes and the picture is opened in the program you've associated with .jpg files. For example, if you've associated the shareware program Paint Shop Pro with .jpg files, Windows Picture and Fax Viewer will close when you click this button, and Paint Shop Pro will open with the picture file ready for editing.

> **Tip**
>
> Some programs have a menu or dialog box option that you can use to specify the file types the programs are associated with. Using this option enables you to avoid having to set the file association in Windows. To find this option, look for a Preferences or Options menu command, and then check the dialog box the command leads to, or check the program's online Help for *file associations* or *file types*.

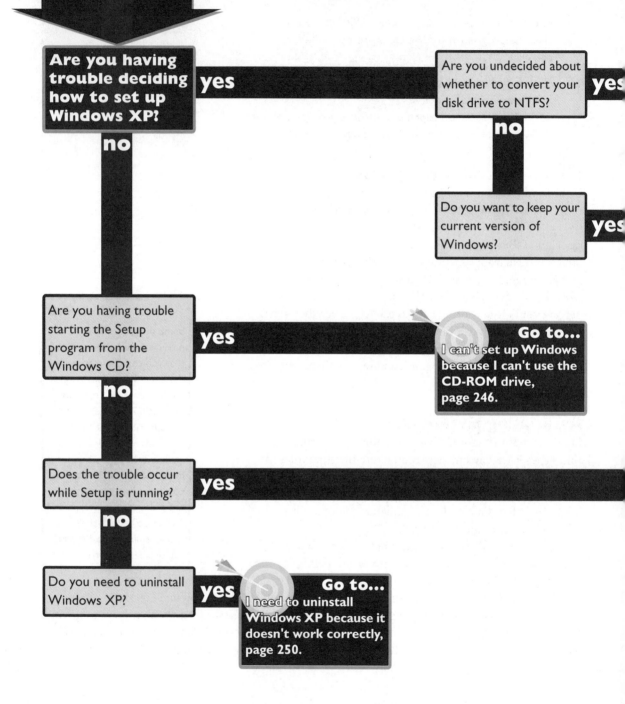

Are you having trouble deciding how to set up Windows XP? **yes** ——→ Are you undecided about whether to convert your disk drive to NTFS? **yes**

no | **no**

Do you want to keep your current version of Windows? **yes**

Are you having trouble starting the Setup program from the Windows CD? **yes** ——→ **Go to...** I can't set up Windows because I can't use the CD-ROM drive, page 246.

no

Does the trouble occur while Setup is running? **yes**

no

Do you need to uninstall Windows XP? **yes** ——→ **Go to...** I need to uninstall Windows XP because it doesn't work correctly, page 250.

Quick fix

I don't know whether to convert my disk to NTFS during setup
NTFS is the best file system to use if you'll have only Windows XP on your computer. NTFS allows you to compress a disk, gaining valuable space, and to assign permissions to the disk or folders on the disk, which provides security for your private files. But if you plan to dual-boot, choosing either Windows XP or an earlier version of Windows each time you start your computer, you should leave the formatting of your disks as FAT or FAT32, which can be used by both Windows XP and earliers versions of Windows, such as Windows 98 or Windows Me.

Go to...
I still need to be able to use my previous version of Windows, page 252.

Does Setup complete its process normally?

no

Go to...
Setup stops responding, page 248.

If your solution isn't here, check these related chapters:

- Hard disks, page 102
- Hardware, page 114
- Optimizing, page 212
- Programs, page 234

Or see the general trouble-shooting tips on page xv.

I can't set up Windows because I can't use the CD-ROM drive

Source of the problem

So you have a Windows XP CD, a computer with a CD-ROM drive, and a hard disk with plenty of space. It looks like you have everything you need to get Windows set up on the hard disk. But you keep getting an *Invalid drive specification* error at the MS-DOS prompt when you try to switch to the CD-ROM drive, or you can't access the CD because your current version of Windows is no longer working. Without the proper commands in your MS-DOS startup files or some version of Windows running, which makes the CD-ROM drive usable, your computer might not be able to read the Windows CD and its installation files.

Fortunately, this problem has several possible solutions. First, you can try setting your computer to boot from the CD-ROM. If that doesn't work, you might able to gain access to your CD-ROM drive if you have MS-DOS or an earlier version of Windows installed on the machine, or if you have another computer nearby whose services you can enlist. Here's how to proceed.

How to fix it

1. Consult your computer's documentation to determine how to start the computer's configuration program, also sometimes called the BIOS configuration program or the CMOS setup, and then follow the instructions to start this program.

    On some computers, you press Ctrl or Esc while starting the computer to start the configuration program.

    Some computers indicate how to start their configuration programs by displaying a message on the screen when they start, such as *Press Ctrl to enter setup*.

2. Use the configuration program to set the CD-ROM drive to be the first boot device, followed by the floppy disk drive, and then the hard disk.

    The method of changing the order of the boot devices is determined by the kind of computer you have. If your computer doesn't give you the option to boot from the CD-ROM drive, skip to the next set of steps.

3. Save the new configuration using the instructions provided in the configuration program.

4. If you successfully made the CD-ROM the first boot device, insert the Windows XP CD in the CD-ROM drive, and restart the computer.

If you have access to another computer that is running Windows 98 or Windows Me, make a startup disk and use it to start your computer by following these steps:

1. Insert a disk in the floppy disk drive of the other computer.

2. Click Start, point to Settings, and click Control Panel.

3. In Control Panel, double-click Add/Remove Programs. (In Windows Me, you might be able to single-click the Add/Remove Programs link.)

4. On the Startup Disk tab in the Add/Remove Programs Properties dialog box, click Create Disk, and follow the instructions on the screen.

5. Take the startup disk to the computer on which you're trying to set up Windows XP, insert it in the floppy disk drive, and start the computer.

```
Microsoft Windows Millennium Startup Menu

1. Normal
2. Start computer with CD-ROM support.
3. Start computer without CD-ROM support.
4. Minimal Boot

Enter a choice: 2
```

6. On the Microsoft Windows Startup Menu, which appears after the computer starts, choose the Start The Computer With CD-ROM Support option. ▶

7. With the Windows CD in the CD-ROM drive, at the MS-DOS prompt, type the drive letter of the CD-ROM drive followed by a colon (:), and press Enter to try to access the drive.

If you don't have access to another computer but an earlier version of Windows was working at one time on your computer, you might be able to use the drivers in the earlier version of Windows to reach the CD-ROM drive by following these steps:

1. Start the computer, and press F8 when you see the *Starting Windows* message.

2. On the Windows Startup Menu, choose Command Prompt Only.

3. At the MS-DOS prompt, type **dosstart.bat**.
   When the MS-DOS prompt reappears, try accessing the CD-ROM drive again.

If Windows wasn't installed on your computer but you do have MS-DOS installed on the hard disk, you must load the MS-DOS driver, which assigns a drive letter to the CD-ROM drive.

If you have the original disk that accompanied the CD-ROM drive, you can run the setup program that installs the driver in your computer's Autoexec.bat and Config.sys files. If you don't have the disk, visit the drive manufacturer's Web site for information about obtaining and installing the driver.

You might also need the Mscdex.exe file, which provides support for CD-ROM drives in MS-DOS. If you don't have this file, you can download it from the following Web page: *support.microsoft.com/support/kb/articles/Q123/4/08.ASP?LN=EN-US&SD=gn&FR=0.*

Setup stops responding

Source of the problem

If your computer has built-in virus protection, the Windows Setup program might be unable to change the boot sector, the small area on the hard disk that the computer needs to read before it can load Windows. Because altering the boot sector can prevent the computer from starting, the boot sector is a likely target for a virus program that seeks to disable your computer. To prevent viruses from altering the boot sector, many computer manufacturers have added boot sector protection to the computer's built-in software, the BIOS.

If this protection is turned on, Windows won't be able to make the necessary modifications to the boot sector, and the Setup program will be unable to continue. The Setup program might simply stop, or the Windows Setup wizard might appear as a black square on the screen as the computer hangs. Or the Setup program will continue and ask whether you want to overwrite the boot sector, but because the Setup program is prevented from changing the boot sector, Windows hangs when it tries to start. To get around this problem, follow these steps.

How to fix it

1. Consult your computer's documentation to determine how to start the computer's configuration program, also sometimes called the BIOS configuration program or the CMOS setup, and then follow the instructions to start this program.

   On some computers, you press Ctrl or Esc while starting the computer to start the configuration program.

   Some computers indicate how to start their configuration programs by displaying a message on the screen when they start, such as *Press Ctrl to enter setup*.

2. In the configuration program, find and disable the built-in virus detection software or antivirus feature.

3. Restart the computer.

4. Run Windows Setup.

5. After Windows is set up, run the computer's configuration program again and reenable the built-in virus detection software.

Performing a clean boot and upgrading Windows from the hard disk

If turning off the computer's antivirus feature doesn't work and Setup still fails, you should perform a *clean boot* of your computer, starting the computer without loading device drivers, utilities, or other programs. When you clean boot your computer, you won't be able to access the computer's

CD-ROM drive because you won't be loading the CD driver, so before you clean boot, you must copy the Windows setup files to the computer's hard disk, using your previous version of Windows, and then run Setup from the hard disk. Here's how to proceed:

1. Insert the Windows CD. When the Welcome To Microsoft Windows XP window opens, click Exit.

2. Double-click My Computer on the desktop, and then double-click the computer's hard disk.

3. Right-click a blank area in the window that's showing the contents of the hard disk, point to New on the shortcut menu, and click Folder.

4. Type a name for the new folder that will hold the Windows setup files, such as *WinXPFiles*, and press Enter.

5. Double-click the new folder to open it.

6. Right-click My Computer, click Explore on the shortcut menu, and arrange the folder window and the new Windows Explorer window so that they don't overlap.

7. In the left pane of the Windows Explorer window, click the plus sign next to the CD-ROM drive containing the Windows CD.

8. Drag the i386 folder from the Windows CD to the window that shows the new folder you created. Also drag the five files that aren't in a folder, including setup.exe, to the new folder you created. ▶

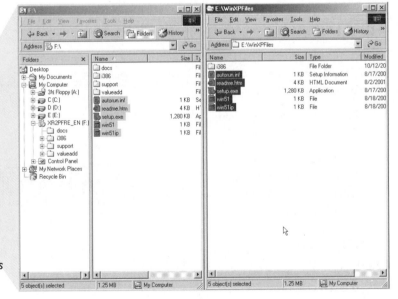

9. Shut down the computer.

10. Press the F8 key repeatedly when you see the *Starting Windows* message.

11. From the Microsoft Windows Startup Menu, choose Safe Mode Command Prompt, and press Enter.

12. At the MS-DOS prompt, type **cd \WinXPFiles** (replace *WinXPFiles* with the name you gave your new folder).

13. Type **setup** and press Enter to start Windows Setup.

I need to uninstall Windows XP because it doesn't work correctly

Source of the problem

Before you install Windows XP on a computer, be sure to choose Check System Compatibility in the Welcome To Microsoft Windows XP screen, an option that appears when you start the Setup program. Choosing Check System Compatibility can tell you, before you install Windows XP, whether your hardware and installed software are compatible with the new operating system. But if you install Windows XP and find that the devices in your computer or the programs you've installed don't work the way they did in Windows 98 or Windows Me, you can uninstall Windows XP and return your computer to its prior state. Here's the easy way to uninstall Windows XP, along with alternatives you can use if an incompatibility keeps you from running Windows XP properly or even from running Windows XP at all.

How to fix it

1. Click Start, and click Control Panel on the Start menu.

2. In Control Panel, click Add Or Remove Programs.

3. In the Add Or Remove Programs dialog box, click Uninstall Windows XP, and click Change/Remove in the Currently Installed Programs list. ▶

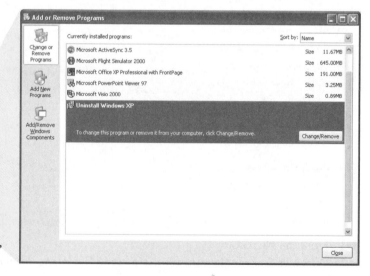

4. Follow the instructions on the screen to return to your previous version of Windows, restarting the computer when you are prompted to do so.

What to do when you can't get to Add Or Remove Programs

If Windows XP won't work well enough to open Control Panel and use Add Or Remove Programs, try getting to Control Panel in Safe Mode by following these steps:

1. Start or, if necessary, restart your computer.

2. While the computer is starting, press F8 to open the Windows Advanced Options Menu.

3. In the Windows Advanced Options Menu, press the up or down arrow key on the keyboard to move the highlight to Safe Mode, and press Enter. ▶

4. When Windows XP displays a message to notify you that Windows is running in Safe Mode, click Yes.

```
Windows Advanced Options Menu
Please select an option:

    Safe Mode
    Safe Mode with Networking
    Safe Mode with Command Prompt

    Enable Boot Logging
    Enable VGA Mode
    Last Known Good Configuration (your most recent settings that worked)
    Directory Services Restore Mode (Windows domain controllers only)
    Debugging Mode

    Start Windows Normally
    Reboot
    Return to OS Choices Menu

Use the up and down arrow keys to move the highlight to your choice.
```

5. Click Start, and click Control Panel on the Start menu.

6. In Control Panel, click Add Or Remove Programs.

7. In the Add Or Remove Programs dialog box, click Uninstall Windows XP, and click Change/Remove in the Current Installed Programs list.

8. Follow the instructions on the screen to return to your previous version of Windows, restarting the computer when you are prompted to do so.

What to do when you can't start Windows XP

If you can't start Windows XP because of a hardware or software incompatibility in your system, you'll need to run a program at a command prompt that will start the uninstall routine.

1. Start or, if necessary, restart your computer, and press F8 while the computer is starting to open the Windows Advanced Options Menu.

2. On the Windows Advanced Options Menu, press the up or down arrow key on the keyboard to move the highlight to Safe Mode With Command Prompt, and press Enter.

3. In the CMD.EXE window, type **c:** at the command prompt, and press Enter.

4. Type **cd \windows\system32**, and press Enter.

5. Type **osuninst.exe**, and press Enter.

6. Follow the instructions on the screen to uninstall Windows XP and restore the previous operating system.

I still need to be able to use my previous version of Windows

Source of the problem

Windows XP can upgrade your computer from Windows 98, Windows Me, or Windows 2000, but that requires giving up your existing Windows installation. Instead of replacing your existing version of Windows with Windows XP, you can set up Windows XP and your old version of Windows side by side and choose one or the other whenever you start your computer. Having multiple versions of Windows on a single computer is called dual-booting, and it requires you to set up different versions of Windows on different drive letters (different disk drives or different partitions on the same disk drive). As long as you install Windows XP on a drive letter that's different from where you have Windows 98 or Windows 2000 installed, you can have two completely non-conflicting versions of Windows on a single computer. Here's how to dual-boot two versions of Windows.

Before you start

- If the free space on your hard disk is less than 1.5 GB (gigabytes), consider installing a second hard disk in your computer, because Windows XP requires that much room, and because you'll need to install Windows XP on a separate drive letter. There are ways to create a second drive letter on a single disk drive, but not if your disk drive is already low on space.

  High-capacity, inexpensive hard disks are readily available from computer mail-order companies and retail stores, and most desktop computers provide the space and connection for a second hard disk.

- If your hard disk has two or more drive letters, such as C:, D:, and E:, check the available space on the drive letter where you want to install Windows XP. This drive letter must be at least 1.5 MB (megabytes) in size. If the drive letter doesn't have sufficient space, delete folders or move them to a different drive letter.

- If your hard disk has sufficient space, but only one drive letter (C:), you can use a partition management program, such as Partition Magic or Paragon Partition Manager, to reduce the size of the C: partition, freeing up space on the disk. After you've freed up space, you can create a second drive letter (partition) in the available space.

How to fix it

1. While running your previous version of Windows, insert the Windows XP CD in the CD-ROM drive.

2. In the Welcome To Windows XP dialog box, click Install Windows XP.

3. In the Windows Setup dialog box, click the Installation Type down arrow.

4. Click New Installation in the list, and click Next. ▶

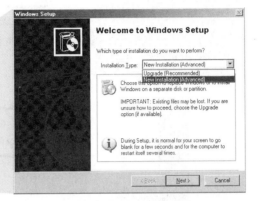

5. Continue the steps of the Windows Setup wizard, accepting the license agreement, and entering your product key.

6. On the Setup Options page of the Windows Setup wizard, click Advanced Options.

7. In the Advanced Options dialog box, click the I Want To Choose The Install Drive Letter And Partition During Setup check box, and click OK. ▶

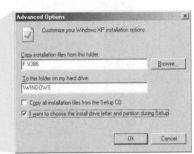

8. After Setup copies the installation files and restarts your computer, select the partition you want to use for the Windows XP installation.

9. Press Enter.

10. If the partition is already formatted, select Leave The Current File System Intact on the next screen, or select one of the options that will format the partition.

    For more information about using the NTFS file system rather than FAT32, see "I can't compress the contents of a hard disk," on page 108.

Warning

During installation, Windows XP can convert a disk drive to the NTFS file system, which provides additional security features, such as the ability to keep others from opening folders. But Windows 98 and Windows Me can't read disks that have been formatted with NTFS—they can read only disks that use FAT or FAT32. So to retain access to the files on a disk where you'll install Windows XP, be sure to leave the disk formatted with FAT32.

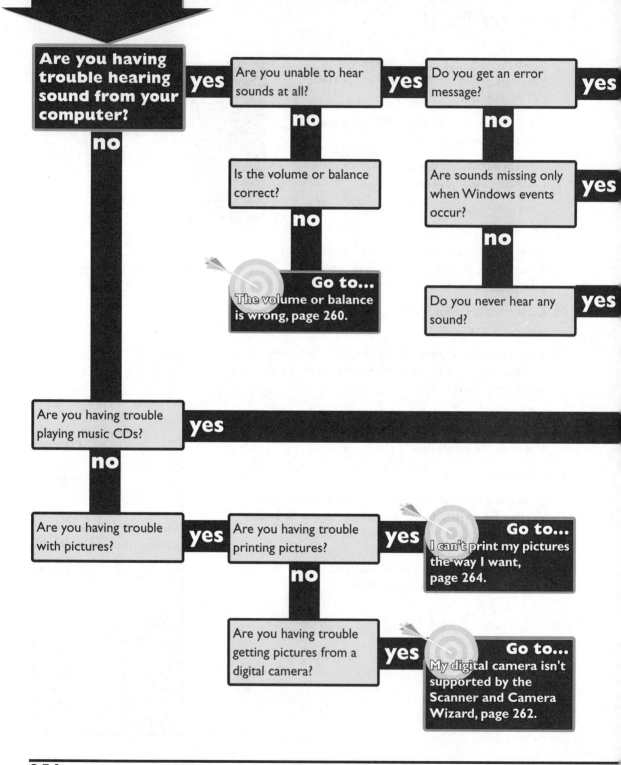

Are you having trouble hearing sound from your computer?

yes → **Are you unable to hear sounds at all?**

yes → **Do you get an error message?**

yes →

no ↓

Is the volume or balance correct?

no ↓

Go to...
The volume or balance is wrong, page 260.

no ↓

Are sounds missing only when Windows events occur?

yes →

no ↓

Do you never hear any sound?

yes →

no ↓

Are you having trouble playing music CDs?

yes →

no ↓

Are you having trouble with pictures?

yes → **Are you having trouble printing pictures?**

yes →

Go to...
I can't print my pictures the way I want, page 264.

no ↓

Are you having trouble getting pictures from a digital camera?

yes →

Go to...
My digital camera isn't supported by the Scanner and Camera Wizard, page 262.

Sound and pictures

Go to...
I can't assign sounds to Windows events, page 261.

Go to...
I don't hear sound, page 256.

Quick fix

I get an error message saying *No wave device that can play files in the current format is installed* Set your audio device to properly play sound by following these steps:

1. Click Start, click Control Panel on the Start menu, click Sounds, Speech, And Audio Devices, and click Sounds And Audio Devices.

2. On the Audio tab of the Sounds And Audio Devices Properties dialog box, make sure your audio device is listed as the Default Device in the Sound Playback area. If it's not, click the Default Device down arrow, and click your audio device in the list.

3. Click OK, and close the Sounds, Speech, And Audio Devices window, and Control Panel.

Does the problem occur only when you use USB speakers??

yes

Go to...
I can't hear music CDs with my USB speakers, page 259.

no

Go to...
My CD or DVD drive won't play music CDs, page 258.

If your solution isn't here, check these related chapters:

- Display, page 40
- Files, page 72
- Hardware, page 114
- Optimizing, page 212

Or see the general trouble-shooting tips on page xv.

I don't hear sound

Source of the problem

If you're trying to play a game, assign sounds to events such as exiting Windows, watch a DVD movie, or play a music CD, and you're not hearing sound from your computer, here are some possible reasons: Windows might not be set to use your sound card, the speakers might not be turned on or connected correctly, some of the software components that Windows needs to play sounds might not be installed, your hardware and software could be conflicting with each other, or your sound card might not be set up properly. You'll need to try a few things until the problem is solved.

How to fix it

- If your computer's speakers are external, verify that they're powered up, that their volume is turned up, and that they're connected to the correct jacks on the back of the computer.
  The sound card or computer documentation should show the location of the speaker jacks.

- If the speakers are built into the monitor, adjust their volume using the controls on the monitor or keyboard. Some monitors have a rotary dial on their front panel. Others have controls hidden behind a door panel you can open, usually on the front face of the monitor.

If checking the volume control and connections for your speakers didn't work, your sound card might be disabled, its volume might be turned down, or it might not be designated as the device to play sounds. To enable the sound card, check its volume, and set it as the device that plays sounds, follow these steps:

1. Click Start, right-click My Computer on the Start menu, and click Properties on the shortcut menu.

2. On the Hardware tab of the System Properties dialog box, click Device Manager.

3. In Device Manager, click the plus sign next to Sound, Video And Game Controllers, right-click your sound card or audio device in the list, and click Enable if it appears on the shortcut menu. ▶

   If Disable is an option on the shortcut menu, your audio device is already properly enabled.

4. Close the Device Manager window, and click OK to close the System Properties dialog box.

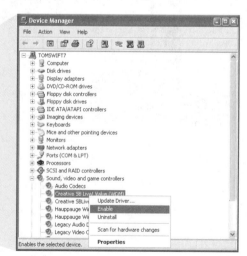

If the device was already enabled, follow these steps:

1. Click Start, and click Control Panel on the Start menu.

2. In Control Panel, click Sounds, Speech, And Audio Devices, and then click Sounds And Audio Devices.

3. On the Volume tab in the Sounds And Audio Devices Properties dialog box, make sure the Device Volume slider is mid-range, between Low and High, and that the Mute check box in the Device Volume area is not selected. ▶

4. In the Speaker Settings area of the Volume tab, click Speaker Volume, make sure the Left and Right sliders are mid-range between Low and High, and click OK.

5. In the Speaker Settings area of the Volume tab, click Advanced.

6. On the Speakers tab of the Advanced Audio Properties dialog box, click the Speaker Setup down arrow, select your speaker setup, and click OK. ▶

7. On the Audio tab of the Sounds And Audio Devices Properties dialog box, click the Default Device down arrow, and make sure your audio device is selected in the list.

If you still don't hear sound, you might need to update the driver for your audio device by following these steps:

1. On the Hardware tab in the Sounds And Audio Devices Properties dialog box, click your audio device in the Devices list, and click Properties.

2. On the Driver tab in the Properties dialog box for the device, click Update Driver.

3. Follow the steps in the Hardware Update Wizard to update the driver for the device.
  Check Windows Update or the audio device manufacturer's Web site for an updated driver for your device. If you download a driver, in the Hardware Update Wizard, click Install From A List Or Specific Location, and then enter the location of the downloaded driver on the next page of the wizard.

My CD or DVD drive won't play music CDs

Source of the problem

Whether you're relaxing at home or stuck on a long flight, the CD or DVD drive in your computer might be just the ticket to keep you entertained. You can pass the time by listening to music or watching your favorite movie. But if you don't hear your favorite music CDs or the sound track of movies even though you do hear other sounds through your speakers or headphones, you should investigate a few causes.

How to fix it

1. Give the CD or DVD drive at least five seconds to read the disc before you try to eject it. The drive can take that long to start producing sound.

2. Try cleaning the disc with a lint-free cloth or playing a different disc altogether to make sure the problem isn't the disc itself rather than the computer.

3. Check the volume and mute settings in Windows. For information about checking these settings, see "The volume or balance is wrong," on page 260.

4. If you installed the CD or DVD drive yourself in a desktop computer, make sure that you ran a cable from the drive's audio-out jack to the audio-in jack on the sound card or on the computer's main circuit board (the *motherboard*).

5. If you installed the cable in step 4, and if the drive has a headphone jack on its front face, plug in headphones and see if you can hear music. If you can, you know the drive is working. You'll need to check the volume control in Windows by following the rest of these steps.

6. Click Start, click Control Panel on the Start menu, click Sounds, Speech, And Audio Devices, and click Adjust The System Volume.

7. On the Volume tab in the Sounds And Audio Devices Properties dialog box, click Advanced in the Device Volume area.

8. In the Play Control dialog box, make sure the CD Audio Mute check box is not selected, and drag the Volume slider up to a higher level before closing the Play Control dialog box.

I can't hear music CDs with my USB speakers

Source of the problem

If you can hear music through headphones when you put an audio CD in your CD-ROM drive, but not through your USB speakers, you need to enable the digital CD playback feature in Windows XP, which sends music as digital information directly from your digital CDs in your digital CD-ROM drive to your digital USB speakers. Your music stays all-digital all the way so it'll sound its best.

After you've enabled digital CD playback, you'll need to turn it off if you want to listen to music through regular headphones plugged into the sound card in your computer.

To enable digital CD playback, follow the steps here.

How to fix it

1. Click Start, right-click My Computer on the Start menu, and click Properties.

2. On the Hardware tab of the System Properties dialog box, click Device Manager.

3. In Device Manager, click the plus sign next to DVD/ CD-ROM drives, and then right-click your CD-ROM drive and click Properties on the shortcut menu.

4. On the Properties tab in the Properties dialog box, select the Enable Digital CD Audio For This CD-ROM Device check box, and click OK. ▶

5. Close Device Manager and the System Properties dialog box.

The volume or balance is wrong

Source of the problem

Whether you find yourself straining to hear the sounds coming from your computer or you're blasted out of your seat, that little Volume icon nestled on the taskbar near the clock is the answer. Clicking it once opens a simple slider that you can drag for overall volume control. Clicking it twice opens a full control panel you can use to change the volume levels of individual sound sources and adjust their balance between left and right. And if the Volume icon isn't visible, this solution describes how to make it appear.

How to fix it

1. Single-click the Volume icon on the taskbar, near the clock, and drag the slider up or down to change the overall volume of all sound, or double-click the Volume icon to open the Volume Control dialog box so that you can adjust individual sound sources in the computer.

   If the Volume icon, which looks like a little speaker, isn't visible, follow the steps in "Displaying the Volume icon," below.

2. In the Play Control dialog box, drag the Balance sliders left or right and drag the Volume sliders up or down to adjust the levels of each sound source.

   The Volume Control slider at the left is the master control. If it's set too low, none of the other sources will be heard.

   If the Mute check box for a device is selected, the device is temporarily turned off. To turn the device back on, clear the Mute check box.

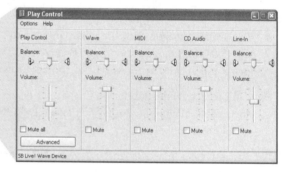

Displaying the Volume icon

1. Click Start, and click Control Panel on the Start menu.

2. In Control Panel, click Sounds, Speech, And Audio Devices, and then click Sounds And Audio Devices.

3. On the Volume tab in the Sounds And Audio Devices Properties dialog box, select the Place Volume Icon In The Taskbar check box, and click OK.

Sound and pictures

I can't assign sounds to Windows events

Source of the problem

A *sound scheme* provides a suite of sounds for Windows events, such as a chime for an error message or a fanfare to proclaim the excitement of emptying the Recycle Bin. But if you don't hear sounds, you can try attaching sounds from a sound scheme to individual Windows events. Using Windows is infinitely more fun when you use sound schemes, so here's how to get them working.

How to fix it

1. Click Start, click Control Panel on the Start menu, and click Sounds, Speech, And Audio Devices.

2. Click Change The Sound Scheme.

3. On the Sounds tab in the Sounds And Audio Devices Properties dialog box, click an event in the Program Events list, click the Sounds down arrow, and click a sound in the list. ▶

    You can preview the sound by clicking the Play (right arrow) button next to the Sounds list.

4. Repeat step 3 for each event for which you want to change the attached sound.

5. After you've changed the assigned sounds for all the events you want, click Save As, and in the Save Scheme As dialog box, type a name for your new sound scheme, and click OK.

6. Click OK again, close the Sounds, Speech, And Audio Devices window, and start using your new sounds.

Getting better sounds

You can download thousands of sounds from file download sites on the Web to create entirely new sound schemes. After you download sounds (as .wav files), copy them to the C:\Windows\Media folder. Now you'll see your new sounds in the Sounds list on the Sounds tab of the Sounds And Audio Devices Properties dialog box.

> **Tip**
>
> To choose an entirely different set of sounds after you've created a few sound schemes, click the Sound Scheme down arrow after step 2, and click a different scheme in the list.

My digital camera isn't supported by the Scanner and Camera Wizard

Source of the problem

Windows XP's Scanner and Camera Wizard can make it extremely easy to transfer pictures from your digital camera to your computer, but for it to work, it needs your camera to have the proper driver for Windows XP. If your digital camera doesn't have such a driver, here's a workaround you can employ. Obtain a Windows XP–compatible reader into which you insert the memory card from your camera. Then you can use the Scanner and Camera Wizard to transfer pictures from the reader to the computer. Small, inexpensive readers that attach to your computer's USB port are readily available for the most popular types of memory cards, both Compact Flash cards and SmartMedia cards.

Here's how to use the Scanner and Camera Wizard with a memory card reader.

How to fix it

1. Connect the memory card reader to the USB port on your computer.

2. Insert the memory card from your digital camera into the card reader.

3. In the window that opens for the memory card reader, click Copy Pictures To A Folder On My Computer Using Microsoft Scanner And Camera Wizard, and click OK. ▶

4. On the first page of the Scanner And Camera Wizard dialog box, click Next.

5. On the Choose Pictures To Copy page of the wizard, click Next if you want to transfer all pictures from the memory card to your hard disk.

    If you'd prefer to select certain pictures to transfer, click Clear All, select the check box for each picture you want to copy, and click Next.

6. In the first box on the Picture Name And Destination page of the wizard, type a name for the group of pictures you'll be copying. ▶

    The picture files will be sequentially numbered in the destination folder with the name you enter used as the prefix. In other words, if you enter July Vacation, the pictures files will be named July Vacation 001, July Vacation 002, and so on.

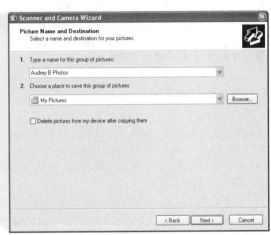

7. In the second box, enter the name of the folder where you want to store the pictures.

    You can also click Browse, select a folder in the Browse For Folder window, and click OK.

    To create a new subfolder in the My Pictures folder, click Browse, click the My Pictures folder in the Browse For Folder dialog box, click Make New Folder, enter a name for the folder in the Folder box, and click OK.

8. Click Next to begin copying the pictures to the folder.

    The wizard shows you the copying progress for each individual file and for all the files collectively. ▶

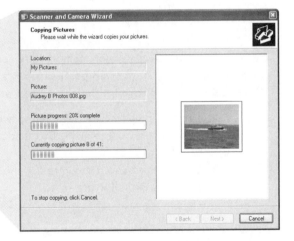

9. On the Other Options page, you can select options to publish the pictures you've copied to a Web site. You can also order prints of the pictures from a photo printing Web site. If you'd rather not choose either of these options, click Nothing. I'm Finished Working With These Pictures, and click Next to go to the last step of the wizard.

10. Click Finish on the last page of the wizard, which notes how many pictures were copied.

    If you'd like to view the pictures, click the link on the last page of the wizard before clicking Finish.

I can't print my pictures the way I want

Source of the problem

If you've struggled with printing pictures in previous versions of Windows, you know how hard it can be to get a proper-sized and neatly centered printout, and you can just about forget printing pictures on 4 x 6 photo sheets that come two to a page. It's not entirely impossible, but it will probably take plenty of trial and error in your favorite image editing program to get photos printed just the way you want.

The Photo Printing Wizard in Windows XP can make your photo printing problems a thing of the past. It makes it a snap not only to select photos in any folder, but also to print them just about any way you could want. Options include printing pictures one to a page (full page), printing two, three, or four to a page, or printing a set of small, wallet-sized pictures that you can pass out to friends and family. And you can decide whether you want to print selected photos from a folder or print a single photo over again to create a set of duplicates.

How to fix it

1. Attach your digital camera or memory card reader to your computer (usually to the USB port), or open a folder in My Computer that contains the photos you want to print.

2. If you've attached a digital camera or memory card reader, click Print The Pictures in the dialog box that opens for the camera. ▶

   If you've opened a folder containing photos, click Print Pictures in the Picture Tasks list in the folder window. ▶

3. On the first page of the Photo Printing Wizard, click Next.

---

4. On the Picture Selection page, click Next if you want to print all the pictures in the folder.

   If you want to select which pictures to print, click Clear All, select the check box at the upper right corner of each picture you want to print, and then click Next. ▶

5. On the Printing Options page, make sure the correct printer is selected.

   If you need to choose a different printer, click the What Printer Do You Want To Use down arrow, and click the printer you want in the list.

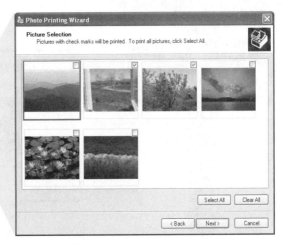

6. Click Printing Preferences, and select the paper and printing quality for the photos. ▶

7. In the Properties dialog box for the printer, select an orientation on the Layout tab.

8. Select a paper type (Media) and quality setting on the Paper/Quality tab.

9. Click OK.

10. On the Printing Options page of the wizard, click Next.

11. On the Layout Selection page, click one of the layouts in the Available Layouts list. ▶

    The Print Preview box shows you how the photos will look when printed.

12. If you'd like to print multiple copies of a certain picture on a Contact Sheet Prints or Wallet Prints page, edit the number in the Number Of Times To Use Each Picture box, and click Next.

13. Click Finish to close the wizard.

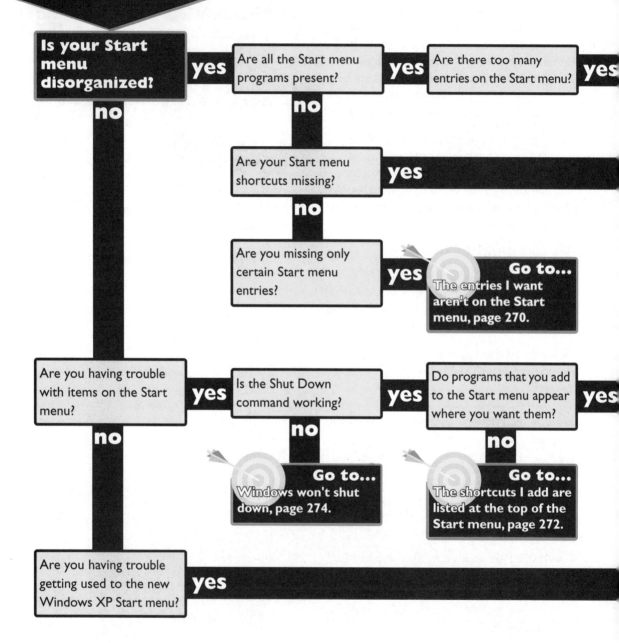

Is your Start menu disorganized?

yes → Are all the Start menu programs present?

yes → Are there too many entries on the Start menu? **yes** →

no ↓

Are your Start menu shortcuts missing? **yes** →

no ↓

Are you missing only certain Start menu entries? **yes** →

Go to...
The entries I want aren't on the Start menu, page 270.

no ↓

Are you having trouble with items on the Start menu? **yes** → Is the Shut Down command working? **yes** → Do programs that you add to the Start menu appear where you want them? **yes** →

no ↓

Go to...
Windows won't shut down, page 274.

no ↓

Go to...
The shortcuts I add are listed at the top of the Start menu, page 272.

no ↓

Are you having trouble getting used to the new Windows XP Start menu? **yes** →

Go to...
My Start menu is too long or too disorganized, page 268.

Quick fix

The Start menu doesn't show my shortcuts If the Start menu does not contain the set of programs you're accustomed to seeing, examine the user name at the top of the Start menu. If your user name is not shown, you are not logged on. Click Off on the Start menu, and log on with your own user name.

Does the Documents list show files you want hidden?

yes

Go to...
The My Recent Documents list shows a file I don't want others to see, page 273.

Quick fix

I can't get used to the new Windows XP Start menu The new Start menu in Windows XP is designed to make your everyday tasks easier, but if you'd prefer to return to the familiar Start menu from Windows 98, Windows Me, or Windows 2000, follow these steps:

1. Right-click the Start button, and click Properties on the shortcut menu.

2. On the Start Menu tab in the Taskbar And Start Menu Properties dialog box, click Classic Start Menu, and click OK.

If your solution isn't here, check these related chapters:

- The desktop, page 12
- Folders, page 82
- Programs, page 234
- The taskbar, page 292

Or see the general troubleshooting tips on page xv.

My Start menu is too long or too disorganized

Source of the problem

Little by little, the Start menu grows as you install new software, until its purpose—to provide quick and easy access to your programs—is nearly defeated. If, like many people, you click Start, point to All Programs, and watch a mile-long menu struggle to find space on your screen, it's time to shorten and organize the Start menu.

In the following steps, you'll create folders in the Start Menu folder for categories of programs, and then you'll group shortcuts and folders in the category folders.

How to fix it

1. Right-click Start, and click Explore All Users on the shortcut menu.

2. In the left pane of the Windows Explorer window, click the Programs folder under Start Menu.

3. Right-click a blank area in the right pane of the Windows Explorer window, point to New on the shortcut menu, and then click Folder.

4. Type a name for the new folder that best describes a category of programs you've installed, such as Games or Graphics, and press Enter.

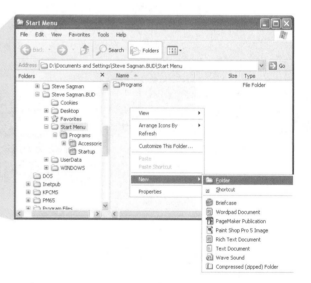

5. Repeat steps 3 and 4, creating additional folders for other categories of programs.

6. Drag a shortcut or folder from the right pane to one of the new category folders you've created. For example, drag all the shortcuts and folders related to graphics to the new Graphics folder.

7. After you finish arranging shortcuts and folders, close the Windows Explorer window. The changes to the Start menu are immediate.

Dragging shortcuts on the Start menu

Another way to rearrange your shortcuts and menus is to drag them around right on the Start menu. This method is simple and direct, and you see the results instantly. You can drag shortcuts and menus onto menus that already exist, but you can't easily create new menus.

To reorganize your Start menu by dragging shortcuts and menus, follow these steps:

1. Click Start, and point to All Programs.

2. On the All Programs menu, position the mouse pointer on a shortcut or menu you want to move. Drag the shortcut or menu to a different submenu on the All Programs menu, and pause until the menu opens. ▶

    If you find that you can't drag a shortcut or menu, right-click the taskbar, and click Properties on the shortcut menu. On the Start Menu tab of the Taskbar And Start Menu Properties dialog box, click Customize. On the Advanced tab in the Customize Start Menu dialog box, select the Enable Dragging And Dropping check box in the Start Menu Items list. Click OK twice to close the dialog boxes.

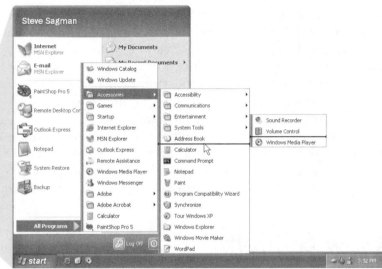

3. Drag the shortcut or menu onto the submenu, and release the mouse button.

The Programs list

As a convenience, the left half of the Start menu displays a list of shortcuts to the programs you use most often. By default, the list shows six programs, but you can increase or decrease this number by right-clicking the Start button, clicking Properties on the shortcut menu, and clicking Customize on the Start Menu tab of the Taskbar And Start Menu Properties dialog box. On the General tab of the Customize Start Menu dialog box, change the number in the Number Of Programs On Start Menu box, and click OK twice to close the dialog boxes.

Tip

The Internet and E-Mail shortcuts take you quickly to your preferred Internet browser and e-mail programs. If the programs these shortcuts lead to are not the programs you want, right-click the Start button, click Properties on the shortcut menu, and click Customize on the Start Menu tab of the Taskbar And Start Menu Properties dialog box. Click the programs you want in the Show On Start Menu area of the General tab in the Customize Start Menu dialog box.

The entries I want aren't on the Start menu

Source of the problem

They were there last week. They were even there yesterday. But now the shortcuts for your programs have disappeared from the Start menu. Has something gone wrong? Is someone tampering with your settings? Assuming you've logged on with your own user name, you're experiencing a feature that's meant to be a convenience. The Start menu evolves as you use Windows, replacing shortcuts for programs you use infrequently with shortcuts for programs you use more often. The shortcuts for these programs appear in the most recently used programs section of the Start menu, on the left side below the horizontal separator line.

If you're less consistent and use a wide variety of programs, you can still create a set of your favorites that will always appear on the Start menu, no matter how much you use them. To do so you pin these programs to the Start menu so they appear on the left side, above the separator line. You can also decide for yourself which folders should appear on the right side of the Start menu. Here's how.

How to fix it

1. Click Start, and make sure that your user name appears at the top of the Start menu.

   If not, click Log Off on the Start menu, and click Log Off in the dialog box that asks whether you're sure you want to log off. Either click your user name on the Welcome screen or, if the Log On To Windows dialog box opens, enter your user name, password, and domain, if necessary, and click OK.

2. Find the shortcut that you want to have stay on the Start menu, either on the list of most recently used programs on the left side of the Start menu or in the All Programs menu or submenus (click All Programs, and point to submenus until you've found the shortcut).

3. Right-click the shortcut, and click Pin To Start Menu on the shortcut menu. ▶

The shortcut appears in the pinned shortcuts area on the left side of the Start menu, above the separator line. To remove a shortcut from the pinned shortcuts area, right-click the shortcut and click Unpin From Start Menu.

Choosing the folders to show on the Start menu

Although Windows picks a starting set of folders to show on the right side of the Start menu, such as the My Pictures and My Music folders, you can customize this list to simplify the Start menu, removing any entries that you rarely use, by following these steps:

1. Right-click the Start button, and click Properties on the shortcut menu.

2. On the Start Menu tab of the Taskbar And Start Menu Properties dialog box, click Customize.

3. On the Advanced tab of the Customize Start Menu dialog box, scroll down the list of Start Menu Items and click Don't Display This Item for each item that you'd like to remove from the Start menu. ▶

4. Click OK to close the Customize Start Menu dialog box, and click OK to close the Taskbar And Start Menu Properties dialog box.

   Some items, such as Help And Support, have check boxes you can clear to remove them.

Turning shortcuts into menus

By making some of the items on the Start menu expandable, you gain more direct access to Windows features, such as the options in Control Panel. For example, when you display the Control Panel shortcut as a menu, you can point to Control Panel and then click a Control Panel item in the Control Panel menu. To make some of the key shortcuts on the Start menu expandable, follow these steps:

1. Right-click the Start button, and click Properties on the shortcut menu.

2. On the Start Menu tab of the Taskbar And Start Menu Properties dialog box, click Customize.

3. On the Advanced tab of the Customize Start Menu dialog box, scroll down the list of Start Menu Items, and click Display As A Menu for each item that you'd like make expandable.

4. Click OK to close the Customize Start Menu dialog box, and click OK to close the Taskbar And Start Menu Properties dialog box.

Tip

To show the Start menu as a scrollable list rather than a multiple-column list, select the Scroll Programs check box in the Start Menu items list on the Advanced tab in the Customize Start Menu dialog box.

The shortcuts I add are listed at the top of the Start menu

Source of the problem

Almost every Windows program setup routine installs a shortcut to the program on the Start menu. Being a good citizen, the setup program creates a new submenu on the All Programs menu for a shortcut to the program and perhaps for some other shortcuts, such as those to a Readme file or a registration routine.

If a program's setup routine doesn't add a Start menu item, you can create one of your own by simply dragging the icon for the program from its folder to the Start button on the taskbar. But this shortcut will go to the top of the Start menu, along with programs you've pinned to the Start menu, not on the All Programs menu where you want it. At least you've gotten the shortcut to the Start menu, but now to get it to the All Programs menu, follow these steps.

How to fix it

1. Click Start.

2. On the Start menu, drag the shortcut you want to move to the All Programs menu and pause until the All Programs menu opens. ▶

3. Drag the shortcut to the position on the All Programs menu where you'd like it to appear, and then release the mouse button.

   To position the shortcut on a submenu of the All Programs menu, drag the shortcut to the submenu, pause until the submenu expands, and then drag the shortcut onto the submenu and drop it wherever you want.

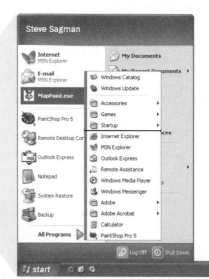

The My Recent Documents list shows a file I don't want others to see

Source of the problem

The My Recent Documents list on the Start menu makes the files you've used recently readily available. But it also leaves a trail that others can follow to see the files you've worked on. If you'd occasionally prefer to sacrifice a little convenience to maintain your privacy, here's how you can clear the entire My Recent Documents list or selectively delete documents from it.

How to fix it

1. Right-click the Start button, and click Properties on the shortcut menu.

2. On the Start Menu tab in the Taskbar And Start Menu Properties dialog box, click Customize.

3. On the Advanced tab of the Customize Start Menu dialog box, click Clear List to clear the entire My Recent Documents list. ▶

4. Click OK to close the Customize Start Menu dialog box, and click OK to close the dialog box.

Deleting a single entry

You can delete a single entry by removing it from the hidden My Recent Documents folder.

To see the folder, you need to click My Computer on the Start menu, click Folder Options on the Tools menu, and in the Folder Options dialog box, click Show Hidden Files And Folders in the Advanced Settings list on the View tab. Now you can open your own folder in the Documents And Settings folder, open the My Recent Documents folder, and delete shortcuts selectively.

Windows won't shut down

Source of the problem

If you click Shut Down and find that the computer goes into limbo when it should either turn itself off or display the message *It is now safe to turn off your computer,* you need to look into several possible causes of shutdown problems. It could be a program that's stopped responding, problems with installed devices, or a BIOS that needs updating. (The BIOS is the software built into the computer that controls its most basic operations.) Follow the steps below to take care of all these potential problems.

How to fix it

1. Press Ctrl+Alt+Del.

2. In the Windows Security dialog box, click Task Manager.

3. On the Applications tab of the Windows Task Manager, look in the list for a program that's accompanied by a *Not responding* message.

4. If you see such a program, click it, and click End Task.

5. If a message box appears telling you that the program is not responding, click End Now to close the dialog box and quit the program. ▶

6. Try shutting down again.

If the computer still won't shut down properly, follow these steps to use System Restore to undo any recent changes that might have caused your computer to stop shutting down.

1. Click Start, point to All Programs, point to Accessories, point to System Tools, and click System Restore.

2. In the System Restore dialog box, make sure Restore My Computer To An Earlier Time is selected, and click Next.

3. On the Select A Restore Point page, click the most recent bold date in the calendar, click a restore point in the list of restore points, and click Next.

4. On the next page of the wizard, click Next to start the restore.
    If Windows is still unable to shut down, run System Restore again and select an earlier restore point.

If the computer still won't shut down properly, use Device Manager to verify that no devices in your computer are having trouble by following these steps:

1. Click Start, right-click My Computer on the Start menu, and click Properties on the shortcut menu.

2. In the System Properties dialog box, click the Hardware tab, and then click Device Manager in the System Properties dialog box.

3. Look for devices whose icons show a yellow exclamation point. A problem with one of these devices might be preventing Windows from properly shutting down.

    If you find that one of your devices is reporting trouble, see "A new device I've installed doesn't work," on page 116, for further troubleshooting steps.

If the computer still won't shut down properly, contact the computer manufacturer, or go to the manufacturer's Web site to look for a program that you can download and run to update the computer's BIOS. Computer manufacturers frequently post BIOS update programs to fix problems that are found only later.

The Shut Down option is missing from the Start menu

If your office computer shows the Log Off option on the Start menu, but not the Shut Down option, you might be prevented from shutting down your computer by the system administrator who has established a policy against it. System Administrators might prevent some computers from shutting down so they can require the computers to run administrative tasks overnight, such as system backups. If your computer is missing the Shut Down option, you can ask to be changed to a group that does have shut down privileges, or you can accept the fact that your computer will stay on at all times, and rejoice in having one less thing to do before leaving the office. But to protect your personal files, be sure to log off before leaving the computer overnight.

My computer won't turn itself off when I use Shut Down

Some computers are able to turn themselves off after you click Shut Down, just as if you turned off their power switch. If your computer has never turned itself off (you've always seen the *It is now safe to turn off your computer* message), you probably can't get it to do so now because the computer is not designed for this feature. But if your computer has turned itself off in the past, the computer has probably had this capability deactivated. To restore automatic shutdown, start the setup program for the computer (usually by pressing a key while the computer is starting), and look for an option that turns on Advanced Power Management (APM). For additional information about APM, see "The battery runs down too fast," on page 154.

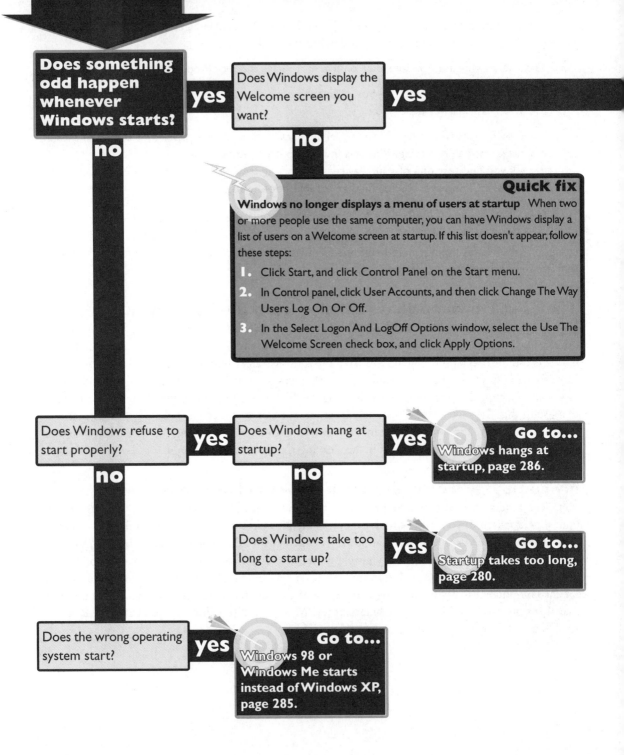

Does something odd happen whenever Windows starts?

yes → Does Windows display the Welcome screen you want?

yes →

no ↓

no ↓

Quick fix

Windows no longer displays a menu of users at startup When two or more people use the same computer, you can have Windows display a list of users on a Welcome screen at startup. If this list doesn't appear, follow these steps:

1. Click Start, and click Control Panel on the Start menu.
2. In Control panel, click User Accounts, and then click Change The Way Users Log On Or Off.
3. In the Select Logon And LogOff Options window, select the Use The Welcome Screen check box, and click Apply Options.

Does Windows refuse to start properly?

yes → Does Windows hang at startup?

yes →

Go to...
Windows hangs at startup, page 286.

no ↓

no ↓

Does Windows take too long to start up?

yes →

Go to...
Startup takes too long, page 280.

Does the wrong operating system start?

yes →

Go to...
Windows 98 or Windows Me starts instead of Windows XP, page 285.

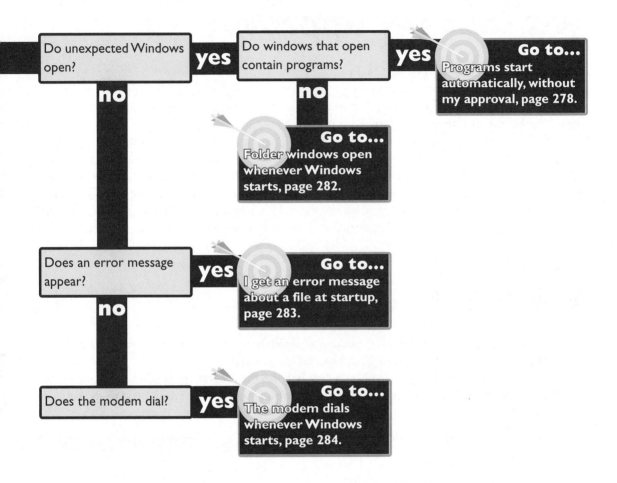

Do unexpected Windows open? — **yes** → Do windows that open contain programs? — **yes** →

Go to...
Programs start automatically, without my approval, page 278.

no →

Go to...
Folder windows open whenever Windows starts, page 282.

no ↓

Does an error message appear? — **yes** →

Go to...
I get an error message about a file at startup, page 283.

no ↓

Does the modem dial? — **yes** →

Go to...
The modem dials whenever Windows starts, page 284.

If your solution isn't here, check these related chapters:

- The desktop, page 12
- Disasters, page 30
- Optimizing, page 212
- The Start menu, page 266

Or see the general troubleshooting tips on page xv.

Programs start automatically, without my approval

Source of the problem

Just by changing an option in the offending program, you can weed out some programs that start themselves whenever Windows starts. But other programs insinuate themselves into your Windows XP installation and need to be yanked out by the roots.

Programs have several ways to start themselves. They can put a shortcut in the Startup folder on the Start menu, which causes them to start each time Windows starts. That makes the Startup folder the first place to look for software that launches itself. But not all programs use the Startup folder. Some software setup programs put a startup command in the Windows registry. These are harder to remove than a simple Startup folder shortcut. Here's how to go through and systematically prevent all unwanted programs from starting up without your express permission—no matter how they've accomplished it.

How to fix it

1. Open the program and examine its options or preferences, looking for an option you can disable such as Run This Program Each Time Windows Starts.

   If you find such an option, you're in luck, because the program gives you a neat and tidy way to disable its automatic startup. But if you can't find such an option, proceed to the rest of these steps.

2. Right-click Start, and click Explore on the shortcut menu.

3. In the left pane of the Windows Explorer window, click the plus sign next to the Programs folder under Start Menu, and then click the Startup folder. ▶

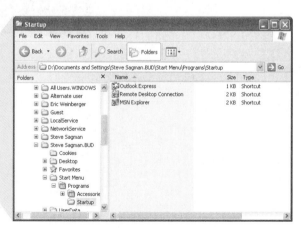

4. In the right pane, drag the icons for the programs you want to prevent from starting to another location on the Start menu.

As long as you know on which submenu their icons reside on the Start menu, you can still start the programs by clicking their icons, if necessary.

5. Close the Startup window.

That takes care of the Startup folder shortcuts. Now here's how to fix the programs that start by using registry settings:

1. Click Start, click Run, and in the Run dialog box, type **msconfig** in the Open box and press Enter.

2. On the Startup tab in the System Configuration Utility window, clear the check box in the Startup Item column for any program that you want to prevent from loading. ▶

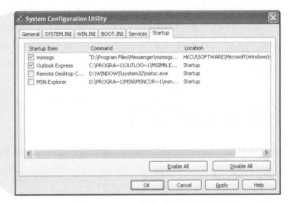

It's not always immediately obvious what these programs accomplish. You might be able to tell by examining the entry in the Command or Location column. These will tell you which folder the program is in.

3. Click OK, and then click Restart when you're asked whether you want to restart your computer.

More about the Startup folder

You might be surprised to find how many entries your Startup folder contains. Each entry corresponds to a program that starts when Windows does. Some programs in the Startup folder open a window and announce their presence—the dialer program for your Internet service provider (ISP) might be an example. Other programs run without fanfare, waiting quietly in the background until it's their turn to provide a service. Some printers have special programs, for example, that pop open to show you the printer's progress through queued-up documents.

How did all those icons get there? Some software setup programs rudely drop icons into the Startup folder without asking. Others have a little more courtesy and ask whether you want their program started each time you start Windows.

Tip

You can specify whether a program opens in a regular window, a full-screen window, or as a button on the taskbar by right-clicking its icon in the Startup folder, clicking Properties on the shortcut menu, clicking the Run down arrow in the Properties dialog box, and then clicking Normal Window, Maximized, or Minimized in the list.

Startup takes too long

Source of the problem

Windows is ready to go when the desktop appears, when all the little icons on the taskbar are visible, and when the mouse pointer no longer shows that wait-just-a-minute hourglass. But if getting to that point requires nothing short of endurance when you have only a little patience, Windows startup is taking too long.

Startup takes time because Windows has a lot of devices to set up, a ton of programs to load, a slew of fonts to install, and a full roster of housekeeping tasks to do before it's ready to go to work for you. Windows XP has made a few strides toward a shorter startup time. You'll find that it gets up and running noticeably faster than previous versions of Windows. But here are steps you can take to minimize startup time so you can get right to work, or play.

How to fix it

Prevent any unnecessary programs from starting at startup by following these steps:

1. Right-click Start, and click Explore on the shortcut menu.

2. In the left pane of the Windows Explorer window, click the plus sign next to the Programs folder under Start Menu, and then click the Startup folder.

3. In the right pane, drag to another location on the Start menu any icons for programs you don't need to have started each time you start Windows.

As long as you know on which submenu their icons reside on the Start menu, you can still start these programs by clicking their icons, if necessary.

4. Close the Windows Explorer window.

If your computer shows a list of operating systems you can choose each time you start the computer, such as Microsoft Windows XP Professional and Microsoft Windows Millennium Edition, you can reduce the length of time this list is shown by following these steps:

1. Click Start, right-click My Computer on the Start menu, and click Properties on the shortcut menu.

2. On the Advanced tab of the System Properties dialog box, click Settings in the Startup And Recovery area.

3. In the Time To Display List Of Operating Systems box, reduce the number of seconds from 30 to 10 or less.

4. Click OK, and click OK again to close the System Properties dialog box.

A pair of related tasks that will help reduce startup time is freeing up space on your hard disk and defragmenting the hard disk. Follow these steps to accomplish both tasks:

1. Click Start, click My Computer on the Start menu, and in the My Computer window, right-click your hard disk and click Properties on the shortcut menu.

2. On the General tab of the Properties dialog box for the hard disk, click Disk Cleanup.

3. In the Disk Cleanup dialog box, select the check boxes for files that you can safely delete, such as temporary Internet files and the contents of the Recycle Bin, and click OK.

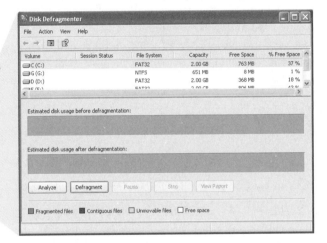

4. On the Tools tab of the Properties dialog box for the hard disk, click Defragment Now, and then click Defragment in the Disk Defragmenter dialog box. ▶

5. After defragmentation is complete, close the Disk Defragmenter, close the Properties dialog box for the hard disk, and close the My Computer window.

In addition, follow these steps to disable scheduled tasks that might be running each time Windows starts.

1. Click Start, and click Control Panel on the Start menu.

2. In Control Panel, click Performance And Maintenance, and then click Scheduled Tasks.

3. Examine the list of tasks in the Scheduled Tasks window, and right-click any task that displays Run At System Startup Or At Logon in the Schedule column.

4. Click Properties on the shortcut menu.

5. On the Task tab in the dialog box for the task, clear the Enabled check box.
　　To keep the task available rather than delete it, you can instead click the Schedule tab in the task dialog box, click the Schedule Task down arrow, and click a different schedule in the list, such as Weekly or Monthly.

6. Click OK to close the task dialog box, and close any open Windows.

> ### Tip
> Before you shut down Windows, remove any CD or removable disk from its drive so its contents won't have to be read the next time Windows starts up.

Folder windows open whenever Windows starts

Source of the problem

Windows can be set to remember how your screen looks whenever it shuts down, so that it can offer you the same open windows the next time you start the computer. Some people find this to be a convenience, but others would prefer to start from scratch each time they start Windows and to open the folders they want.

If you'd rather have Windows stop remembering which folders were open the last time you used the computer and reopening them on your behalf, follow these steps.

How to fix it

1. Click Start, and click My Computer on the Start menu.

2. In My Computer, click Folder Options on the Tools menu.

3. On the View tab of the Folder Options dialog box, clear the Restore Previous Folder Windows At Logon check box. ▶

4. Click OK to close the Folder Options window, and close My Computer.

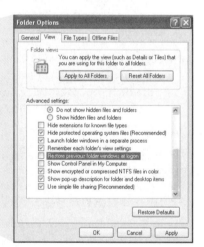

Keeping network drive windows from reopening

Windows might also display the contents of a network drive when it starts if you've set it to restore a network connection each time it starts. To disconnect a network drive, follow these steps:

1. Click Start, and click My Computer on the Start menu.

2. In My Computer, right-click an entry in the Network Drives list, and click Disconnect on the shortcut menu.

   To avoid this problem in the future, do not select the Reconnect At Logon check box the next time you use Map Network Drive to map a drive to a folder on a network computer.

I get an error message about a file at startup

Source of the problem

If you get an error message about a file when you start Windows, a software program or hardware device that you've installed might have added a file to your installation that's preventing Windows from a trouble-free startup. You can use the System Configuration Utility to disable this file so Windows won't try to load it at startup.

Conversely, a program you've removed might also be causing an error message at startup if you tried to delete the program manually without using the Add Or Remove Programs option in Control Panel. If you follow this procedure and find that it disables a software program or hardware device, make sure the program or device is compatible with Windows XP by checking the Hardware Compatibility List at this address: *www.microsoft.com/hcl/default.asp*. If the program or device is not compatible, check the manufacturer or the manufacturer's Web site for an available update.

How to fix it

1. Click Start, and click Run on the Start menu.

2. In the Run dialog box, type **msconfig** in the Open box, and press Enter.

3. In the System Configuration Utility, click the SYSTEM.INI and WIN.INI tabs, and look for a line that refers to the file name reported in the error message. ▶

    On the SYSTEM.INI and WIN.INI tabs, click the plus sign next to a category to expand and view its entries.

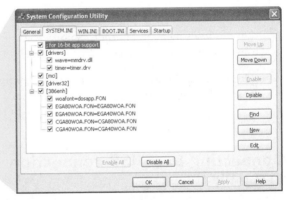

If you're unsuccessful at finding the file that's causing the error message, consider whether you've removed a program from your computer recently without using Add Or Remove Programs. If so, follow these steps:

1. Reinstall the program by running its setup program.

2. Click Start, click Control Panel on the Start menu, and click Add Or Remove Programs.

3. In the Add Or Remove Programs dialog box, click the program and click Change or Change/Remove.

4. Click Yes when you're asked whether you want to remove the program.

The modem dials whenever Windows starts

Source of the problem

If your Web browser or e-mail program starts whenever you start Windows, it can push the modem into trying to connect to the Internet because it wants to retrieve a Web page or an e-mail message.

If you'd rather maintain tighter control of your modem and phone line and prevent Internet Explorer or your e-mail program from dialing a connection whenever it starts, follow these steps.

How to fix it

● If your Internet service provider or online service has provided software that establishes a connection, look in the software's options for an autodial feature, and disable it.

If you've used the Create A New Connection options to set up a connection to connect to an ISP, follow these steps:

1. Click Start, and click Internet on the Start menu to open Internet Explorer.

2. On the Tools menu in Internet Explorer, click Internet Options.

3. On the Connections tab in the Internet Options dialog box, click Never Dial A Connection. ▶

4. Click OK.

Connecting to an ISP connection manually

After you select Never Dial A Connection on the Connections tab of the Internet Options dialog box, you'll need to connect to your ISP manually before you can browse the Web with Internet Explorer or exchange e-mail with Outlook Express.

To connect to your ISP manually, follow these steps:

1. Click Start.

2. Point to Connect To.

3. Click your ISP connection on the menu.

Windows 98 or Windows Me starts instead of Windows XP

Source of the problem

When your computer is set up to boot into either Windows XP or a previous version of Windows, it displays a menu of operating systems when the computer starts. If your previous version of Windows is set as the default operating system and the menu is displayed only momentarily, you might not have the chance to choose Windows XP before Windows 98 or Windows Me starts. Here's how to fix it.

How to fix it

1. Start the computer, and press F8 while the computer is restarting.

2. On the Windows Advanced Options Menu, press the down arrow to move the highlight to Return To OS Choices Menu, and press Enter.

3. Press the down arrow to move the highlight to Microsoft Windows XP Home Edition or Microsoft Windows XP Professional, and press Enter.

4. After Windows starts, click Start, right-click My Computer on the Start menu, and click Properties on the shortcut menu.

5. On the Advanced tab of the System Properties dialog box, click Settings in the Startup And Recovery area.

6. Click the Default Operating System down arrow, and click Microsoft Windows XP Home Edition or Microsoft Windows XP Professional in the list. ▶

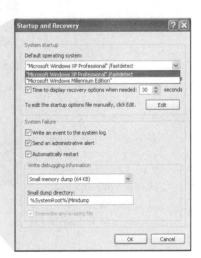

7. Select the Time To Display List Of Operating Systems check box, and increase the number of seconds to at least 10 seconds.

8. Click OK, and then close the System Properties dialog box.

Windows hangs at startup

Source of the problem

If you're ready to start, but Windows just stops—it gets stuck at the logo screen, never gets to the desktop, and displays no error messages—you could be encountering any one of several problems that can keep Windows from starting properly. You might have a bad driver, or a program that hangs when it loads automatically at startup. To fix the problem, you need to investigate possible causes until you've determined what's going on by disabling configuration files and programs that automatically launch at startup and then gradually reenabling them until the computer no longer starts. After you've found the file or program that's causing Windows to hang, you can disable it.

If these steps don't produce a working system, you might need to have the Windows Setup program repair your Windows installation. Or you might need to check your hard disk to find and repair a disk problem. Here, in sequence, are the steps you should go through.

How to fix it

1. Turn on the computer, and press F8 while the computer is starting.

2. When the Windows Advanced Options Menu appears, press the Down Arrow key to move the highlight to Safe Mode, and then press Enter. ▶

    After Windows starts, you see the words *Safe Mode* in each corner of the desktop. The Safe Mode Troubleshooter opens in the Microsoft Help And Support window. Close this window so that you can follow the steps here.

```
Windows Advanced Options Menu
Please select an option:

    Safe Mode
    Safe Mode with Networking
    Safe Mode with Command Prompt

    Enable Boot Logging
    Enable VGA Mode
    Last Known Good Configuration (your most recent settings that worked)
    Directory Services Restore Mode (Windows domain controllers only)
    Debugging Mode

    Start Windows Normally
    Reboot
    Return to OS Choices Menu

Use the up and down arrow keys to move the highlight to your choice.
```

3. When Windows reports that it's running in safe mode, click Yes.

4. When Windows starts in safe mode, click Start, and click Run on the Start menu.

5. In the Run dialog box, type **msconfig** in the Open box, and press Enter.

6. In the System Configuration Utility, click Selective Startup on the General tab.

7. Clear the Process SYSTEM.INI File check box, click OK, and click Yes when you're asked whether you want to restart your computer. ▶

8. When the computer restarts, enter your password if necessary, and click OK in the message box telling you that you're using Selective Startup.

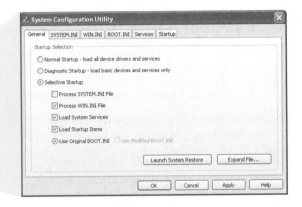

If Windows starts normally, skip to "My SYSTEM.INI File is keeping Windows from starting," on page 288.

If Windows doesn't start normally, turn off the computer and follow steps 1 and 2 on the previous page. After Windows starts in safe mode, follow these steps:

1. Click Start, click Run, type **msconfig** again, and press Enter to restart the System Configuration Utility.

2. On the General tab, reselect the Process SYSTEM.INI File and clear the Process WIN.INI File check box. ▶

3. Click OK, and click Yes when you're asked whether you want to restart your computer.

   If Windows now starts normally, skip to "My WIN.INI file is keeping Windows from starting," on page 289. If Windows doesn't start normally, follow steps 1 through 4, beginning on the previous page, to start the computer in safe mode again and reselect the Process WIN.INI File check box, and then skip to "A startup program is keeping Windows from starting," on page 289.

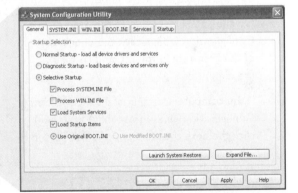

If this solution didn't solve your problem, go to the next page.

Windows hangs at startup

(continued from page 287)

My SYSTEM.INI file is keeping Windows from starting

The SYSTEM.INI file contains configuration information that Windows uses to start itself properly. To determine which item in the file is keeping Windows from starting, follow these steps:

1. Click Start and click Run on the Start menu.

2. In the Run dialog box, type **msconfig** in the Open box, and press Enter.

3. On the SYSTEM.INI tab of the System Configuration Utility, click Disable All, and click OK. ▶

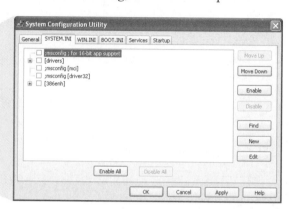

4. In the System Configuration dialog box, click Restart.

5. When Windows restarts, click Start, and click Run on the Start menu.

6. In the Run dialog box, type **msconfig** in the Open box, and press Enter.

7. On the SYSTEM.INI tab of the System Configuration Utility, click the check box of the first item in the list, and restart the computer. ▶

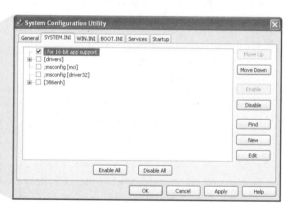

8. If the computer restarts, start the System Configuration Utility (msconfig) again and click the next check box on the SYSTEM.INI tab, and then restart the computer.

9. When the computer fails to start, you've found the problem item. Start the computer again in Safe Mode, start the System Configuration Utility, clear the last check box you selected, and reselect all the other check boxes on the SYSTEM.INI tab.

10. Restart the computer.

My WIN.INI file is keeping Windows from starting

Like the SYSTEM.INI file, the WIN.INI file contains configuration information that Windows uses to start itself properly. To determine which item in the file is keeping Windows from starting, follow these steps:

1. Click Start, and click Run on the Start menu.

2. In the Run dialog box, type **msconfig** in the Open box, and press Enter.

3. On the WIN.INI tab of the System Configuration Utility, click Disable All, and then click OK.

4. In the System Configuration dialog box, click Restart.

5. When Windows restarts, click Start, and click Run on the Start menu.

6. In the Run dialog box, type **msconfig** in the Open box, and press Enter.

7. On the WIN.INI tab of the System Configuration Utility, click the check box of the first item in the list, click OK, and restart the computer. ▶

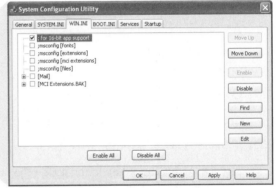

8. If the computer restarts, start the System Configuration Utility (msconfig) again and click the next check box on the WIN.INI tab, and then restart the computer.

9. When the computer fails to start, you've found the problem item. Start the computer again in Safe Mode, start the System Configuration Utility, clear the last check box you selected, reselect all the other check boxes on the WIN.INI tab, and restart the computer.

A startup program is keeping Windows from starting

If Windows seems to hang just as it's finally getting started—when the desktop starts to appear, or as the icons on the taskbar next to the clock fall into place—a program that launches automatically at startup might be keeping Windows from starting. You can determine whether this is the cause, and isolate the program and prevent it from starting.

1. Start Windows in safe mode by pressing F8 while the computer is starting and then choosing Safe Mode from the Windows Advanced Options Menu.

If this solution didn't solve your problem, go to the next page.

Windows hangs at startup

(continued from page 289)

2. Click Run on the Start menu, and in the Run dialog box, type **msconfig** in the Open box and press Enter.

3. On the Startup tab in the System Configuration Utility window, click Disable All. ▶

4. Click OK, and click Yes when you're asked whether you want to restart your computer.

5. Start the System Configuration Utility (msconfig) again.

6. On the Startup tab, select the first check box in the list.

7. Click OK, and click Yes when you're asked whether you want to restart the computer.

8. If Windows starts normally, start the System Configuration Utility (msconfig) again.

9. Select the next check box in the list on the Startup tab and click OK.

10. Click Yes when you're asked whether you want to restart your computer.

11. Continue this process until Windows hangs when it tries to restart.
   The last program you selected is the one that's keeping Windows from starting.

12. Clear the check box next to the last program you selected, but select all the other check boxes in the list, including the untested programs below this program, and restart Windows once again, just to confirm that you've really found the offender.

If you can readily identify the startup program you've disabled, check the manufacturer's Web site for updated software or technical support. If you can't easily determine the program you've disabled, you might find out only when a device no longer works, a program fails, or a capability (such as a special shortcut key combination that starts your Web browser) is no longer available.

If you've found that none of the startup programs is causing Windows to hang, you should repair your installation of Windows XP by following the steps in "Repairing Windows XP," on the facing page.

Repairing Windows XP

The Windows Setup program can detect and repair a damaged Windows installation if you follow these steps:

1. Insert the Windows XP CD in the CD-ROM drive.

2. Turn off the computer, and then turn it back on.

3. When Windows XP Setup starts, press Enter.

    If your computer is unable to boot from a CD, go to "I can't set up Windows because I can't use the CD-ROM drive," on page 246.

4. Press Enter again to choose To Set Up Windows XP Now, Press Enter.

5. Press F8 to accept the licensing agreement.

6. When Setup finds your previous installation of Windows XP, press R to repair the selected installation.

7. Choose your Windows XP installation from the list, and then press R to repair it.

8. Follow the steps on the screen.

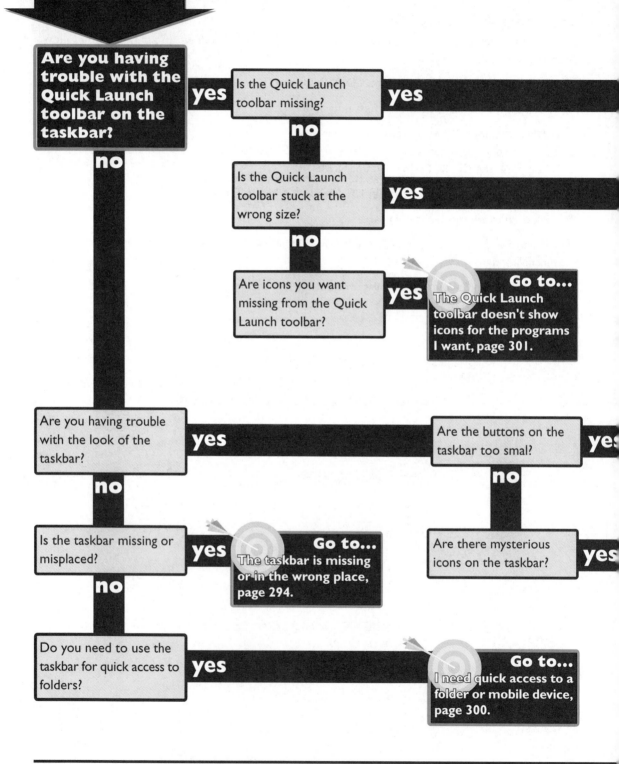

Are you having trouble with the Quick Launch toolbar on the taskbar?

yes → Is the Quick Launch toolbar missing? **yes** →

no ↓

Is the Quick Launch toolbar stuck at the wrong size? **yes** →

no ↓

Are icons you want missing from the Quick Launch toolbar? **yes** →

Go to...
The Quick Launch toolbar doesn't show icons for the programs I want, page 301.

no ↓

Are you having trouble with the look of the taskbar? **yes** → Are the buttons on the taskbar too smal? **yes**

no ↓ **no** ↓

Is the taskbar missing or misplaced? **yes** →

Go to...
The taskbar is missing or in the wrong place, page 294.

Are there mysterious icons on the taskbar? **yes**

no ↓

Do you need to use the taskbar for quick access to folders? **yes** →

Go to...
I need quick access to a folder or mobile device, page 300.

Quick fix

The Quick Launch toolbar isn't visible When you set up Windows XP, the Quick Launch toolbar might not be visible. If you've found the Quick Launch toolbar useful in a previous version of Windows, you can regain its use by following these steps:

1. Right-click the taskbar, and click Properties on the shortcut menu.

2. On the Taskbar tab of the Taskbar And Start Menu Properties dialog box, select the Show Quick Launch check box.

3. Click OK.

Quick fix

I can't make the Quick Launch toolbar wider to see all its icons A double-arrow at the right end of the Quick Launch toolbar indicates that the toolbar contains more icons than it has the space to show. But if you can't widen the Quick Launch toolbar to show all its icons, follow these steps:

1. Right-click the taskbar, and click Lock The Taskbar on the shortcut menu to clear its check mark.

2. Drag the dotted border at the right edge of the Quick Launch toolbar to widen the toolbar.

3. Right-click the taskbar again, and click Lock The Taskbar on the shortcut menu.

Go to...

The taskbar buttons are too narrow, page 296.

Go to...

The notification area near the clock shows mysterious icons, page 298.

If your solution isn't here, check these related chapters:

- The desktop, page 12
- The display, page 40
- Folders, page 82
- The Start menu, page 266

Or see the general troubleshooting tips on page xv.

The taskbar is missing or in the wrong place.

Source of the problem

It's an unnerving feeling to lose the taskbar when you've come to rely on it while working in Windows. The taskbar is the home of the Start menu, the clock, and buttons that tell you which programs are running. It's also the place where the Quick Launch toolbar can reside, offering you one-click access to your favorite applications.

But if the taskbar repeatedly seems to disappear, a number of things could be happening. The taskbar might be set to allow other windows to cover it. Or it might have its Auto-Hide option turned on, which removes the taskbar from the screen when it's not being used. Another possibility is that you've inadvertently flattened the taskbar, making it nearly impossible to see. And while working with the mouse, it's not too hard to drag the taskbar from the bottom of the screen to one of the sides, where it looks more like a task pane.

So if you can't find the taskbar, here are a number of things you can do to track it down, and steps you can take to keep it from disappearing again.

How to fix it

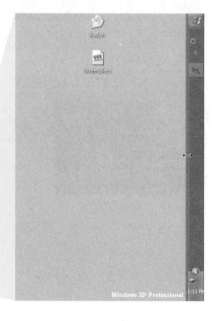

● Press Ctrl+Esc to open the Start menu and display the taskbar.

Be prepared for the taskbar to appear at either side of the screen, or even along the top. If the taskbar is still missing when the Start menu opens, it's been flattened to a thin strip that's very hard to see. To restore the taskbar to full size, follow these steps:

1. Click the Minimize button in the upper right corner of every window you have open.

Normally you could right-click the taskbar and click Show The Desktop on the shortcut menu to quickly minimize all open windows, but that trick won't help you this time!

2. Move the mouse pointer to each of the four edges of the screen until the pointer changes to a two-headed arrow— you've found the taskbar.

3. Drag the edge of the taskbar toward the center of the screen until the taskbar is the height you want (or width, if the taskbar is along the side of the screen). ▶

Usually the taskbar has room for just one row or column of buttons, but you can make it any height or width you want using this method.

After you find the taskbar, follow these steps to make sure it won't vanish again.

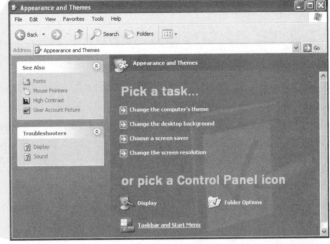

1. Right-click the taskbar, and click Properties on the shortcut menu.

   Alternatively, you can click Start, click Control Panel on the Start menu, click Appearance And Themes in Control Panel, and then click Taskbar And Start Menu. ▶

2. On the Taskbar tab in the Taskbar And Start Menu Properties dialog box, make sure the Keep The Taskbar On Top Of Other Windows check box is selected. ▶

   The taskbar will now remain visible, even if you maximize a program's window.

3. Clear the Auto-Hide The Taskbar check box, if necessary.
   The taskbar will no longer disappear when you move the mouse pointer away from it.

4. Select the Lock The Taskbar check box.
   Now you'll no longer be able to drag the taskbar out of position or inadvertently squash the taskbar into a flat strip.

What if my taskbar has moved?

In Windows, it's not all that hard to dislodge the taskbar from its normal location by accident. While you won't actually lose the taskbar by moving it (unless of course you also somehow resize it so that it's flat), you might end up scratching your head wondering why the taskbar is now standing vertically along the side of the screen rather than lying neatly along the bottom.

To get the taskbar back where you want it, position the mouse pointer in any empty area on the taskbar and drag the taskbar back to the bottom of the screen. If you can't seem to get ahold of the taskbar, you're probably grabbing it by one of its toolbars—reposition the mouse pointer and try again.

The taskbar buttons are too narrow

Source of the problem

The icon on each taskbar button identifies the program that's open, but the text description next to the icon gives you more useful information, such as the name of the folder or document that's open. But as more and more buttons occupy the limited real estate of the taskbar, the text description on each button gets shorter and shorter, eventually becoming useless.

If the taskbar is crowded with buttons, you can increase the space for buttons on the taskbar, which in turn increases the width of the text area in each button. Another option is to increase the size of the text on buttons. To try out these alternatives, follow these steps.

How to fix it

1. Position the mouse pointer on the handle at the left end of the row of taskbar buttons (at the top if the taskbar is oriented vertically).

2. Drag the handle to the left (or up if the taskbar is oriented vertically). ▶
   This expansion might encroach on the Quick Launch toolbar if it's displayed, but you'll have more room for the taskbar buttons.

If you want still more room on the taskbar, you can remove the Quick Launch toolbar:

1. Right-click anywhere on the taskbar where there's no button or icon.

2. On the shortcut menu, point to Toolbars, and click Quick Launch to clear the check mark.

Tip

To have Windows display the entire text for any button on the toolbar, just hold the mouse pointer over the button for a second or two. A pop-up description will appear that gives you information about the file, folder, or Web page that's open and the name of the program in which it's open.

If you want still more room, you can increase the height or width of the taskbar. This option is only useful if you have plenty of screen resolution (at least 1024 by 768 pixels), which gives you enough screen space for windows and icons.

1. Move the mouse pointer to the top edge of the taskbar (or the right or left edge if the taskbar is vertical).

2. Drag the edge of the taskbar up (or to the right or left) so that the taskbar becomes twice the width or height.

   If you find that you can't resize the taskbar, right-click the taskbar, and click Lock The Taskbar on the shortcut menu to clear the check mark.

To further maximize the button area, you can help Windows XP hide some of the icons in the system tray at the end of the taskbar, near the clock. For more information, see "The notification area near the clock shows mysterious icons," on the next page.

Another way to increase the size of the taskbar buttons is to increase the size of the text they display. The attractive Windows XP style fixes the size of taskbar buttons, but reverting back to the Windows Classic style, which make Windows and buttons look the way they did in previous versions of Windows, allows you to increase the size of the taskbar text. To try this, follow these steps:

1. Right-click the desktop, and click Properties on the shortcut menu.

2. On the Appearance tab in the Display Properties dialog box, click the Windows And Buttons down arrow, and then click Windows Classic Style in the list.

3. On the Appearance tab, click Advanced.

4. In the Advanced Appearance dialog box, click the Item down arrow, and click Active Title Bar in the list.

5. Make a note of the current setting for the active title bar's font and text size so that you can reset the buttons to their original state if you need to.

6. Click the Size down arrow next to Font, and click a size that's larger than the current size by 2 or 3. ▶

   This number represent size in *points* (a unit of measurement in typography).

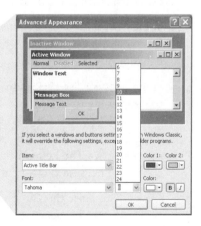

7. Click Apply, and take a look at the taskbar to see the change.

   Try different settings until you find the one you want. Keep in mind that changes you make here will also affect the title bar of each window.

8. Click OK to close the Display Properties dialog box.

The notification area near the clock shows mysterious icons

Source of the problem

If you've had your computer for a while, you might notice a slow buildup of icons in the notification area next to the clock. These icons notify you about the workings of programs and utilities you've installed. If you want to rid the taskbar of icon clutter, you need to identify these icons and either have their programs cease and desist from displaying the icon or tell Windows XP that you want the icons hidden, because Windows XP can hide some of these icons when their associated programs are inactive.

You can discover what many of these icons do by moving the mouse pointer onto each one and waiting. A pop-up description will identify the icon. You can also discover what these icons do from their shortcut menus. Sometimes you can even use the shortcut menus to remove the icons or instruct the associated program for an icon not to show the icon in the notification area. Here are the steps to follow to identify icons and hide or remove those that aren't useful to you.

How to fix it

1. Right-click the taskbar, and click Properties on the shortcut menu.

2. On the Taskbar tab of the Taskbar And Start Menu Properties dialog box, click Customize.

3. In the Customize Notifications dialog box, click the name of an icon in the Current Items or Past Items list, and click the Behavior down arrow. ▶

4. In the Behavior list, click Hide When Inactive or Always Hide to remove the icon.

   After you've made this choice, the items in the Current Items list are those that are visible because they've been recently active. The items in the Past Items list are those that are hidden because they've been inactive.

5. Click OK to close the Customize Notifications dialog box, and click OK to close the Taskbar And Start Menu Properties dialog box.

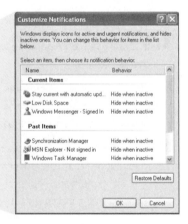

Another option is to investigate an icon's shortcut menu to see whether it contains an option to turn off the icon:

1. Right-click an icon in the notification area.

2. Review the options on the shortcut menu to identify the program and determine what it does. If you decide you don't need the program, continue to step 3.

3. If you see a Properties command on the shortcut menu, or another command that lets you adjust the program's options, click it and look for an option in the Properties dialog box named something like Show Icon On The Taskbar. Clear this option, and click OK.

   If there's no command on the shortcut menu that leads to a Properties dialog box, look for a Close or Exit command to click on the shortcut menu. After you click Close or Exit, follow the instructions on the screen to quit the program.

   Remember, quitting a program might not prevent the same program from starting again the next time you start Windows.

If you can't find a Properties, Close, or Exit command on the shortcut menu, look in Control Panel for an icon for the program:

1. Click Start, and click Control Panel on the Start menu.

2. In Control Panel, click the category that the program is associated with.

   ● To remove the Volume icon, which looks like a speaker, click Sounds, Speech, And Audio Devices, and then click Sounds And Audio Devices. On the Volume tab of the Sounds And Audio Devices Properties dialog box, clear the Place Volume Icon In The Taskbar check box. Click OK.

   ● To remove the Power Management icon, which looks like a power plug or a battery, click Performance And Maintenance and then Power Options in Control Panel. On the Advanced tab in the Power Options Properties dialog box, clear the Always Show Icon On The Taskbar check box, and click OK.

   ● To remove the Infrared icon if it appears, click Printers And Other Hardware, click Wireless Link, and clear the Display An Icon On the Taskbar Indicating Infrared Activity check box.

Deciding which icons to remove

Most icons on the taskbar are there to remind you that a program is running, to give you a convenient way to access their features, and to notify you of an urgent condition, such as the arrival of new e-mail. Be sure to explore an icon's benefits before removing it—you might find it's worth keeping. Also, consider carefully before you disable a service just to get rid of the icon, and make sure you know how to start the service again. Even if you disable a program to rid yourself of its icon, a shortcut to the program might still be in your Startup folder and the icon might reappear when you next start Windows. For more information about the Startup folder, see "Programs start automatically, without my approval," on page 278.

I need quick access to a folder or mobile device

Source of the problem

The folder system neatly organizes files on your hard disk, but it doesn't always provide quick access to your files, especially when they're buried several folder levels deep. You can solve this problem, gaining quick access to files without having to open folder after folder, by creating a custom toolbar for a folder and its subfolders on the taskbar. To quickly open a file in the folder, you can click its button on the toolbar. You can also create custom toolbars for Control Panel options, printer options, and scheduled tasks—all by following these steps.

How to fix it

1. Right-click the taskbar, point to Toolbars on the shortcut menu, and click New Toolbar.

2. In the New Toolbar dialog box, navigate to the folder you want to show as a toolbar. ▶
   You can select a disk drive, a folder, a mobile device, or Control Panel, among other items to show as custom toolbars.

3. Click OK.
   To see contents of a toolbar, click the double-arrow button (>>) at the right end of the toolbar. ▶

Tip

To gain quick access to resources in your computer, you can create a new tool-bar that contains the disks, folders, and other items shown in My Computer. To do so, in step 2, select My Computer in the New Toolbar window.

The Quick Launch toolbar doesn't show icons for the programs I want

Source of the problem

The default Quick Launch toolbar displays only a few icons for programs that come with Windows, such as Internet Explorer, Windows Media Player, and the Show Desktop utility. To get shortcut icons for the programs you use most frequently on the Quick Launch toolbar, you need to place them there. Fortunately, this task is easy. Here are the steps.

How to fix it

1. Right-click the taskbar, and if the Lock The Taskbar option is selected, click it to clear it.

2. Drag the dotted border at the right edge of the Quick Launch toolbar to widen the toolbar and make space for new icons.

3. Click Start to open the Start menu.

4. Click All Programs to open the All Programs menu, and then point to other submenus until you see the icon for the program you want.

   Shortcuts for the programs you use most often appear in the most recently used section on the left side of the Start menu.

5. Hold down the Ctrl key while you drag the icon for a program you want to add the Quick Launch toolbar. ▶

   A vertical bar indicates where the icon will drop when you release the mouse button.

6. Release the mouse button to place the icon on the Quick Launch toolbar. After you place an icon on the Quick Launch toolbar, you can drag it left or right to change its position on the toolbar.

Glossary

active window The window you're currently using. Windows always applies the next command you choose to the active window.

administrator For Windows XP Professional, the person responsible for setting up and managing computers and their user and group accounts, assigning passwords and permissions, and helping users with networking problems. Administrators are members of the Administrators group and have full control over the domain or computer.

For Windows XP Home Edition, a person who can make system-wide changes to the computer, can install software, and has access to all files on the computer. A person with a computer administrator account has full access to other user accounts on the computer.

Advanced Configuration and Power Interface (ACPI) A power management specification for computers, usually portable computers.

background The image used on the Windows desktop.

background program A program that runs while you're working on other tasks.

basic input/output system (BIOS) The built-in software program that tests the computer's hardware at startup, starts the operating system, and transfers data among hardware devices.

baud rate The speed at which a modem communicates. Two modems must operate at the same baud rate in order to communicate with each other.

bits per second (bps) The number of bits transmitted across a phone line every second, used as a measure of the speed at which a modem transfers data.

boot The process of starting or resetting a computer. When you cold boot a computer (first turn it on) or warm boot the computer (reset it), the computer runs the software that loads and starts the computer's operating system.

boot files The system files needed to start Windows. The boot files include Ntldr and Ntdetect.com.

broadband connection A high-speed connection, such as a cable modem or a DSL modem. Broadband connections are typically 256 kilobytes per second (KBps) or faster.

browser A program that interprets HTML instructions, text, and pictures on the Web and formats them into Web pages on the screen. Some browsers also permit you to play sound or video files embedded in Web documents.

cable modem A device that connects your computer to the cable company's high-speed line.

clear To turn off an option by removing the X or check mark from a check box. You clear a check box by clicking it, or by selecting it and then pressing the Spacebar.

client Any computer or program connecting to, and requesting the services of, another computer or program (a host or server), usually on a local area network. Client can also refer to the software that enables the computer or program to establish a network connection.

color depth The number of colors per pixel your monitor and video adapter can display.

command prompt window A window displayed on the desktop that gives you an MS-DOS command prompt.

compatibility mode A feature of Windows XP that allows it to run programs written for a previous version of Windows. Programs often run more slowly in compatibility mode.

defragmentation The process of moving parts of files to contiguous areas on a hard disk to increase retrieval speed. Files become fragmented when the computer saves parts of them in available spaces on the hard disk. To retrieve the files, the computer must search the hard disk to find all of the file's parts, which slows down retrieval time.

desktop The on-screen work area on which windows, icons, menus, and dialog boxes appear.

device Any piece of equipment that can be attached to a network or computer; for example, a computer, printer, joystick, adapter, or modem. Each device normally requires a device driver to function in Windows XP.

device conflict A conflict that occurs when the same system resources are allocated to two or more devices.

device driver A program that allows a device, such as a network adapter or printer, to communicate with the operating system.

Device Manager A program that you can use to manage the devices in your computer, viewing and changing device properties, updating device drivers, and uninstalling devices.

Digital Subscriber Line (DSL) A type of high-speed Internet connection using standard telephone wires.

direct cable connection A link between the serial or parallel ports of two computers created with a cable.

DirectX A software component within Windows XP that helps games and other programs use the multimedia capabilities of your computer.

DLL (dynamic-link library) A Windows feature that allows parts of programs to be stored separately as files with .dll extensions. These parts are loaded only when needed by the program.

document   Any piece of work created with a program and, when saved on disk, given a unique file name by which it can be retrieved.

domain   A group of computers that are part of a large, corporate, or organizational network. A domain is given a name, and it's administered as a unit, with common rules and procedures. Each domain has a unique name.

dots per inch (dpi)   The standard used to measure screen and printer resolution. The number of dots that a device can display or print per inch. The greater the number of dots per inch, the better the resolution.

drag   To move an item on the screen by selecting the item, pressing and holding down the mouse button, and moving the mouse.

drive letter   The naming convention for disk drives. Drives are named by letter, beginning with A, followed by a colon.

dual boot   A configuration that can start two different operating systems when you start the computer, usually Windows XP and your previous version of Windows.

enable   To make a device functional. For example, if a device in your hardware configuration is enabled, the device is available for use when your computer uses that hardware configuration.

FAT, FAT32   File allocation table. FAT and FAT32 are file systems used by Windows to organize and manage files on disk drives. The file allocation table (FAT) stores information about and the location for each file so that the hard disk can retrieve it.

file system   The structure in which files are named, stored, and organized. NTFS, FAT, and FAT32 are types of file systems.

File Transfer Protocol (FTP) A protocol used to copy files between two computers on the Internet.

file type   Identifies the program, such as Microsoft Word, that is used to open the file. File types are associated with a file name extension. For example, files that have the .doc extension are the Microsoft Word Document type and can be opened using Microsoft Word.

firewall   A combination of hardware and software that provides a security system to prevent unauthorized access from the Internet to the computers on a local area network.

folder   A means of organizing programs and documents on a disk. A folder can hold both files and additional folders and is symbolized by an icon of a file folder.

gigabyte (GB)   1024 megabytes, or approximately one billion bytes.

group   A collection of users and computers. Groups are used to grant access to resources on a network.

guest account   A built-in account used for logging on to a computer running Windows XP when a user does not have an account on the computer or domain.

hardware configuration   Resource settings that have been allocated for a specific device. Each device on your computer has a hardware configuration, which may consist of IRQ lines, DMA, an I/O port, or memory address settings.

host A computer that runs a server program or service, such as Internet connection sharing, used by one or more clients on a network.

hyperlink Colored and underlined text or a graphic that you click to go to a file, a location in a file, a Web page, or an FTP site. In Windows folders, hyperlinks are text links that appear in the folder's left pane. You can click these links to perform tasks, such as moving or copying a file, or to go to other places on your computer, such as the My Documents folder or Control Panel.

Hypertext Markup Language (HTML) A text language used to create hypertext documents on the Web. HTML files are simple text files with codes embedded (markup tags) to denote formatting and hyperlinks.

Hypertext Transfer Protocol (HTTP) The protocol used to transfer information on the World Wide Web. An HTTP address is in the form: *http://www.microsoft.com.*

infrared file transfer Wireless file transfer between a computer and another computer or device using infrared light.

insertion point The place where text will be inserted when typed. The insertion point usually appears as a flashing vertical bar in a program's window or in a dialog box.

install To add program files and folders to your hard disk and related data to your registry so that the software runs properly, or to connect a hardware device to your computer and load the appropriate device drivers into Windows XP.

Integrated Device Electronics (IDE) A type of disk drive interface in which the controller electronics reside on the drive itself, eliminating the need for a separate adapter card.

Internet address An address for a resource on the Internet that is used by Web browsers, such as *www.microsoft.com.* Internet addresses are also called Uniform Resource Locators (URLs).

Internet service provider (ISP) A company that provides individuals or companies access to the Internet and the Web. An ISP provides a telephone number, a user name, a password, and other connection information so users can connect their computers to the ISP's computers.

interrupt request (IRQ) lines Hardware lines over which devices can send signals to get the attention of the processor when the device is ready to accept or send information. Each device must have a unique IRQ line.

intranet A network within an organization that uses Internet technologies and protocols, but is available only to certain people, such as employees of a company. An intranet is also called a private network.

IP address A four-part number that identifies a computer on an IP network or the Internet, such as 192.168.23.3.

liquid crystal display (LCD) A type of display used in digital watches and many portable computers.

local area network (LAN) A communications network connecting a group of computers, printers, and other devices within a limited area, such as an office or home.

local printer   A printer that is directly connected to one of the ports on your computer.

log on   To begin using a network by providing a user name and password that identifies you to the network.

multiple boot   A computer configuration that runs two or more operating systems. Also called dual boot.

Musical Instrument Digital Interface (MIDI)   An interface standard that allows you to connect music synthesizers, musical instruments, and computers.

My Documents   A folder that provides you with a convenient place to store documents, graphics, or other files you want to access quickly. When you save a file in a program such as WordPad or Paint, the file is automatically saved in My Documents, unless you choose a different folder.

network   A group of computers and other devices, such as printers and scanners, connected by a communications link, enabling all the devices to interact with each other.

network adapter   A device that connects your computer to a network. This device is sometimes called a network interface card or NIC.

network administrator   The person responsible for planning, configuring, and managing the day-to-day operation of the network. The network administrator is also called a system administrator.

non-Plug and Play   A device, such as a printer, modem, or game controller, that requires manual configuration of hardware settings before it can be used. Non-Plug and Play typically applies to older pieces of equipment.

notification area   The area on the taskbar to the right of the taskbar buttons and to the left of the clock. The notification area displays the time and can also contain shortcuts that provide quick access to programs, such as Volume Control and Power Options. Other shortcuts can appear temporarily, providing information about the status of activities.

NT file system (NTFS)   An advanced file system that provides performance, security, reliability, and advanced features that are not found in the FAT file system, such as file and folder permissions, and disk compression.

partition   A portion of a disk that has its own drive letter and functions as though it were a physically separate disk.

PC Card   A removable device, about the size of a credit card, that you can plug into a PC card slot or PCMCIA slot in a portable computer. PCMCIA devices can include modems, network cards, and hard disk drives.

permission   A rule associated with an object to regulate which users can gain access to the object and in what manner. Permissions are granted or denied by the object's owner.

ping   A utility that verifies connections to one or more remote computers on a network or the Internet.

pixel   Short for picture element. One spot on a display.

Plug and Play   A set of specifications developed to allow a computer to automatically detect and configure a device and install the appropriate device drivers.

POP3 (Post Office Protocol 3) A popular protocol used by ISPs for delivering e-mail messages to you.

power scheme   A group of preset power-management options. For example, you can set elapsed times for putting your computer on standby and for turning off your monitor and hard disk. You save these settings as a named power scheme.

print queue   The print queue is the list of documents waiting to be printed on a printer.

printer driver   A program designed to allow programs to work with a particular printer without worry about the specific capabilities and language used by the printer. By using printer drivers that handle the subtleties of each printer, programs can communicate properly with a variety of printers.

printer window   The printer window shows information about any pending print jobs for the printer, such as who sent them, and how large they are.

program   A set of computer instructions that you use to perform a specific task, such as word processing, Internet browsing, or e-mail management. Programs are also called applications.

protocol   A set of rules governing how information is transmitted over a network.

queue   A list of programs or tasks waiting for execution, such as the documents waiting to be printed.

Quick Launch toolbar   A customizable toolbar that lets you start a program with a single click. You can add buttons to the Quick Launch toolbar to start your favorite programs.

Recycle Bin   The place where Windows XP stores deleted files. You can retrieve files you deleted in error, or you can empty the Recycle Bin to create more disk space.

refresh rate   The frequency with which the screen is updated. The image area of most monitors is refreshed at least 60 times per second.

registry   A database of information about a computer's hardware and software configuration. The registry contains information that Windows XP continually references during operation.

removable storage   A service used for managing removable media (such as tapes and discs) and storage devices (libraries).

resource   Any part of a computer system or network, such as a disk drive, printer, or memory address, that can be allotted to a running program.

restore point   A representation of a stored state of your computer. A restore point is created by System Restore at specific intervals and when System Restore detects the beginning of a change to your computer.

Glossary

screen resolution The setting that determines the amount of information that appears on your screen, measured in pixels. Low resolution, such as 640 x 480, makes items on the screen appear large, although the screen area is small. High resolution, such as 1280 x 1024, makes the screen area large, but individual items appear small.

screen saver A moving picture or pattern that appears on your screen when you haven't used the mouse or keyboard for a specified period of time.

security On a network, protection of a computer system and its data from harm or loss, implemented so that only authorized users can gain access to shared files.

select To specify a block of data or text on screen by highlighting it or otherwise marking it, with the intent to perform some operation on it.

server In general, a computer that provides shared resources to network users.

service A program, routine, or process that performs a specific system function to support other programs.

share To make resources, such as folders and printers, available to others.

share name A name that refers to a shared resource on a computer. Each shared folder on a server has a share name used by others to refer to the folder.

shared folder A folder on a computer that has been made available for other people to use on the network.

shared resource A resource on a computer that is available to network users.

shortcut A link to any item accessible on your computer or on a network, such as a program, file, folder, disk drive, Web page, printer, or another computer. You can put shortcuts in various areas, such as on the desktop, on the Start menu, or in specific folders.

Simple Mail Transfer Protocol (SMTP) A protocol that governs sending e-mail messages. Computers that transmit your e-mail at ISPs are called SMTP servers.

Small Computer System Interface (SCSI) A high-speed interface used for connecting computers to peripheral devices such as hard disks and printers.

sound card An expansion board for computers that permits recording and playing back sound.

sound file A sound file contains information that Windows uses to play sounds on your computer. Sound files have the file name extension .wav.

spooling A process in which print documents are stored on a disk until a printer is ready to process them. A spooler accepts each document from each client, stores it, and then sends it to the printer when the printer is ready.

standby A state in which your computer consumes less power when it is idle, but remains available for immediate use. While your computer is on standby, information in computer memory is not saved on your hard disk. If there is an interruption in power, the information in memory is lost.

status bar A line of information, usually at the bottom of a window, related to the current program.

System Restore A tool that tracks changes to your computer and creates a restore point when it detects the beginning of a change. You can use the System Restore Wizard to select a restore point to restore your computer to an earlier state, at a time when your computer was functioning properly.

Task Manager A utility that provides information about programs and processes running on the computer. Using Task Manager, you can end or run programs and end processes, and you can display an overview of your computer's performance.

taskbar The bar that contains the Start button and appears by default at the bottom of the desktop. You can click the taskbar buttons to switch between programs. You can also hide the taskbar, move it to the sides or top of the desktop, and customize it in other ways.

text box In a dialog box, a box in which you type information needed to carry out a command. The text box may be blank or may contain text when the dialog box opens.

theme A set of visual elements that provide a unified look for your computer desktop. A theme determines the look of the various graphic elements of your desktop, such as the windows, icons, fonts, colors, and the background and screen saver pictures. It can also define sounds associated with events such as opening or closing a program.

thumbnail A miniature version of an image that is often used for quick browsing through multiple images.

title bar The horizontal bar at the top of a window that contains the name of the window. On many windows, the title bar also contains the program icon and the Maximize, Minimize, and Close buttons.

toolbar A row, column, or block of on-screen buttons or icons. When clicked, these buttons or icons activate certain functions, or tasks, within the program. Users can often customize toolbars and move them around on the screen.

Transmission Control Protocol/Internet Protocol (TCP/IP) A protocol that has become the standard for data transmission over networks.

Uniform Resource Locator (URL) An address that identifies a location on the Internet. A URL for a World Wide Web site is preceded with http://, as in *http://www.microsoft.com/*. A URL can contain more detail, such as the name of a page of hypertext, usually identified by the file name extension .html or .htm.

uninstall To remove program files and folders from your hard disk, removing related data from your registry, so the software is no longer available, or to remove a device from your computer, removing the corresponding device drivers from your hard disk.

USB port An interface on the computer that enables you to connect a universal serial bus (USB) device. USB enables data transfer rates of 12 Mbps (12 million bits per second).

user A person who uses a computer. If the computer is connected to a network, a user can access the programs and files on the computer as well as programs and files located on the network (depending on account restrictions determined by the network administrator).

user profile   A file that contains configuration information for a specific user, such as desktop settings, network connections, and program settings. Each user's preferences are saved to a user profile that Windows XP uses to configure the desktop each time a user logs on.

video adapter   An expansion board that plugs into a personal computer to give it display capabilities. Video adapters, also called display adapters, often have their own graphics coprocessor for performing graphics calculations. These adapters are often called graphics accelerators.

virtual memory   Temporary storage used by a computer to run programs that need more memory than the computer can provide. For example, programs can have access to many gigabytes of virtual memory on a computer's hard drive, even if the computer has only 128 megabytes of RAM.

virus   A program that attempts to spread from computer to computer and either cause damage (by erasing or corrupting data) or annoy users (by printing messages or altering what's displayed on the screen).

Web server   A computer used to store Web pages and provide them to a user's browser.

window   A portion of the screen where programs and processes can be run. You can open several windows at the same time. Windows can be closed, resized, moved, minimized to a button on the taskbar, or maximized to take up the whole screen.

workgroup   A grouping of computers that helps users find printers and shared folders within that group. Workgroups in Windows XP do not offer the centralized user accounts and authentication offered by domains.

Quick fix index

Connections

I don't know how to protect
my child's privacy on line 3

The desktop

Unexpected Web pages open
on my desktop 12
I need to restore the old
Windows look 12

Desktop icons

My desktop icons have
become enormous 20
I don't see the icons on the
taskbar that I use to start
my favorite programs 21

Disasters

The power at my location
goes out periodically 31

The display

The colors on my display
momentarily distort when
I change Web pages 41
The Windows desktop doesn't
fill the display on my
LCD monitor 41

Downloading files

Downloading is very slow 51

E-mail

The Inbox doesn't show
all my e-mail messages 58
I get a Relay error from my ISP
when I try to send a message ... 59

Files

I can't open a file after I
rename it 73
I can't see all the details about
files in My Computer 73

Folders

Folders don't show all the
information about my files 83
I can't open or modify a folder
or its contents 83
I have Mscreate.dir files in a
lot of my folders 83

Games

I can't play Internet games
through my network 93
I can't connect to other players
on my home network 93

Hard disks

I hear my hard disk working
even when I'm not at
my computer 103

Hardware

I get a message about
permissions when I try
to install a new device 115

I installed a new driver for a
device and now the device
doesn't work 115

Internet connections

I don't know how to make
my full-time Internet
connection secure 126

My modem dials too slowly 127

Internet Explorer

When I search for a site,
Internet Explorer goes
directly to a site without
showing me alternatives 139

I can't change the home page
on my office computer 139

The text on Web pages is too
small to read easily 139

Laptops

I don't want to forget to print
a document when I return
home or to my office 153

The mouse

The mouse is too sensitive 163

Multiple users

A folder I want to make secure
doesn't have a Security tab in
its Properties dialog box 171

Networks, home

The host computer won't hang
up an Internet connection
when a client computer is
done with it 181

Networks, office

I can't find a computer in
My Network Places 201

Optimizing

My computer seems slow
at drawing graphics 213

I never know when an
update is available from
Windows Update 213

Printing

Windows doesn't get status
information from my printer . . . 225

Programs

A program starts in a window
that's the wrong size 235

A program used to work
correctly but now it doesn't
in Windows XP 235

Setting up Windows

I don't know whether to
convert my disk to NTFS
during setup 245

Sound and pictures

I get an error message saying
*No wave device that can
play files in the current
format is installed* 255

Start menu

The Start menu doesn't show
my shortcuts 267

I can't get used to the new
Windows XP Start menu 267

Startup

Windows no longer displays
a menu of users at startup 276

The taskbar

The Quick Launch toolbar
isn't visible 293

I can't make the Quick Launch
toolbar wider to see all
its icons 293

Index

acceleration, hardware, 43
ACPI (Advanced Configuration and Power Interface) specification, 154, 155, 215, 303
Active Desktop. *See also desktop*
  disabling unwanted Web pages, 12
  showing/hiding Web pages, 15
  turning on/off, 223
active window, 303
Add Hardware Wizard, 117, 119
Add Or Remove Programs dialog box, 218, 240–41, 250, 251
Add/Remove Windows Commponents, 218
administrators, 115, 116, 122, 136, 210, 303
Advanced Configuration and Power Interface (ACPI) specification, 154, 155, 215, 303
Advanced Power Management (APM), 154, 155, 215, 275
antivirus programs, 36–37, 248
AOL Instant Messenger, 8–9
APM (Advanced Power Management), 154, 155, 215, 275
applications. *See programs*
ASR (automated system recovery) disks, 37
assistance. *See Remote Assistance*
associating file types with programs, 242–43
attachments, e-mail
  limiting their size, 68
  receiving, 60
  undeliverable, 63
automated system recovery (ASR) disks, 37
automatic dialer, disabling, 136, 284

background
  adding to desktop fom My Pictures folder, 16, 17
  adding to e-mail messages, 67
  borrowing Web page images for desktop, 17
  glossary definition, 303
  turning off, 23
  ways to add to desktop, 16–17
background programs, 303
basic input/output system (BIOS), 245, 248, 274, 303
batteries, laptop, 154–55
baud rate, 303
BIOS (basic input/output system), 245, 248, 274, 303
bits per second (bps), 303
boot devices, changing order, 246
boot files, 303
booting, 303. *See also dual booting*
boot sector, 248
broadband, 303. *See also high-speed Internet access*
browsers, 304

cable modems, 8, 69, 129, 133, 137, 304
cables, network, 187
cables, printer, 225
caching, 216–17

call waiting, 134, 135
cameras. *See digital cameras*
canceling printing, 226
CD-ROM drives
  changing drive letter, 111
  enabling digital CD playback for USB speakers, 259
  installing driver, 247
  playing music CDs, 258
  problems using to install Windows XP, 246–47
  setting up to be first boot device, 246
  ways to access, 246–47
centering desktop pictures, 19
Check Disk utility, 38, 104, 110
children. *See also* games
  checking game suitability, 97
  protecting privacy online, 3
clean boots, 248–49
clearing, 304
client computers
  access to Internet, 194, 196–98
  defined, 194
  glossary definition, 304
  and IP addresses, 197–98
  need for, 28
Client for Microsoft Networks, installing, 28, 203
Client Service for Netware, installing, 203
clock, computer, changing, 214
clutter, desktop, cleaning up, 22–23
CMOS, 245, 248
color depth, 304
color distortions when switching among Web pages, 41
command prompt window, 304
compatibility mode, 235, 304
compressed folders, creating, 106, 109
compressing files, 68
computer clock, changing, 214
computer games. *See* games
computer viruses
  getting rid of, 36–37
  glossary definition, 310
  hoaxes, 37
  obtaining second opinion, 37
  overview, 36
  protecting against, 37
  symptoms, 36
connections. *See Internet connections*
Content Advisor, 221
cookies
  accepting/rejecting, 144, 145
  as privacy issue, 145
  role in troubleshooting Internet Explorer crashes, 147
  selecting which ones to accept, 145

copying
  files and folders, 80–81
  vs. moving, 80–81
cropping pictures, 19
Ctrl+Alt+Del, 236, 237

Data Error Reading Drive message, 110
decluttering desktop, 22–23
Default Monitor driver, 44
defragmentation, 112–13, 216, 217, 304
desktop. *See also* Active Desktop
  adding picture as background, 16–17
  arranging icons, 24
  borrowing Web page images for background, 17
  changing screen resolution, 23
  changing screen saver interval, 47
  changing spacing between icons, 26
  clearing open windows, 23
  creating folder for downloaded files, 53
  creating new folders, 23
  decluttering, 22–23
  deleting icons, 22
  determining size, 18
  determining user name, 15, 24, 25
  extending across two display monitors, 48–49
  flowchart, 12–13
  as folder, 81
  glossary definition, 304
  missing My Network Places icon, 28
  moving documents to My Documents folder, 23, 25
  removing unwanted Web pages, 23
  resizing icon labels, 26, 27
  resizing icons, 20
  restoring icons, 14
  selecting theme, 27
  switching users, 15, 24, 25, 173
  turning off background, 23
  viewing on LCD displays, 41
Desktop Cleanup Wizard, 15, 22
device conflicts, 304
device drivers
  defined, 116
  for displays, 44–45, 94, 96
  glossary definition, 304
  for printers, 227
  reinstalling, 98–99, 116, 117, 227
  rolling back, 115
  for sound cards, 98–99

device drivers *(continued)*
uninstalling, 115, 116
updating, 44–45, 94, 96, 116, 118, 257
ways to find, 118, 119, 121
Device Manager, 304
devices, 304. *See also* device drivers; hardware
dial-up Internet connections, controlling, 70
digital cameras
and memory card readers, 262–63
and Photo Printing Wizard, 264–65
and Scanner And Camera Wizard, 262–63
Digital Subscriber Line (DSL), 8, 69, 129, 133, 137, 304
direct cable connection, 304
directory services, 63
DirectParallel cable, 159
DirectX, 95, 304
disabled devices, 120
disasters. *See also* error messages
computer viruses, 36–37
flowchart, 30–31
hard disk crashes, 38
Windows XP failure to start, 32–33
Disk Cleanup, 107
Disk Defragmenter, 112–13, 216, 217
displays
changing power management settings, 46
changing refresh rate, 42–43
changing screen resolution, 23
color distortions when switching among Web pages, 41
eliminating flicker, 42–43
flowchart, 40–41
increasing number of colors, 41
LCD, 41
multiple monitors, 48–49
turning off to save power, 46
unusual, 44–45
updating drivers, 44–45, 94, 96
DLLs (dynamic link libraries), 304
documents
finding, 78
glossary definition, 305
moving from desktop to My Documents folder, 23, 25
printing problems, 226–27
recently used, 78
saving on desktop, 25
sharing with other users, 174–75
documents folder type, 89. *See also* My Documents folder
domains, 305
dots per inch (dpi), 305
double-clicking, 79

downloaded files
confirming opening, 54
finding, 52–53
opening without asking first, 54–55
organizing, 54–55
downloading
after changing filenames, 55
error message, 56
files from Web sites, 57
flowchart, 50–51
stopping unexpectedly, 56
transfer rates, 56
updated device drivers, 44–45, 94, 96, 116, 118, 257
Web pages for viewing offline, 150–51
dragging, 80–81, 87, 305
drive letters
changing, 111
for dual Windows versions, 252
glossary definition, 305
drivers. *See* device drivers
DSL (Digital Subscriber Line), 8, 69, 129, 133, 137, 304
dual booting, 108, 245, 252–53, 305
DVD drives, 258

Edit File Type dialog box, 54
e-mail
checking server settings, 60
flowchart, 58–59
forwarding messages to other e-mail accounts, 61
inviting Remote Assistance help, 7
managing multiple accounts, 64–65
receiving messages when ISP mail server is down, 61
searching for addresses, 62, 63
setting up separate Outlook Express identities for multiple users, 178–79
undeliverable messages, 62–63
e-mail addresses
changing reply default, 65
creating MSN account, 5
linking to need for plain text messages, 67
multiple, 64–65
for .NET Passport, 5
searching for, 62, 63
selecting among From addresses, 64
viewing default account, 65
emptying Recycle Bin, 104

enabling devices, 120, 305
Entertainment Software Rating Board (ESRB), 97
error messages
    after installing new programs, 34–35
    from deleted programs, 240–41
    hard disk-related, 110
    No wave device that can play files in the current format is installed message, 255
    at startup, 283
    troubleshooting *The page cannot be displayed* message, 140–42
    when downloading, 56
ESRB (Entertainment Software Rating Board), 97
Ethernet adapters, 8

FAT and FAT32 file systems, 108–9, 245, 305
File And Printer Sharing for Microsoft Networks, 184
file extensions, 73, 242–43
files
    associating with programs, 242–43
    changing names before downloading, 55
    compressing, 68
    copying between folders, 80–81
    downloaded, finding, 52–53
    downloaded, opening without asking first, 54–55
    downloaded, organizing, 54–55
    downloading from Web pages, 57
    dragging, 80–81, 87
    finding via Search Companion, 53, 74–75
    flowchart, 72–73
    hidden, 79
    indexing, 77
    losing, 74–75
    missing, 74–75
    moving between folders, 52, 53, 80–81
    moving vs. copying, 80–81
    opening, 79
    organizing, 75, 76
    permission to open, 83
    problems opening after renaming, 73
    renaming, 73
    right-clicking vs. left-clicking, 80–81
    setting to confirm opening after downloading, 54
    sharing, 68
    sharing with other users, 174–75

files *(continued)*
    sorting folder list, 84
    transferring between laptop and desktop computers, 158–59
    types of, 79
    viewing details in folders, 83, 84
file systems, 305. *See also* FAT and FAT32 file systems; NTFS (NT File System)
File Transfer Protocol (FTP), 305
file types, 242–43, 305
Filmstrip view, 17, 88, 89
finding. *See also* Search Companion
    device drivers, 118, 119, 121
    documents, 78
    downloaded files, 52–53
    files, 53, 74–75
    network printers, 230–31
firewalls, 305. *See also* Internet Connection Firewall
flicker, display, eliminating, 42–43
Folder Options dialog box, 84–85, 86, 242–43
folders
    compressed, creating, 106, 109
    creating quick access on taskbar, 300
    customizing for specific file types, 88–89
    desktop as, 81
    for downloaded files, 52, 53, 55
    dragging, 80–81, 87
    flowchart, 82–83
    glossary definition, 305
    list of types, 89
    making secure, 171
    moving files between, 52, 53
    moving vs. copying, 80–81
    new, creating, 23, 88–89
    opening in same vs. many windows, 86
    organizing files in, 75, 76
    permission to open, 83
    resetting view memory, 85
    right-clicking vs. left-clicking, 80–81
    saving view settings, 85
    selecting to show on Start menu, 271
    setting uniform view, 84
    sharing contents, 174–75
    sorting list of files, 84
    viewing file details, 83, 84
font, for desktop items, changing, 26, 27
Found New Hardware Wizard, 119
free ISPs, 129
FTP, when to use, 56
FTP (File Transfer Protocol), 305
full-time Internet access. *See* high-speed Internet access

Internet service providers (ISPs) *(continued)*
 local vs. national, 129
 and .NET Passport, 5
 problems connecting, 130–31
 problems downloading files, 56
 Relay errors, 59
 role in high-speed Internet access, 129
 sending e-mail messages via, 59
 signing up for service, 129
 and undeliverable messages, 62–63
 what to look for, 129
interrupt request (IRQ) lines, 122, 306
intranets, 306
I/O addresses, 122
IO Error **message,** 110
IP addresses, 8, 9, 197, 198, 306
IRQ addresses, 122, 306

.jpg files, 68, 243

kids. *See also* **games**
 checking game suitability, 97
 protecting privacy online, 3
Kids Passport accounts, 3

LANs (local area networks), 183, 306
LapLink, 159
laptops
 adding external display monitor, 49
 built-in power management, 155
 changing power management properties, 154–55
 enabling/disabling standby mode, 156–57
 extending battery life, 154–55
 flowchart, 152–53
 importance of saving work, 157

laptops *(continued)*
 phone line issues when traveling, 160
 printing files offline, 153
 transferring files to and from desktop computers, 158–59
Last Known Good Configuration option, 32
LCD displays, 41
legacy devices, 122–23
liquid crystal displays (LCD), 306
local area networks (LANs), 183, 306
local ISPs, 129
local printers, 307
logging on, 4, 25, 173, 202–3, 307

memory, adding, 217
memory card readers, 262–63, 264
messages, e-mail
 decorative backgrounds, 67
 forwarding to other e-mail accounts, 61
 making HTML the default format, 67
 receiving when ISP mail server is down, 61
 saving copies in Sent Items folder, 69
 selecting HTML format, 66
 sending immediately vs. waiting, 69
 turning off HTML, 66–67
 undeliverable, 62–63
microprocessors, and gaming needs, 95
Microsoft Office
 Find Fast feature, 77
 transferring Outlook .pst file between computers, 159
 using data between laptop and desktop computers, 159
Microsoft Outlook. *See also* **Outlook Express**
 transferring .pst file between computers, 159
 using data between laptop and desktop computers, 159
Microsoft Paint, 19
Microsoft Photo Editor, 18
modems
 increasing dialing speed, 127
 phone line issues when traveling, 160
 troubleshooting ISP connection problems, 131
 troubleshooting to optimize Internet connection, 221–23
 troubleshooting to reduce connection delays, 133
monitor resolution, changing, 23. *See also* **displays**

mouse
  adjusting double-click timing, 169
  adjusting sensitivity, 163
  changing pointer, 166
  cleaning, 165
  customizing, 167
  finding pointer on screen, 166
  flowchart, 162–63
  left-handed use, 167
  reducing need for double-clicking, 168
  role of mouse pad, 165
  switching buttons, 167
  troubleshooting installation, 164–65
moving
  vs. copying, 80–81
  files and folders, 80–81
  files between folders, 52, 53, 80–81
Mscdex.exe file, 247
Mscreate.dll file, 83
MS-DOS, 90–91, 247
MSN.com, 5, 61, 68
MSN Online File Cabinets, 158
multiplayer games, 100
multiple booting, 307. See also dual booting
multiple display monitors, 48–49
multiple e-mail addresses, 64–65
multiple users
  creating separate user accounts, 172–73
  designating default identity, 178
  flowchart, 170–71
  rules for managing desktop, 25
  setting up separate e-mail identities, 178–79
  switching identities, 179
music album folder type, 89
Musical Instrument Digital Interface (MIDI), 307
music artist folder type, 89
music CDs, playing, 258, 259
music folder type, 89. See also My Music folder
My Computer folder
  changing text size or font, 27
  setting uniform view, 84
  showing/hiding icon on desktop, 14
  specifying path in Address bar, 90–91
  vs. Windows Explorer, 86–87
My Documents folder
  creating My Laptop subfolder, 159
  as default storage folder, 78
  glossary definition, 307
  moving files from desktop to, 23, 25
  moving to NTFS disk drive, 177
  organizing files within, 76
  protecting, 176–77
  showing/hiding icon on desktop, 14
  subfolders, 78

My Music folder, 78, 88
My Network Places folder
  accessing Network Tasks list, 9
  displaying computers on home network, 182
  displaying computers on office network, 204–7
  icon missing, 28
  searching for computers in, 201
  showing/hiding icon on desktop, 14
My Pictures folder
  selecting pictures for desktop background, 16–17
  as subfolder of My Documents, 78
  viewing pictures as filmstrip, 17, 88
  viewing pictures as thumbnails, 17, 88, 89
My Recent Documents folder, 78, 273
My Videos folder, 78

NetBEUI protocol, 184, 185
.NET Passport
  Kids Passport accounts, 3
  obtaining, 5
  recognition, 4
  signing in, 5
  sign in problems, 4
  Web site, 4
  and Windows Messenger, 4–5
.NET Passport Wizard, 5
network adapters
  checking, 205–6
  glossary definition, 307
  installing, 187
  need for, 28
network administrators, 307. See also administrators
network client, need for, 28
Network Diagnostics, 207
network printers, 230–31
networks. See also home networks; office networks
  glossary definition, 307
  and laptops, 158
  My Network Places icon missing from desktop, 28
  need for permission to install new hardware, 115
  role of proxy settings, 141
  sharing files, 174–75
  troubleshooting high-speed connection problems, 137
Network Setup Wizard, 182, 186, 188–89, 195, 196–97
New Connection Wizard, 128–29, 186
new folders, creating, 23

non-Plug and Play devices, 122–23, 307
notification area, 298–99, 307
No wave device that can play files in the current format is installed message, 255
NTFS (NT file system)
compared to FAT/FAT 32 file systems, 245, 253
converting FAT/FAT32 file systems to, 108–9, 177
deciding whether or not to convert, 108, 245
glossary definition, 307
moving folders to, 177
security issues, 171, 176, 253

office networks
enabling Remote Desktop feature, 210–11
flowchart, 200–201
logging on, 202–3
repairing configuration, 206–7
sharing resources, 208–9
Offline Favorite Wizard, 150–51
online databases, 63
online help. *See Remote Assistance*
opening files, 73, 79
operating systems menu, 285
optimizing, flowchart, 212–13
Outbox, Outlook Express, 69
Outlook Express
checking e-mail server settings, 60
controlling ISP dial-up frequency, 70
finding e-mail addresses, 62
selecting e-mail address to send messages from, 64
sending messages immediately vs. waiting, 69
setting up separate identities for multiple users, 178–79
using default e-mail account, 65

Paint program, 19
Paint Shop Pro, 243
parallel ports, 159
partitions, 252–53, 307
Passport. *See .NET Passport*
path, specifying, 90–91
pcAnywhere, 159
PC Cards, 307

performance, flowchart, 212–13
permissions
assigning to folders, 171
checking, 209
glossary definition, 307
for hardware installation, 115
overview, 83, 208
for viewing Web pages, 149
phone lines
analog vs. digital, 160
and hotel room data ports, 160
outside North America, 160
testing for dangerous conditions, 160
photo album folder type, 89. *See also Filmstrip view*
Photo Editor program, 18
Photo Printing Wizard, 228, 264–65
photos. *See also My Pictures folder*
online communities, 68
printing, 228–29, 264–65
viewing online, 68
pictures, background. *See also images; photos*
adding to desktop, 16–17
adjusting size, 18–19
borrowing from Web pages, 17
centering, 19
cropping, 19
downloading from Web pages, 57
editing in image editing program, 18–19
in My Pictures folder, 16, 17
scanning, 16
turning off, 23
pictures folder type, 89. *See also My Pictures folder; Thumbnail view*
ping, 100, 307
pinned shortcuts, 270–71
pixels, 307
Plug and Play
glossary definition, 308
installing devices, 119
vs. legacy devices, 122–23
what it means, 120
Plug And Play Monitor driver, 44
POP (Post Office Protocol), 308
port numbers, 8, 9
Post Office Protocol (POP), 61
power management
changing settings, 46
for laptops, 154–55
and uninterruptible power supply, 31
power schemes, 46, 308
printer drivers, 227, 308

printers
bidirectional cables, 225
getting status information from, 225
network, 230–31
offline use, 153
overriding default settings, 233
problems printing, 226–27
quality settings, 228–29
reinstalling drivers, 227
searching networks for, 230–31
speeding up printing, 232

printing
canceling, 226
flowchart, 224–25
offline, 153
overriding default settings, 233
photos, 228–29, 264–65
speeding up, 232
troubleshooting, 226–27
via network printers, 230–31
Web pages, 229

print queue, 227, 232, 308

privacy
and cookies, 145
protecting children online, 3

processors, and gaming needs, 95

programs
associating with file extensions, 242–43
avoiding mishaps, 337
displaying icons on taskbar, 21, 238
error messages after installing, 34–35
error messages after removal, 240–41
failure to respond, 236–37
finding favorites easily, 21, 238–39
flowchart, 234–35
glossary definition, 308
preventing automatic startup, 278–79
problems running in Windows XP, 235
reducing steps needed to start, 238–39
removing, 34, 218, 240–41
specifying window size at startup, 235, 279
starting from Quick Launch toolbar, 238
starting from Start menu, 239
ways to start, 238–39

protocols, 308. See also TCP/IP protocol

proxy settings, 141

.pst files, 159

Q

queue, 308. See also print queue

Quick Launch toolbar
adding icons, 238, 301
vs. desktop icons, 22
glossary definition, 308
rearranging icons, 239
reducing steps needed to start programs, 239
showing/hiding, 21, 22, 239, 293, 296
viewing as folder for managing shortcuts, 239
widening, 293

R

Recent Documents folder, 78, 273

Recycle Bin, 104, 308

refresh rate, 42–43, 308

registry, 241, 308

Relay errors, 59

Remote Assistance
enabling in System Properties dialog box, 6
establishing connection, 6–7
how it works, 7
inviting help via e-mail, 7
taking control of computer, 7
terminating connection, 7
and Windows Messenger, 6–7

Remote Desktop
changing options, 211
enabling, 210
for file transfer between desktop and laptop computers, 159
installing, 210
running, 211

removable drives
changing drive letter, 111
role in file transfer between laptop and desktop computers, 159

removable storage, 308

removing programs, 34, 218, 240–41

renaming files, 73

resizing
desktop icons, 20
icon labels on desktop, 26, 27
pictures, 18–19

resolution, display screen, changing, 23
resources, 208–9, 308. *See also* hardware, resource conflicts
restore points, 33, 35, 308
right-clicking, 80–81
rolling back drivers, 115

Safe Mode, 33, 249, 251
Save As dialog box, 52
Scanner And Camera Wizard, 262–63
scheduled tasks
  enabling/disabling at startup, 281
  running, 214–15
screen resolution, 23, 309. *See also* displays
screen savers, 47, 309
SCSI devices, 125, 309
Search Companion. *See also* finding
  basic use, 74
  customizing, 75
  removing animation, 75
  searching for computers in My Network Places folder, 201
  searching for downloaded files, 53
  searching for files, 74–75
  as tool for organizing files, 75, 76
security. *See also* privacy
  glossary definition, 309
  and NTFS file system, 171, 176, 253
Seek Error **message, 110**
selection, 309
Sent Items folder, Outlook Express, 69
servers
  downloading problems, 56
  for e-mail, 61
  glossary definition, 309
services, 309
Service Settings dialog box, 9
Shared Documents folder, 174, 175
shared folders, 174–75, 309
shared resources, 208–9, 309
share names, 309
sharing
  computer resources, 208–9
  files, 68, 174–75
  glossary definition, 309
  Internet connections on home network, 190–93

shortcuts. *See also* icons, desktop
  creating by dragging files and folders, 81
  glossary definition, 309
  pinned, 270–71
  positioning on Start menu All Programs menu, 272
  selecting to show on Start menu, 270–71
Show Hidden Icons button, 4
Show The Desktop command, 23
shutdown problems, 274–75
Simple File Sharing, 174, 175
Simple Mail Transfer Protocol (SMTP), 61, 309
sizing. *See* resizing
Small Computer System Interface (SCSI), 125, 309
software. *See* programs
sorting file lists, 84
sound
  adjusting balance, 260
  adjusting volume, 260
  assigning to Windows events, 261
  built-in, 99
  downloading .wav files, 261
  flowchart, 254–55
  game problems, 98–99
  troubleshooting failure to hear, 256–57
sound cards
  enabling/disabling, 256
  glossary definition, 309
  reinstalling drivers, 98–99
sound files, 255, 309
sound schemes, changing, 261
speakers
  adjusting volume, 256, 260
  troubleshooting, 256
  USB vs. other, 259
spooling, 309
standby, 309
Start menu
  changing text size or font, 27
  creating shortcuts that will always appear, 270–71
  customizing list of folders, 271
  vs. desktop icons, 22
  dragging shortcuts to rearrange, 269
  flowchart, 266–67
  Log Off option vs. Shut Down option, 275
  positioning shortcuts on All Programs menu, 272
  Programs list, 269
  reducing steps needed to start programs, 239
  removing documents from My Recent Documents list, 273
  reverting to Windows Classic style, 267
  scrollable vs. multiple-column, 271
  Search Companion, 53, 74–75

Start menu *(continued)*
  shortening and organizing, 268–69
  specifying each program's window size at startup, 235, 279
  switching users, 15, 24, 25
  turning shortcuts into menus, 271
  wrong user name, 267
start page, changing default, 148
startup
  creating startup disks, 257
  disabling automatic dialer, 284
  displaying list of users, 276
  enabling/disabling scheduled tasks, 281
  error messages, 283
  keeping windows from reopening automatically, 282
  minimizing time it takes, 280–81
  preventing programs from starting automatically, 278–79
  problem of Windows XP hanging, 286–91
  setting Windows Messenger to run, 5
  specifying program window size, 235, 279
startup disks, creating, 257
Startup folder, 278–79, 280
status bar, 310
synchronizing files, 159
System Configuration Utility, 283
SYSTEM.INI file, 283, 287, 288
System Restore window, 33, 35, 310

taskbar
  changing button text size or font, 27
  creating custom toolbars, 300
  flowchart, 292–93
  glossary definition, 310
  increasing space for buttons, 296–97
  moving, 295
  reverting to Windows Classic style, 297
  selecting Keep On Top option, 295
  Show Hidden Icons button, 4
  showing/hiding, 294–95
  showing/hiding notification area icons, 298–99
  showing/hiding Quick Launch toolbar, 21, 22, 239, 293, 296
  viewing pop-up descriptions of buttons and icons, 296, 298
Task Manager, 236, 237, 310

tasks
  disabling scheduling, 281
  moving and copying files and folders, 81
  scheduling, 214–15
Task Scheduler, 214–15
TCP/IP protocol, 132, 147, 184, 185, 198, 310
TCP ports
  for AOL Instant Messenger, 8
  defined, 8
  determining needs, 8
  specifying, 9
text
  adjusting Web pages for viewing, 139
  changing size or font, 27
text boxes, 310
themes, desktop
  choosing, 27
  downloading, 27
  glossary definition, 310
Thumbnail view, 17, 88, 89, 310
title bars, 27, 310
toolbars, 300, 310. *See also* Quick Launch toolbar
Transmission Control Protocol/Internet Protocol (TCP/IP), 132, 147, 184, 185, 198, 310

UDP ports, 9
uncluttering desktop, 22–23
undeliverable e-mail messages, 62–63
Uniform Resource Locators (URLs), 310
uninstalling
  drivers, 115, 116
  glossary definition, 310
  programs, 240–41
  Windows XP, 250–51
uninterruptible power supply (UPS), 31
Unused Desktop Shortcuts folder, 15
unwanted Web pages on desktop, 12, 23
USB devices
  enabling digital CD playback for speakers, 259
  installing, 120
USB ports, 310
user accounts
  creating, 172–73
  determining whose desktop is visible, 15, 24, 267
  displaying list of users at startup, 276
  logging off and back on, 15, 24, 25
  logging on, 4, 25, 173

user accounts *(continued)*
  multiple users, 25, 172–73
  naming, 172
  and .NET Passport, 4–5
  obtaining .NET Passport, 5
  requiring user name and password, 177
  switching users, 15, 24, 25, 173
  turning off Welcome screen, 177
  and Windows Messenger, 4–5
user profiles, 25, 310
users
  displaying list at startup, 276
  glossary definition, 310
  sharing files, 174–75

video adapters, 310
videos folder type, 89. *See also* My Videos folder
virtual memory, 310
Virtual Private Networking (VPN), 159
viruses. *See computer viruses*
Volume icon, 260

wallpaper. *See background*
.wav files
  downloading, 261
  setting audio devices to play, 255
Web browsing, 220–23
Web pages
  accepting/rejecting cookies, 144–45
  adjusting text size for viewing, 139
  borrowing images for desktop background, 17
  changing default home page, 148
  color distortion when switching among, 41
  deleting downloaded pages, 151
  displaying single picture when graphics disabled, 143
  downloading files from, 57
  downloading for viewing offline, 150–51
  downloading pictures, 57
  enabling/disabling multimedia and graphics, 143, 220
  enabling/disabling transitions, 221
  printing graphics, 229

Web pages *(continued)*
  printing quality, 229
  saving for later viewing, 150–51
  scheduling offline updates, 151
  showing/hiding on desktop, 15
  troubleshooting *The page cannot be displayed* message,
    140–42
  unwanted, on desktop, 12, 23
  viewing offline, 150–51
  You are not authorized to view this page message, 149
Web servers, 310
Web sites, 63, 149. *See also* Web pages
windows, 310
Windows Components Wizard, 105, 218
Windows Explorer
  changing text size or font, 27
  vs. My Computer folder, 86–87
Windows Media Technologies Web page, 27
Windows Messenger
  blocking others, 10, 11
  changing My Status setting, 10
  establishing Remote Assistance connection, 6–7
  flowchart, 2–3
  and .NET Passport, 4–5
  opening window, 6
  setting to run at startup, 5
  signing in, 4–5
  unblocking others, 10
  and user accounts, 4–5
  using Remote Assistance, 6–7
  ways to minimize interruptions, 10–11
Windows operating system, earlier versions
  creating startup disks, 257
  as default operating system, 285
  dual-booting with Windows XP, 252–53
  and Internet Connection Sharing, 193
  and Network Setup Wizard, 195
  restoring look, 12, 267
Windows Setup program
  checking system compatibility, 250
  detecting and repairing damaged Windows XP
    installations, 291
  failure to respond, 248–49
  flowchart, 244–45
Windows Update Web site, 118, 121, 213
Windows XP. *See also* Windows Setup program
  and automated system recovery (ASR), 37
  built-in indexing service, 77
  compatibility mode, 235
  as default operating system, 285
  detecting and repairing damaged installations, 291
  device drivers, 121

Windows XP *(continued)*
  dual-booting with previous Windows version, 252–53
  failure to start, 32–33, 251
  Last Known Good Configuration option, 32–33
  logging on to user accounts, 4, 25, 173
  minimizing startup time, 280–81
  preventive maintenance, 214–15, 237
  problem with hanging at startup, 286–91
  reasons for mishaps, 237
  and Remote Assistance, 6–7
  restoring look of Windows 98 or Windows 2000, 12, 267
  restoring responsiveness, 218–19
  restoring to earlier time, 33, 35
  setting Windows Messenger to run at startup, 5
  shutdown problems, 274–75
  starting in Safe Mode, 33, 251
  switching users, 15, 24, 25, 173
  uninstalling, 250–51
WIN.INI file, 283, 287, 289
Winsock.dll file, 142
WinZip, 68
wizards
  Add Hardware Wizard, 117, 119
  Desktop Cleanup Wizard, 15, 22
  Found New Hardware Wizard, 119
  Hardware Update Wizard, 44–45, 165
  Internet Connection Wizard, 178–79
  .NET Passport Wizard, 5
  Network Setup Wizard, 182, 186, 188–89, 195, 196–97

wizards *(continued)*
  New Connection Wizard, 128–29, 186
  Offline Favorite Wizard, 150–51
  Photo Printing Wizard, 228, 264–65
  Scanner And Camera Wizard, 262–63
  Windows Components Wizard, 105, 218
workgroups, 310
write caching, 216–17

Yahoo!, 68
Yahoo! Mail, 61
***You are not authorized to view this page* message, 149**
young people. *See also* games
  checking game suitability, 97
  protecting privacy online, 3

Zip drives, changing drive letter, 111
.zip files, 109

About the author

Steve Sagman is the author of more than 20 books on the subjects of graphics, Microsoft Windows, business applications, and online communcations, and he has contributed to several more. For Microsoft Press, he has also written *Troubleshooting Microsoft Windows, Running PowerPoint, Microsoft PhotoDraw 2000 At a Glance*, and *The Official Microsoft Image Composer Book*. His book *Traveling The Microsoft Network*, also published by Microsoft Press, was the recipient of the Award of Excellence from the Society of Technical Communication. His books have sold well over a million copies worldwide, and they have been translated into Bulgarian, Chinese, Dutch, German, Greek, Hebrew, Japanese, Portuguese, Russian, Spanish, and Thai.

When he's not writing books, Steve runs Studioserv (www.studioserv.com), a technical communication company that offers book editing and production, creation of user documentation, software training, and user interface design.

And when he's not writing or running his business, Steve plays jazz piano and sails his IP320, Offline. He can be reached by e-mail at steve@studioserv.com.

The manuscript for this book was prepared and galleyed using Microsoft Word 2000. Pages were composed by Studioserv (www.studioserv.com) using Adobe PageMaker 6.52 for Windows, with text in ACaslon Regular and display type in Gill Sans. Composed pages were delivered to the printer as electronic prepress files.

Cover designer

Landor Associates

Interior graphic designer

James D. Kramer

Principal compositor

Sharon Bell, Presentation Desktop Publications

Principal proofreader

Gail Taylor

Indexer

Julie Kawabata

Target your problem and
fix it yourself—
fast!

When you're stuck with a computer problem, you need answers right now. *Troubleshooting* books can help. They'll guide you to the source of the problem and show you how to solve it right away. Get ready solutions with clear, step-by-step instructions. Go to quick-access charts with *Top 20 Problems* and *Preventive Medicine*. Find even more solutions with handy *Tips* and *Quick Fixes*. Walk through the remedy with plenty of screen shots. Find what you need with the extensive, easy-reference index. Get the answers you need to get back to business fast with *Troubleshooting* books.

Troubleshooting Microsoft® Office XP
ISBN 0-7356-1491-1

Troubleshooting Microsoft® Access Databases
(Covers Access 97 and Access 2000)
ISBN 0-7356-1160-2

Troubleshooting Microsoft® Access Version 2002
ISBN 0-7356-1488-1

Troubleshooting Microsoft Excel Spreadsheets
(Covers Excel 97 and Excel 2000)
ISBN 0-7356-1161-0

Troubleshooting Microsoft Excel Version 2002
ISBN 0-7356-1493-8

Troubleshooting Microsoft® Outlook®
(Covers Microsoft Outlook 2000 and Outlook Express)
ISBN 0-7356-1162-9

Troubleshooting Microsoft Outlook Version 2002
(Covers Microsoft Outlook 2002 and Outlook Express)
ISBN 0-7356-1487-3

Troubleshooting Your Web Page
(Covers Microsoft FrontPage® 2000)
ISBN 0-7356-1164-5

Troubleshooting Microsoft FrontPage Version 2002
ISBN 0-7356-1489-X

Troubleshooting Microsoft Windows®
(Covers Windows Me, Windows 98, and Windows 95)
ISBN 0-7356-1166-1

Troubleshooting Microsoft Windows 2000 Professional
ISBN 0-7356-1165-3

Troubleshooting Microsoft Windows XP
ISBN 0-7356-1492-X

Troubleshooting Your PC
ISBN 0-7356-1163-7

Microsoft
microsoft.com/mspress

Tune in and turn on to the *ultimate digital media experience!*

U.S.A. **$29.99**
Canada $43.99
ISBN: 0-7356-1455-5

Listen to Internet radio. Watch breaking news over broadband. Build your own music and video playlists. With the MICROSOFT® WINDOWS MEDIA® PLAYER FOR WINDOWS® XP HANDBOOK, you control the airwaves! Personalize the way you see, hear, and experience digital media with this all-in-one kit of tools and how-tos from the Microsoft Windows Media team. You get everything you need to bring cutting-edge music and video everywhere your PC, laptop, or portable device goes!

microsoft.com/mspress

Get a **Free**
e-mail newsletter, updates,
special offers, links to related books,
and more when you
register on line!

Register your Microsoft Press® title on our Web site and you'll get
a FREE subscription to our e-mail newsletter, *Microsoft Press
Book Connections.* You'll find out about newly released and upcoming
books and learning tools, online events, software downloads, special
offers and coupons for Microsoft Press customers, and information
about major Microsoft® product releases. You can also read useful
additional information about all the titles we publish, such as detailed book descriptions, tables of contents and indexes, sample
chapters, links to related books and book series, author biographies,
and reviews by other customers.

Registration is easy. Just visit this Web page and fill in your information:
http://www.microsoft.com/mspress/register

Microsoft

- -